BOY
TALK

How You Can Help Your Son Express His Emotions

MARY POLCE-LYNCH, PH.D.

FOREWORD BY MICHAEL GURIAN

New Harbinger Publications, Inc.

Publisher's Note

This publication is designed to provide accurate and authoritative information in regard to the subject matter covered. It is sold with the understanding that the publisher is not engaged in rendering psychological, financial, legal, or other professional services. If expert assistance or counseling is needed, the services of a competent professional should be sought.

Distributed in the U.S.A. by Publishers Group West; in Canada by Raincoast Books; in Great Britain by Airlift Book Company, Ltd.; in South Africa by Real Books, Ltd.; in Australia by Boobook; and in New Zealand by Tandem Press.

Copyright © 2002 by Mary Polce-Lynch
New Harbinger Publications, Inc.
5674 Shattuck Avenue
Oakland, CA 94609

Cover photo: Luc Beziat/Stone
Cover design by Amy Shoup
Edited by Kayla Sussell
Text design by Tracy Marie Powell

ISBN 1-57224-271-X Paperback

Printed in the United States of America

New Harbinger Publications' Web site address: www.newharbinger.com

04   03   02

10   9   8   7   6   5   4   3   2   1

First printing

Dedication

This book is dedicated with love to my parents, Esther B. Polce and Anthony H. Polce, Sr.

Author's Notes

It is important for readers and mental health consumers to know that although many names and stories fill this book, I have respected the confidentiality of the boys and families in my clinical practice by creating composite narratives. Thus, none of the names and/or situations reveal true identities. If similarities arise, they are due to coincidence. When information about research participants is presented, it is only with their permission. I have also included stories from my own life, and although the events are true, some identifying information has been changed to respect the privacy of others.

◆   ◆   ◆   ◆   ◆

I reviewed the final proofs for this book one week after the September 11, 2001, tragedy that befell the United States. It was difficult to refocus on the book. Not only was it hard just to concentrate, I also wondered if anything in the book could possibly still be relevant after such a life-changing and horrible event. But as I, and countless psychologists across the nation, guided parents in how to talk with their children about the terrorist attacks, there was a consistent message: Parents should listen to children's thoughts and feelings. This message, along with witnessing many women and men openly express their emotions during the tragedy, helped me begin to refocus on the book. Regardless of the presence of terrorism in our lives, or perhaps because of it, emotions matter and must be heard. Children are our future leaders and diplomats. So let us continue to support boys' emotions—during times of war and times of peace.

Contents

Foreword

The book you are about to read offers essential practical tools for helping boys to access that often mysterious part of themselves: their emotions and feelings. But *Boy Talk* does more than just inform. It invites you to think carefully, perhaps even differently, about boys' emotional development. Then it inspires you to talk and listen to boys in broader ways.

How does a book accomplish this? The author, Dr. Mary Polce-Lynch, uses the lenses of developmental psychology and psychotherapy to bring us a unique and highly practical perspective on raising healthy boys. By connecting the dots between temperament, socialization, cognitive development, and emotional intelligence skills, she shows us how to support boys' emotional development from birth through adolescence. She also helps us see the cultural rules that can shape whether boys tell us—or even know—their feelings.

There is a common but mistaken fear that supporting boys' emotions will lessen their masculinity. This is simply not true. *Boy Talk* gives us all a reason to transcend this fear by challenging either/ or beliefs, such as a boy must be macho *or* he's a wimp. Indeed, boys can be both strong *and* sensitive, both emotionally expressive *and* logical . . . and still be boys.

In addition to many helpful tools, perhaps the greatest gift of *Boy Talk* is that it gives us permission to talk with boys about how they're feeling. Let this book be a guide as you choose to support boys' emotional development. Regardless of your philosophical perspectives on masculinity, you will discover a practical wisdom in *Boy Talk* that is essential to the raising of our sons.

—Michael Gurian
October 9, 2001

Acknowledgments

I begin by thanking my publisher, New Harbinger, for publishing a book about boys' emotions. Many wonderful books already exist on this important topic. I appreciate New Harbinger's belief that I could add to the discussion, especially Kristin Beck and Catharine Sutker, who believed in *Boy Talk* from the very beginning.

I had the privilege of working with gifted clinicians for a dozen years, the Child and Adolescent Team of Hanover County Community Services Board (CSB) in Ashland, Virginia. Their expertise and understanding of children's emotions has helped thousands of children and families; their professional consultation and support was just as important to me. When the team gave me a farewell gift of wind chimes last year, I promptly hung them near my writing desk. Each time the wind blew I felt encouraged. Thanks to Barbara Smith, Karen Rice, Carol Hughes, Loucinda Long, Pat Purcell, Jane Yurina, Allison Sibley, and friends of the team, Dot Livingston, Millie Hycner, and Diane Story. Tom White and Stewart Callahan were also part of the CSB family (still are) and for that I remain very grateful.

Somewhere during the challenges of being a parent, working, and graduate school, I considered not finishing the Ph.D program. It was a sane option in the midst of a crazy time. One of the reasons I decided to continue was Barbara J. Myers, chair of the developmental psychology department at Virginia Commonwealth University, my dissertation chair, and *mentor extrordinaire*. Barbara encouraged me to follow my own research path into gender and emotional expression, which eventually led to this book.

I want to acknowledge the work of pioneers in the boys' movement: Michael Gurian, William Pollack, James Garbarino, and Daniel Kindlon. I especially thank Mike Gurian for writing the foreword and for important discussions about masculinity. Similarly, I thank Bill Pollack for reading an early version of the manuscript and for his support of *Boy Talk*.

Meetings with my writing group were valuable and supportive, often giving me the courage to publish (it's never easy). Authors themselves, their laserlike feedback was right on target. I remain grateful to Leslie Wright, Mindy Loiselle, and Renee Cardone for believing.

Patti Atkins Noel and Kim Forbes Fisher, two friends who are also psychotherapists, were supportive despite the fact that we live in distant cities. Sometimes their support was to tolerate my brief e-mails or far too few phone calls; other times it was to say "hang in there." Patti and Kim's friendship, often in spirit, made the past year bearable—as friendships often do.

My parents, Esther and Anthony Polce, provided the kind of support that only parents can. They believed in me and they prayed for me every day. I thank them lovingly.

This book, of course, wouldn't be possible without the boys I have had the privilege of working with in therapy. I applaud these boys, young and old, for having the courage to break the rules and tell me how they feel. Their stories echoed in my mind and heart when I was their therapist, and always as I wrote this book.

What does one say about the best "emotions teachers" in the world? My children, Rachel and Morgan, are feelings experts. I continue to be impressed with how clear they are about their feelings. I want to thank them for their gifts of time and understanding. They know how important writing this book was, yet they bravely interrupted me when they needed their mom. Their presence, understanding, and courage made the book a reality.

I must thank John Lynch, my life partner, clinical psychologist, and very best friend. He frequently held up my "half of the sky" so I could write this book. John is an intelligent and creative person who has chosen not only to break the Pack Rules, but also to teach other boys and men the value in doing so. I respect John and am grateful to him for all of this and more.

A writing project is rarely the result of one person's efforts, and this book is no exception. The staff at New Harbinger supported *Boy Talk* every step of the way. I appreciate Amy Shoup's incisive work on the cover and title, and Carole Honeychurch's midpoint guidance and support. Finally, it is the work of Kayla Sussell, my editor at New Harbinger, that I must spotlight. Kayla's editorial experience and wizardry with words steadily guided the final stages of this book. The combination of her sagacity and attention to detail is a writer's dream. I am grateful for her skills and I know that readers will benefit as well.

Introduction: The Big Picture

The first chapters of this book present an important context for discussing boys' emotions. They are very comprehensive and may even be a tough read at times, but necessarily so. Boys' emotions are complicated: they are not merely feelings, not just physiological sensations, and not just in their heads. Furthermore, specific cultural rules restrict boys' access to and expression of their own emotions. I call these rules the Pack Rules, a distortion of healthy masculinity that can even cause boys' emotions to "disappear."

Although chapters 1, 2, and 3 start out comprehensively, the remaining chapters provide you with specific interventions to remedy some of the resistance to boys' emotions. Because there have been centuries of cultural resistance to boys' emotions, I think it's necessary to discuss the bigger picture. Not looking at the bigger picture is like trying to stop a leak without locating the source. I don't provide an historical analysis of resistance to boys' emotional expression, nor do I provide a complete biological analysis, but I do present as much psychoeducational information as possible to help you consider how and why boys' emotions matter.

If you see an interesting chapter in any part of the book, go ahead and read it first. Chapters can be read out of sequence because each one can stand on its own. However, I do encourage you to read chapters 1, 2, and 3 at some point, because they provide a pithy overview of the biology, socialization, and development of boys' emotions in a readable format.

To underscore the importance of boys' emotions, chapter 1 introduces the subject "Why Boys' Emotions Matter." This chapter starts to unravel boys' emotional straitjackets. I begin by tugging at the threads that affect boys' emotions. One important thread is the physiology of emotions. Although it is a rather technical read, this information legitimizes boys' emotions in a way that cannot be denied. Another important thread is the social resistance to boys' expression of their emotions that seems to be pervasive throughout mainstream culture.

I focus on different content in chapters 2 and 3, but there is one overlapping theme: socialization affects how boys express their emotions. A major part of this socialization is found in the Pack Rules, a restricted code of behavior that many boys follow to become "real" boys and men. Although allegiance to these rules may or may not be conscious, the outcome is the same: Boys often give up their emotions to comply with an unhealthy, distorted version of masculinity (i.e., boys can *only* be confident and *never* feel scared). I detail this process in chapter 2, "Boys' Socialization: The Pack Rules," by expanding on the idea that boys try, and sometimes succeed, in making their emotions "disappear" in order to comply with rigid cultural expectations.

In chapter 3, "Developing Boys and Their Emotions," the focus is on the developmental progression of boys' emotions from birth through late adolescence, paying specific attention to temperament. Regardless of the age you're interested in, this chapter should be read from beginning to end because the content builds upon itself. Reading about only one age group won't give you all the information you need. To get the big picture, you must connect the dots from one age to the next because past and future perspectives are needed to fully understand and support boys' emotional development. In many ways, chapter 3 is the cornerstone of the book because I describe boys' emotions from the very beginning through early adulthood. This chapter gives you the perspective of where boys have been and where they're headed, emotionally.

Although it's not possible to "see" what boys feel inside, it is possible to observe how they express their emotions on the outside. Chapter 4, "Boys and Emotional Expression," describes what healthy and unhealthy emotional expression looks like and the consequences of both. Results from a recent study are presented, showing the pattern of how boys restrict the expression of their emotions. Responses from surveys and interviews with adults about boys' emotions are also described. These responses provide perspectives about boys' emotional expression and perhaps clues on how to go about changing current patterns.

Chapter 5, "Boys Empathy: A Hallmark of Emotional Health," is a must read. The ability to feel one's own emotions and the emotions of another is called empathy–and it is this ability that is so critical to the development of healthy interpersonal relationships. It is also the ability that sets humans apart from monsters and machines. Without the inner compass of empathy, boys cannot be fully present in their relationships with themselves or others. I believe that empathy for the self precedes empathy for others. How empathy develops and how it gets "snuffed out" of boys is discussed in detail. Perhaps most importantly, ways to promote empathy in boys are provided.

Chapter 6, "Boys and Anger," begins with a rhetorical question, "Must boys' anger always end in aggression?" I believe there is a real answer; that answer is, "Yes, boys' anger will continue to end in aggression unless current norms change." In this chapter, I present a model for understanding boys' interpersonal anger and aggression in the context of fear (an emotion that boys aren't "allowed" to feel). I refer to this model as the Fear→Anger→Aggression Cycle. Discussed in detail and presented as a visual graphic, the model links boys' fear and anger to the importance of clear and conscious thinking. Indeed, such thinking can interrupt the cycle of interpersonal violence in a way that allows boys to make choices within themselves to manage their anger without causing it to "disappear" inside of them, or turn into aggression.

Chapters 7 and 8 were written for the change agents that we all can be for boys. In chapter 7, I focus exclusively on how parents can contribute to boys' emotional development in the family. I present ideas that can help families become a safe place for boys to feel and express their emotions. Specific suggestions are presented that can create and sustain boys' emotions on a day-to-day basis at home, in school, and with friends. What parents do at home is so important, for this is how—and where—boys' emotions begin to develop.

Chapter 8 is for the many different men and women who influence boys' lives. Parents are also encouraged to read this chapter since it provides a description of the larger environment surrounding boys, one that can support (or not support) their emotions. This chapter provides separate sections about foster parents, teachers, coaches, grandparents, aunts and uncles, therapists, medical doctors, mentors, and religious or spiritual leaders in boys' lives. Practical guidelines and suggestions are provided to assist these adults in helping boys develop in emotionally healthy ways. The focus is on emotional expression, since this is an effective way to send the message to boys that their emotions matter. Specific suggestions are given to reinforce emotional expression skills. This includes being a role model for healthy emotional expression and helping boys to express emotions in daily life.

The ultimate goal of this book is to allow boys to have both their emotions and their masculinity. I hope you will engage in a dialogue with others about boys' emotions. Boy Talk is an important conversation to have.

Why Boys' Emotions Matter

Emotions don't feminize boys, they humanize *boys to be fully connected to themselves and to others.*

—John Lynch, *The Pain Behind the Mask*

Jeremiah was an active four-year-old boy who kept hitting his newborn sister. After he was encouraged to use these words, "I'm mad because Mommy can't play with me now," Jeremiah's aggressive acts decreased by half in just two days. His parents couldn't believe it. They had been telling him to stop for weeks, but nothing had helped. Similarly, when twelve-year-old Michael finally disclosed to his parents that his girlfriend had "dumped him" and that he felt bad, his crankiness stopped. Immediately. His parents also noticed how the muscles in Michael's face looked different, more relaxed, after he had talked with them about his feelings.

Identifying and expressing emotions can be learned at any age. Very young children use their behaviors to express their feelings because they haven't acquired verbal skills yet. But even two-year-olds will use feeling words instead of behaviors *if these words are taught to them.* Jeremiah and Michael first expressed their emotions behaviorally. But this didn't persist because their parents paid attention and responded. It is in this kind of day-to-day living that boys learn lessons about their emotions. Small steps such as teaching

Jeremiah what to say to express his feelings, and listening to Michael express his sadness, had significant and positive effects.

When emotions are blocked from conscious verbal expression, they seek behavioral or somatic expression. Indeed, physical symptoms such as headaches and digestive problems ("tummy aches") are quite common to children and teens. This mind and body connection is receiving increasing attention in behavioral medicine, so a major part of this chapter focuses on the physiology of the brain-emotion-body relationship.

When Terrance Real (1999) asked an African elder what makes a good man, the elder replied that a good man is one who laughs, cries, and protects—*and does each when needed*. This broad view of masculinity is different from the way our culture restricts boys' and men's emotions. And while our culture may be more emotionally expressive than many others, boys' emotions still aren't as valued as girls' emotions are in the United States today. An understanding of this resistance to boys' emotions is needed so you'll be free to teach boys the skills they need to identify and express emotions effectively. But before I focus exclusively on boys' emotions, it's important to examine the general purpose of emotions in the human experience.

The Purpose of Emotions

Although it is accurate to say that throughout recorded history human beings have always had emotions and expressed them in one form or another, this statement isn't enough. Researchers and clinicians continue to identify what happens when emotions are ignored, as well as describe the skills and approaches needed to deal effectively and productively with emotions. Without a clear understanding of the *purpose* of emotions, resistance can take over, and rather easily at that. One form of this resistance is seen in the way that boys' emotions are covertly neglected and overtly rejected in our culture.

Think for a moment. Why do *any* of us have emotions? What is their purpose? One answer is that emotions exist in the service of human survival to promote full human growth. With this overarching function in mind, I think there are at least four purposes for the existence of emotions. These involve needs, identity, connection, and thought.

Emotions communicate needs. Babies could starve if they couldn't communicate their distress by crying. Born with the innate ability to recognize and respond to the human face, they also need comfort. As babies grow older, their needs continue to develop. And their emotions will continue to signal these needs throughout their lives.

Emotions individualize us. They are part of life experience and help to create the uniqueness of one's identity. Each person can experience the moment only in the way that he or she does. While we mainly come to know others through "seeing" them, we come to know ourselves through "feeling." These feelings validate our individual identities.

Emotions communicate and connect people with each other. You know you're not alone (or that you are) because of your emotions. Everyone shares these experiences, even if those experiences are sometimes completely internal. Emotions help us to live more connected and meaningful lives.

Emotions are integrated with thoughts. Some theorists argue that it isn't possible to have a thought without a coexisting emotion. Among many functions, this powerful teamwork results in emotions aiding (or interfering with) memory and other cognitive abilities that help us to regulate our emotions.

Boys to Men

What would boys' lives be like if they couldn't signal their needs, if they didn't fully understand their uniqueness, if they weren't connected to others, and if their thoughts and emotions weren't integrated? If any or all of these scenarios were the case, boys would have to become artificially self-sufficient and never ask for help. They would experience doubt and fear about their basic identity and competence. They'd feel alone and have only partial responses (ones that lack emotion) to the events in their lives.

Indeed, many writers in the field of men's studies argue that this is *exactly* how many boys grow into their adulthood (Kimmel 1987; Levant 1995; Lynch and Kilmartin 1999). Men find themselves detached from others, unable to identify or express their emotions, and often not fully present to the connection between their thoughts and emotions. These problems don't result from *masculinity* per se, but rather from *strict adherence to traits associated with masculinity* (i.e., strength, independence, competitiveness, unemotionality, etc.). Being athletic or being a breadwinner are other examples of gender roles and behaviors that define masculinity in our culture. Masculinity as such is valuable to boys and our larger society.

Somewhere along the way, though, distortions occur. One distortion is the way that being "strong" and "not talking about feelings" have mistakenly become synonymous not only with each other, but with masculinity. I don't think that masculinity is responsible for this. Rather it is the *polarization* of masculinity. This lack of flexibility in our perceptions of masculinity and the norms surrounding these perceptions are pervasive for boys. Simply put, girls can be both masculine and feminine, but boys can only be masculine. By complying with these rigid norms in order to fit in or be accepted, many boys lose the freedom to experience and express a fuller range of human behaviors and traits (i.e., nurturance, vulnerability, interdependence, emotionality, etc.). The result is that boys may grow into men who have lost some of their humanity.

The Resistance to Boys' Emotions: Uncovering the Fear

Resistance to boys' emotions is everywhere and affects everyone. Whenever I talk about the topic of this book, I observe how parents, colleagues, girls, women, and men all seem to feel uncomfortable. (The only ones who are not made uncomfortable are boys—they actually seem relieved.) Those with the strongest resistance are the parents of boys. It's almost as if saying the words "boys" and "emotions" together isn't okay ... or it's against some kind of rule.

Initially, this resistance surprised me. However, when I considered the cultural rules that dictate how boys should deal with their emotions, it made sense. As I interviewed the parents of boys, I learned a great deal about what boys' emotions represent to their parents. It seems that parents' resistance is rooted in their *fear about what might happen to their sons if they expressed their emotions*. Parents want to protect their sons from rejection, ridicule, and other forms of abuse they might encounter *for not being masculine enough*. Everyone knows that boys who aren't "masculine enough" (using narrowly defined masculinity as the yardstick) are at the bottom of the peer pecking order. These boys can be hurt, both physically and psychologically.

Of course, culture defines what is masculine. In the United States, the cultural rules for displaying emotions have always been more restrictive for boys than for girls. It comes as no surprise, then, that this culture associates the absence of emotional expression with being masculine. So, although parents have the positive intention of protecting their sons from other boys' ridicule, the unfortunate result is that parents' resistance to their boys' emotions keeps the whole cycle going. The following stories illustrate how this cycle of resistance to boys' emotions, even in the form of well-intended parental protection, can adversely affect boys.

Jeremy

Sam is an intelligent and articulate father of two sons, Steven, age fifteen, and Jeremy, age fourteen. Sam is also a man who understands the importance of boys being able to express their emotions.

But in raising his own sons, he relied on the parental default of protecting Jeremy from rejection, rather than protecting Jeremy's ability to express his emotions. As Sam explains it, he made a "conscious choice to respect Jeremy's temperament." The older boy, Steven, was very sensitive and showed his feelings easily, while Jeremy rarely displayed positive *or* negative emotions. Added to this was the fact that Jeremy made friends with a close-knit group of rough-and-tumble boys in preschool. They didn't show their emotions, either. These boys, who became known as "the pack," continued to be friends throughout middle school.

I listened carefully as Sam recalled how Jeremy had stopped kissing his parents good-bye at preschool. Both Sam and his wife, Teri, had watched with envy as the little girls freely kissed their parents good-bye and the little boys did not. Their rough-and-tumble boy would have nothing to do with their hugs and kisses, and neither would the rest of the pack. Sam and Teri didn't insist that Jeremy kiss them good-bye. Rather, they respected his need not to show affection in public. Because the pack didn't approve of such behavior, all signs of affection in public ceased on that autumn preschool day. Unfortunately, affection to and from Jeremy was also expressed less and less at home.

Relinquishing Jeremy's physical affection was a sacrifice for Sam and Teri because they were both very affectionate people physically. They enjoyed sharing hugs with their older "sensitive" son, who also enjoyed physical signs of affection. As Jeremy's parents explained it to themselves, Jeremy and his pack of friends just had a different type of temperament. Although this may have been accurate at some level, this form of temperament doesn't mean that the boys' emotions don't matter. It does mean they had a harder time expressing emotion.

During this discussion, I pondered out loud about what it must be like for a four-year-old child *not to be able to show his feelings freely.* Especially toward his parents, whom he dearly loved. After I said this, we were all silent for a moment. Sam responded first by saying that they (the parents) had respected their son's boundaries. They thought it would have been difficult and inappropriate to *force* their then four-year-old boy to kiss them good-bye. Indeed, respecting boundaries is critically important to the development of a healthy sense of self. But so is the ability to feel and express emotion. Then, it was as if we all realized what had happened at the same time. Sam and Teri had done just what most other parents do. They had resisted encouraging their son to express his emotions because if they had done so, his behavior would not have matched the behavioral display rules of the Pack.

Michaela

The parents of Michaela, Sam's neighbor, shared a similar story but with a different outcome. When their daughter had turned four years old, she refused to hug or kiss her parents at preschool *or* at home either. Michaela's parents described her as being a rough-and-tumble kid who would rather run away from a hug than give or receive one. Like Sam and Teri, these parents also respected Michaela's boundaries and didn't force her to express affection. But by the time she was eight, she was freely hugging and kissing her parents, and she continued to do so through middle school. What made the difference?

How Children Become Emotionally Expressive—or Not

Of course, it's impossible to identify a single factor, or even several factors, that definitively create personality traits or human behaviors. Nevertheless, developmental psychology theories provide some clues. Although the following theories may seem abstract, I think they're a helpful and hopeful guide through boys' emotional development.

Developmental Perspectives

A general tenet in developmental psychology is that of "continuity and change." Some traits and behaviors continue throughout life span development, while some change. The transactional theory (Sameroff and Chandler 1975) and the genotype-environment theory (Scarr and McCartney 1983) combine to suggest that, as children's development changes, so does the environment. Thus, the child and the environment continually affect each other throughout the individual's life span in a coordinated dance. Children's development (cognitive, emotional, temperamental, etc.) elicits specific responses from their environment (parents, family, peers, school, etc.), and that environment, in turn, responds and has an effect on the children's development. But it doesn't stop there. The child then again affects the environment and the process continues functioning back and forth. This transactional process takes place within a specific culture or context, which shapes both the environment and children's responses. Although this may all seem rather complicated, I see it as very hopeful: the child and environment continue to develop and change together.

Applying Theory

Now, let's apply this theoretical construct to Michaela and Jeremy. When Michaela was adamant about not showing affectionate emotions, her parents (part of her environment) responded in kind. They didn't force the issue. So, she continued not showing affection to them. However, Michaela's parents *didn't stop showing affection to her* the way that Sam and Teri did with their son, Jeremy. Rather than stopping all affection, or forcing Michaela to hug them, her parents would "blow" her hugs and kisses at night, at preschool, and then later at elementary school. They also created special names for each other that conveyed affection. The familial environmental response to Michaela continued to promote expression of affection, while also respecting her desire not to be touched or kissed.

The outcome to Michaela's and Jeremy's aversion for expressing affection clearly differed. It could be that, initially, their temperament or sensory integration prevented them from enjoying physical affection. It's not exactly clear what unique part of *them* caused the initial rejection. It also is not clear whether the way their parents and peers responded resulted in their different behaviors around affection in later childhood.

What is clear is that Michaela eventually showed affection toward her parents and Jeremy did not. If Michaela's parents had stopped sending her signals of affection, figuring "she's just not the sensitive type," her behavior might not have changed and she might have remained unaffectionate, like Jeremy. Yet if emotional development is an ongoing process throughout the life span (and it is), there are endless opportunities to change the familial environment and teach boys like Jeremy the rewards of identifying and expressing their feelings.

Facing the Fear

When both Michaela's and Jeremy's situations are considered, the part that is clearest to me involves the intention of both sets of parents. They were doing what they believed was best for their child in a culture that has different emotional display rules for boys and girls. This is where the fear begins. There is increasing pressure from the larger culture for parents to protect boys from being viewed as "emotionally sensitive." Having a wimpy son can be dangerous for the boy and embarrassing for the parents. The same is not as true for the parents of girls. Michaela's parents had much more cultural permission to continue "wooing" their daughter's affection over the years of her childhood than Jeremy's parents did.

It doesn't take much thought to decide which child has the richer life experience. One might even argue the healthier experience. And it doesn't take much looking to see how *fear* lurks beneath parents' resistance to their sons' emotional expression. I believe that parents who try to "toughen up" their "sensitive" sons or who see them as the rough-and-tumble type, and let it go at that, are good parents. They have the best of intentions. However, I also believe it is this same fear that prevents parents from considering the importance of their sons' emotions.

Telescoping

Some of the fear the parents feel may be related to the tendency to "telescope." This is a phrase I use to describe how parents look at children as they are in the present, but see them in the future. For example, a three-year-old boy may cry often and his parents may worry that he'll be a "crybaby" when he's in middle school. Rather than seeing him as he is (at the young and vulnerable age of three) and responding to him in appropriate ways *for his age*, parents who telescope will ignore the crying to toughen up their little boy. If such parents put their telescopes away, they would see that the developmentally appropriate way to respond to a crying three-year-old boy is first to comfort him, and then to teach him how to comfort and soothe himself. (The same is true for raising emotionally healthy girls.) But many parents try to toughen up their son for fear he'll be "too emotional" or wimpy when he's older.

Telescoping isn't fair to children for any sound reason. We all behave differently when compared to how we were when three years old. Yet the fear on which telescoping is based is not irrational. What parent isn't familiar with the cultural punishment and rejection that boys receive for expressing their emotions? Especially their vulnerable and tender emotions. *Parents' fear is honestly rooted in a prevalent and reinforcing cultural belief that boys' emotions are at best unnecessary, and at worst, not to be felt or expressed.* This belief is right in line with "The Pack Rules" that I discuss at length in the following chapter and throughout the book.

Naming the Resistance

When considering parents' resistance to boys' expressions of emotion, the real issue isn't what did Michaela's parents do differently than Jeremy's parents that contributed to different levels of emotional expression. The real issue is this: *Do boys' emotions matter?* If they do, then parents and other interested adults must overcome their fear and pay more attention to boys' emotions. This includes parents, grandparents, teachers, coaches, friends . . . everyone.

It is the *cultural resistance* to boys' expressing their emotions that gets in the way of allowing boys to express—or simply feel—their emotions. This resistance must be addressed head-on. Cultural resistance requires a countercultural response. That response is to encourage and help boys feel, own, and express their emotions. Furthermore, if their emotional lives are left unattended or untaught, boys will deal with feelings they don't know how to express through unhealthy outlets such as tummy aches, stoicism, and aggressive behavior.

How and Why We Feel Emotions

The physiology of emotions is critical to any discussion of emotions. Why? One reason is that physiology makes an otherwise intangible experience—a fleeting feeling, for example—more concrete. Another is that when the physiological bases for emotions are understood, boys' emotions are less likely to be dismissed as unimportant. Indeed, the entire human body is wired for emotional arousal and receptivity. Because the human body is hardwired to feel emotions, and since boys have both bodies and emotions, it's useful to know something about the complex physiology involved in emotions.

The purpose of this overview is to introduce you to the complexities of emotional behavior, rather than to present a comprehensive course. With some knowledge of the physiology of emotions, you'll be better equipped to understand why it's difficult to reason with boys when they're upset, why helping boys express sadness is important to their mental and physical health, and why a physical workout can help regulate emotions.

Although I tried to make the following material readable for nonscientists, it contains a lot of scientific "shop talk." So feel free to skip over any scientific words that interrupt the flow of reading. You can even skip the entire section and just read the summary ("The Physiology of Hiding Behind the Mask") instead. But before you skip ahead, please understand that I included information about the "hardwiring" of emotions to underscore the *reality* of human emotion. With all the cultural pressure there is for boys not to feel or express their emotions, I thought an equally powerful counterforce was necessary: Enter science!

The Physiology of Feelings

The word *emotion* comes from a Latin word that means "to move." In psychology, the word emotion refers to feelings, physiological reactions, and behavioral response patterns. Volumes of research have been written about the specific origins of emotion in the brain and throughout the body (yes, emotions are located all over your body!). Most people are familiar with the central nervous system, but not with this "second nervous system," which is located throughout the body (Pert and Chopra 1997). This second nervous system consists of many ligand-to-receptor circuits.

Ligands are chemical messengers, typically made up proteins, that carry information to cells located in organs throughout the body. *Receptors* are special spaces on these cells that receive the information from the ligands. These ligand-to-receptor circuits may be responsible for most of the emotional information communicated to various organs and body systems (Pert and Chopra 1997). A large number of emotion receptors are located in the stomach. No wonder that stressed children get tummy aches, or that we all have "gut feelings" on occasion.

Many respected neuroscientists (e.g., Damasio 1994; LeDoux, 1992; 1996) have conducted research to help chart some of this emotional circuitry in humans. So far, the most persuasive research I have found for the "brain-emotion-behavior connection" comes from brain surgery patients. These patients remained conscious while their brains were probed with medical instruments; later they described their experiences under the surgeon's knife. For example, when part of a patient's cortex was stimulated and the patient reported feeling rage or fear, it is highly likely that the part of the brain that was stimulated was responsible for the patient feeling those emotions.

An Owner's Manual: How Emotions Work

What's currently known about the brain-emotion-behavior connection is roughly analogous to the way that computers operate. Both the central nervous system and autonomic nervous system are analogous to a computer's hardware. The central processing system of a computer is analogous to the *limbic system* in the brain. The limbic system consists of several brain structures, including: the amygdala, cingulate gyrus, thalamus, and hypothalamus and their interconnections. The system is activated by behavior and arousal, which influences the endocrine and autonomic motor systems. To continue the computer analogy here, our experiences and behaviors are like the software that we load into our computer's hardware. Messages are sent via neurotransmitter and hormone circuits, and they are received at various cites throughout our body system.

The amygdala has been linked to processing anger and fear (Whalen, Shin, McInerney, Fischer, Wright, and Rauch 2001), while the cingulate gyrus appears to process both positive and negative emotions (Damasio 1994). Research by LeDoux (1992; 1996) also links the prefrontal cortex (the thinking and reasoning part of the brain) and the limbic system to emotions. All of these parts of the brain receive sensory information (visual, auditory, tactile, kinesthetic, taste) from the environment and then process an emotional response. So, as you can see, each structure may have specific functions, but each structure is also interconnected with other brain structures in complex ways.

Specific Brain-Emotion-Behavior Circuits: How We Feel

The connection between the prefrontal cortex and the limbic system is an important interface. Why? Because this is where thoughts link to feelings. Boys' brains, like everyone else's, are wired in such a way that their conscious thoughts can influence the physiological aspects of their emotions and vice versa. Boys can be taught emotional intelligence skills because of the presence of this interface. Simply put, the presence of this interface can help boys to understand and regulate their emotions.

The *autonomic nervous system* (ANS) is a major circuit that affects human emotions. It works through two separate systems: the sympathetic and parasympathetic. (Did you notice the emotional word "sympathy" in both?) The sympathetic nervous system (SNS) speeds up heart rate, blood flow, and muscle energy. Are you afraid of speaking in public, or of a Rottweiler chasing you on your daily walk? The physiological sensations you feel when frightened (dry mouth, butterflies in stomach, heartbeat pounding in your chest) are all communications from your SNS. When you are frightened, it automatically sends chemical messengers throughout your body, priming it for action. And it's all about the "feeling" or emotion of fear.

The *parasympathetic nervous system* (PNS) counterbalances its speedy counterpart. The PNS slows down heart rate, lowers blood pressure, and soothes a nervous stomach . When you feel your body relax it's because the PNS has been activated by a complex mix of chemical messengers. The PNS appears to play a major role in "the relaxation response." It is also known to reduce the negative effects of long-term stress on the human body (Benson 1975).

In addition to the autonomic nervous system and its two subsystems (PNS and SNS), the other important system that regulates everyone's emotional reactions is the *endocrine system*. Endocrine glands secrete hormones that are carried by the blood, lymph system, or nerve cells and transported to the target organ. Endocrine glands include the adrenals, thyroid, parathyroid, pituitary, hypothalamus, pineal, pancreas, testes, and ovaries.

Emotions in Action

Now, let's consider how the ANS and the endocrine system might work together in a real-life situation. Let's suppose a young boy has a baseball purposely smashed into his face. His automatic SNS reaction will signal his distress. His heart will race and blood pressure rise. His adrenal glands will send more energy to his muscles for easier movement. If all his systems are working properly, the well-known sympathetic "fight or flight" response will be activated.

With so much happening internally in addition to the pain and shock of being hit in the face, it's easy to see why the boy would cry, run away, or hit back. However, once all of these physiological effects have been activated, how he responds depends upon his individual temperament and social conditioning. Some boys would have a strong reaction, some might not. But the older boys get, regardless of their individual temperaments, the more likely it is that they will hide or mask how they really feel.

In this situation, an injury and a perceived threat activated his SNS. To relax, this boy needs to be comforted. He needs to feel a sense of safety to stimulate his PNS. His ability to perceive safety helps to engage the calming PNS. Once safety has been established, the PNS slows his heart rate and decreases blood pressure while his endocrine system stops the adrenaline pump. Activating the PNS is especially critical in helping boys learn how to interrupt the all too often automatic Fear→Anger→Aggression Cycle (see chapter 6).

A Closer Look at the Chemical Messengers

The James-Lange theory suggests that we experience our emotions through physiological feedback that's mediated through the limbic system, resulting in behavioral responses (Carlson 1992). This relationship between physiology, brain structures, and behavioral responses relies upon the individual cells that communicate with and between each other via chemical messengers. There are several different types of chemical messengers. So far, two types have been identified as related to emotions. They are hormones and neurotransmitters.

As mentioned, hormones are secreted by the endocrine glands and are sent through the bloodstream to receptor cites all over the body (including stress and sex hormones). Neurotransmitters are chemicals released by the brain. These include serotonin, dopamine, epinephrine (adrenaline), and acetylcholine. Receptor sites in the brain detect these chemical messages. This chemical activity in the brain appears to play an important role in emotions and moods.

Also, cells throughout the body contain different types of receptor sites. Some parts of the body, such as the stomach, shoulders, back, and chest have cells with a higher than average concentration of emotion receptors. Other areas of the limbic system, located in the brain, such as the hippocampus (linked to memory), have a huge *variety* of receptor sites, while the amygdala (linked to fear and anger) carries *less variety* but a *higher concentration* of cells with receptors for emotions. One estimate states that when you're aware of an emotion, 98 percent of the information comes from cells located throughout your body and only 2 percent from receptors in your brain (Pert and Chopra 1997).

The type of chemical messenger sent appears to depend on the type of message that you receive from your environment. For instance, a particular event can stimulate the amygdala and you may feel anger or fear in your body. A different event may stimulate the cingulate gyrus and you may feel happiness. To be sure, emotions unfold within a complicated and finely tuned network orchestrated by chemical messengers.

When Feelings Become Foreign: The Physiology of *Not* Feeling Emotions

Now, with some of the "hardware" and "software" explained, it's important to consider the following question: *What happens to boys when they learn to turn off their feelings?* Flipping the switch to off can result in familiar behaviors. Many boys' voices come to mind, especially at the beginning of therapy sessions: *"I don't care"* (after displaying several bruises earned from the school bully); *"It doesn't bother me"* (after his parents' divorce); *"It was the best thing that happened to me"* (after recalling a childhood beating given to him by his stepfather).

Emotional Energy Must Go Somewhere

In the preceding brief examples, boys genuinely may not have felt their fear or anger. When ignored over long periods, it is possible not to *feel* an emotion. Yet you now know that chemical messengers and neural circuits create a range of physiological responses within the body when the environment activates those responses. So, all of the resulting physiological energy must go *somewhere*. I believe that it either comes out "sideways" in behavioral problems or as somatic (physical) symptoms.

Indeed many boys' stories throughout this book echo this very pattern. Boys' feelings were ignored by themselves and others—only to come out later in a different form, as an unhealthy symptom.

Another important issue is this: what happens to the other nervous system, the parasympathetic system that calms boys down, when emotional messages are ignored? One generalized answer to this question is that boys are turning off a very valuable part of themselves. Whether at school or playing sports, it seems that boys' ability to calm and regulate themselves is critical to paying attention and learning, as well as to the more obvious skills of getting along with others. Boys who don't feel their emotions may be less able to activate their parasympathetic nervous systems and may not be able to calm themselves down. Boys, like all human beings, receive benefits from being able to feel their emotions so that they can learn to use these inner signals to regulate the physiological aspect of their emotions.

Turning Boys' Emotional Circuits Off—and On!

If emotional circuits exist to help us feel our emotions, and if everything is wired correctly, the boy who is sad or scared about his parents' divorce actually will *feel* this experience. But cultural conditioning also can affect physiology and thinking. Boys who learn to ignore their feelings can "short-circuit" their brain-emotion-behavior systems. This can result in boys learning to misread their internal body signals, thus developing a skewed sense of what is normal or healthy. For example, boys who ignore their sadness again and again may adjust to this physical state. Rather than express sadness and then go back to a normal (not sad) set point, they may stay sad, perhaps even become depressed. This same process also can happen with fear and anger. Unless boys learn to recognize when they are feeling fear and anger and how to express these emotions in healthy ways, they may be negatively affected by a constantly firing nervous system.

Basic Awareness Helps

It takes an awareness of physiological states, emotions, and thoughts to regulate emotions. If boys learn how to turn off feeling their emotions, they won't be able to calm themselves down. Such boys may be described as having a "short fuse," as not being able to sit still, or as being "all boy." Attention and behavior problems are not uncommon with boys who have learned to ignore their emotions, mainly because they haven't learned to regulate them.

Fortunately, boys *can* learn to regulate their emotions. A multisystem approach is needed to make this happen. In general, it's important to know that thoughts and behaviors influence how the brain and body respond. Cognitive interpretations (thoughts) are a very important part of the brain-emotion-behavior circuitry. This includes the way that boys can learn to reason with their emotions. For example, learning to say to another student, "I'm upset because you teased me at lunch, don't do that again," is anger shaped by reason, while clobbering the kid over the head with a textbook is not.

It Goes Both Ways

Many of the following chapters include specific ways to help boys regulate, rather than be hijacked by, their emotions. Here, it's important to just get the "big picture." Most people were taught to see how the brain affects behaviors. But few consider how behaviors and experiences have an impact on how the brain works and responds to the environment. Scientists have known for a long time that environmental experiences affect the brain. The general public has been slower to catch on to this concept. I'm not sure why. But the relationship between the brain and the environment is definitely *bi-directional* (i.e., it goes both ways):

Brain ◄─────► Environment

(Emotions and Body)   (Behaviors and Experiences)

This bi-directional relationship is especially relevant to boys' emotions. Why? Well, if you consider how boys are taught to hide their emotions from a very early age, then it's very likely that the behavioral practice of hiding emotions has a physiological effect on the brain-emotions-behavior circuit. Simply put, it *is* possible for boys to learn how *not* to feel their emotions. A psycholgocial condition known as alexithymia ("without words for feelings") is more prevalent in men than in women (Lynch and Kilmartin 1999). This suggests that adult men learn their lessons well. Not only do they stop telling their feelings to others, they stop feeling them. They stop being able to name them—even to themselves.

The Physiology of Hiding Behind the Mask

So, boys emotions are as real as the organs in their bodies. If something happens to a twelve-year-old boy like a baseball thrown too hard, a physical threat, constant teasing, angry looks, or social rejection, he will feel threatened or angry. Immediately, his brain communicates to receptors in the stomach. Hormones and neuro-transmitters do their jobs, facilitating communication from cell to cell, from organ to organ. The symathetic nervous system is engaged. His muscles tighten and his breathing changes. Neurochemical activity increases between his limbic system, autonomic nervous system, and endocrine system. His brain-emotion-behavior circuit system is engaged. His parasympathetic nervous system is alerted and ready to respond, to calm things down.

Yet the expression on the boy's face may not show much, if any, of this activity. If you ask this boy what he's feeling, he may say, "Nothing." Then, if you ask, "Are you okay?" he will respond, "Yeah." And he may not be lying. He really may not feel any of this physiological activity. *This is what can happen when boys' emotions don't matter.*

Emotional Intelligence Skills

Mayer and Salovey (1997) have created a theoretical model for understanding emotional intelligence skills. They identifiy four broad skill categories that go a long way toward providing you with a map of the emotional skills that boys need. These are (1) perceiving and expressing emotions, (2) integrating emotions with thoughts, (3) analyzing emotions, and (4) regulating emotions.

Perceiving and Expressing Emotions

The ability to accurately identify and express one's own emotions, to identify the emotions of others, and to perceive emotions in abstract forms such as art, literature, music, and so forth is important. To be fully open emotionally, boys need to be able to see emotion in all of these ways. An inability to perceive emotion in one area can become a missing link in an important chain of experiences. The interpersonal aspect of perceiving emotions in others has obvious daily implications for school and family life ... the boy who can *accurately* "read" the feelings of others is more likely to get along well with his teachers and peers. Thus, the accuracy with which boys' read their own emotions and those of others is critical. The more practice a boy has doing this, the more likely he will discriminate accurately. Simply put, for boys to express their needs, they must be able to perceive feelings accurately. Also, the ability to identify one's own emotions is closely related to the ability to identify the emotions of others.

Integrating Emotions with Thoughts

Integration refers to the way that perceiving one's own emotions helps to prioritize thinking and aid judgment, memory, and performance: "I really want to do well on this test, so I'll study instead of watching the last quarter of the game," and "I don't want to get kicked out of school, so I won't blow up and let Ricky push me over the edge again," are two examples of integrating emotions with thinking to aid judgment.

Emotional mood states also affect thinking and performance, as is clearly the case when a boy is feeling happy and he's more creative or productive. Similarly, when he feels depressed, he doesn't want to study or do his homework. Moods can affect thinking, just as thinking can affect moods. Pessimism and optimism are frequent travelers on this two-way street.

It appears that the ability to integrate thoughts and feelings automatically, as well as to understand the relationship between the two, is an emotional skill that develops as cognitive abilities develop. It's obvious that a two-year-old boy cannot reason his way out of a tantrum when he sees it's not getting him the toy he wants. But as the frontal cortex (the seat of higher reasoning) continues to grow and develop (up to approximately age eighteen), boys "collect" more reasoning power along the way. When cognition is integrated with emotion, there's more data to make informed and healthy decisions.

Analyzing Emotions

The ability to name complex emotions and to determine the relationship between different feelings and experiences develops with age and practice. For example, seven-year-old Mikey feels hurt when Grandpa can't go on their regular Sunday fishing trip, but Mikey also understands that Grandpa is sick. Three years ago, Mikey could only feel mad or sad. To be sure, most relationships are emotionally complex and multilayered. "I'm angry but I still love you, Dad," or "Mom loves me even though she's mad at me right now," illustrate this well. (You can see how this is linked to integrating skills.)

Another aspect of the ability to analyze complex emotions involves anticipating probable shifts among emotions. Fear can shift to relief when safety arrives; anger can change to empathy when the other person's point of view is considered; and anxiety can shift suddenly to pride and joy when a school project is deemed successful. Because analyzing this anticipated shift involves abstract cognitive skills, younger boys typically can't do it independently. However, as with any emotional skill, this can be taught and boys can be coached to learn it. It's well worth the time, because the ability to recognize that one is feeling love and anger at the same time is a hallmark of mental health.

Regulating Emotions

Being able to regulate emotions is a sign of maturity. It involves observing your positive and negative emotions and thinking about how these emotions can be best expressed. If a boy continually ignores either his positive or his negative emotions, he won't *feel* them (see the section on Physiology above). To regulate, control, or act on their feelings in an informed way, boys must first be able to feel, perceive, and analyze these feelings.

The ultimate goals are to control negative emotions and to enjoy the positive ones. Effective emotional regulation requires the ability to intensify, maintain, and control emotions as needed. So the boy who can feel very angry without needing to explode, or who can feel excited about the upcoming school dance and still focus on his science project, is regulating his emotions successfully.

Different "Kinds" of Emotions

At this point, you may be wondering what the *basic* emotions are? Theorists, clinicians, and researchers have different answers to that question. Although it's difficult to know precisely what new-borns feel, current developmental researchers (Shaffer 1999) have concluded that before they are two and one-half months old, babies appear to show interest, distress, disgust, and contentment. Then, between the ages of two and one-half months and seven months, the primary emotions of anger, sadness, joy, surprise, and fear emerge. These primary emotions all appear at approximately the same time. After the age of one year, a second tier of emotions arrive. These are pride, shame, guilt, and envy.

Everyone has experienced different kinds of emotion and few people cannot distinguish between them. However, the reason there are quote marks in the head above, "Different 'Kinds' of Emotions," is that the *theoretical* orientations of psychologists, as well as the purpose and application of their work, can and do differ. For example, Heidi Kadusan (1998), a clinical psychologist and play therapist, insists that the minimum four emotions children need to express in therapy are happy, sad, mad, and scared.

Other psychotherapists, however, like to add "hurt" to this list. The phrase "he hurt my feelings" is a common experience that every-one understands without needing a scientific translation. Often we feel this hurt viscerally in our stomach or chest (thanks to emotion receptors), and the phrase certainly captures a real emotional and physiological experience. However, I usually find that when I look further, the emotion of fear is beneath hurt feelings.

Clearly, what emotions eventually "look like" depends upon *internal* factors like age and individual temperament. Then, as children grow older, *external* factors such as peer group display rules and the particular situation appear to shape what the child's emotions will look like to the outside observer. As suggested throughout this book, boys' emotions receive so much of this shaping that we sometimes don't even see boys' different feelings.

Challenging the Belief That Boys' Emotions Are Not Important

Recent research suggests that feeling and expressing emotions, rather than holding them in or making them "disappear," is critical to healthy functioning. For example, Richards and Gross (2000) conducted a study that compared the effects of expressing versus suppressing emotions on memory. These researchers concluded that constantly monitoring oneself to hide emotions such as anger, anxiety, and sadness can divert our attention and impair our reasoning skills.

Two other very relevant studies measured the physiological effects of hiding strong negative and positive emotions. In the first study, when emotions were hidden, measurable changes in the cardiovascular system were recorded. These changes were not observed in the control group who did not hide their emotions (Gross and Levenson 1997). Similar physiological changes were observed in another study that asked participants to hide their disgust. Decreased somatic (physical) activity and decreased heart rate were noted, along with increased blinking and sympathetic nervous system activity (Gross and Levenson 1993).

What Does This Research Mean for Boys?

Research suggests that suppressing or hiding emotions can interfere with thinking, remembering, and physical health. So, when boys learn to make their emotions "disappear," they may experience negative physiological effects. Given the physiological basis of emotions, this makes good sense. It's important to highlight how it is not *emotions* per se that interfere with thinking and health (as *Star Trek's*

Mr. Spock suggests); what interferes with clear thinking and good health is the *lack of expressing* emotions.

Over the past decade, clinical attention has focused on the relationship between emotional expression and physical health (Pennebaker 1995; 1997), as well as between emotions and psychological disorders such as anxiety, depression, and conduct disorders (Gross and Munoz 1995). Although the findings from these studies cannot be generalized to *all* boys, this research can inform our thinking about what happens when emotional expression is blocked. Given the apparent relationship between suppressing emotion, cognitive functions, and health, more research is needed to explore the relationship between suppressing emotions and disorders commonly diagnosed in boys such as attention deficit/hyperactivity disorder (AD/HD), learning disabilities, and substance abuse.

Conclusion

Recently, I saw a six-year-old boy get hit in the face by a bad pitch at a Little League game. The boy sobbed freely because it hurt so badly. As his pain peaked, he ran to his father. I watched the father cradle the boy in his arms and whisper soothing, comforting words. It took only a few seconds of feeling "all better" for the hurt boy to stop crying. When the father put his son down on the well-worn grass near the dugout, the boy eagerly ran back onto the field, ready to play ball again. Everything was okay.

Watching this father rock his son in midair, I thought about how this little boy hadn't been told, "Big boys don't cry," or "It's not that bad, it doesn't hurt," or "C'mon, get back out there and play ball!" Instead, he was allowed to feel and express his pain and to be comforted. As I write this, I recall the many men and boys I've worked with in therapy who no longer know how to cry or how to receive such comfort. Instead, they've learned how to make their feelings disappear. Like Bobby, age eight, who said that he didn't cry when his father died . . . or eleven-year old Michael, whose best friend taught him "how to not cry" by pushing him down onto the asphalt, over and over again, until Michael could get hurt and not cry.

If one purpose of emotions is to signal basic human needs, then it's important for those signals not to be ignored. The next logical step is then to communicate those needs to others who can respond or assist. This is where the disconnect often takes place for boys. Boys need to be able to express and regulate their emotions in appropriate ways. This is true for girls and adults as well. But the display rules for emotions are so rigid for boys that the ways and situations in which they can freely express their emotions are certainly unfair and arguably inhuman.

Challenging the beliefs that boys' emotions aren't important goes against the dominant culture's grain. These challenges make parents feel anxious because they don't want to intentionally hurt their son by setting him up to be socially rejected for not being "masculine enough." These parents are afraid that they'll contribute to their son being seen by his peers as a wimp, mama's boy, or sissy if they encourage his emotional development. But all the scientific studies in the world cannot prove to parents what they intuitively know to be true: Boys' emotions do matter, and the playing field isn't level yet.

Fortunately, emotional expression is a very teachable skill. Parents and other adults need to know how to socialize little boys who can both feel and express their emotions—and how to intervene when older boys have learned to make their emotions "disappear."

CHAPTER
2

Boys' Socialization:
The Pack Rules

*Though the stereotypes about what boys are
and how boys should behave continue to be
perpetuated, in our hearts many of us know
that these outdated ideas are simply untrue.*

—William Pollack, *Real Boys*

Boys Are People, Too

I recently watched a second-grade boy at dismissal time in a local
elementary school. He was standing in the school's entrance hall
with a group of other little boys and girls who looked eager to go
home. This second-grader broke into a sprint at the sight of his father
in the school hall. Backpack bouncing with each step, he jumped up
into his father's arms. The boy's eagerness had turned into complete
delight. And the father looked just as delighted. I had the sense that
this type of "hello" happened often between them.

This boy and his dad broke what I call the Pack Rules, a distorted view of healthy masculinity that requires boys and men to
mask their feelings, even positive ones. Far too often adults forget
that boys are people, too. Just as often, adults don't realize that boys

and girls are more alike than different with regard to their psychological needs. This similarity is rooted in the simple fact that both boys and girls are alive and human.

In this chapter, I provide a picture of boys' inner emotional lives while also exposing how culture influences boys' psychological needs. I discuss how socialization inside and outside the family, and the consequences of this socialization, affect boys. The first section describes the Pack Rules, a major socializing agent of boys' emotions. The term *Pack Rules* has a dual meaning. As a noun, it is a list of mandates about how boys should act. As a verb, when the "pack rules," it describes how boys' inner lives become dominated by these mandates. Both usages are apt descriptions of how boys often learn to become men in mainstream American culture.

Although there are many variations of the Pack Rules, I focus primarily on restricted emotional experience and expression. Other rules are discussed, but these two stand out as the main threads in boys' emotional straitjackets. Socialization forces and the punishment for "out role" behaviors (actions outside culturally prescribed masculine gender roles) are also described, as well as boys' sexuality. The main goal of this chapter is to reinforce the value of boys' expressing their emotions and to show how social influences affect boys' emotions and behaviors.

The Pack Rules

The *Pack* is an accurate metaphor for a primary agent in boys' socialization. This term refers to that band of boys who swoop into your kitchen, den, basement, or garage with a guttural hello and minimal eye contact, only to swoop back out again, mount their bikes, and head off to the next outpost of civilization (food, heat, video games). The Pack can also be a few boys who form a small, tightly knit group in a classroom or other group setting, following each other's lead on whether to pay attention, laugh, or raise their hands. The Pack reflects being psychologically and physically together, i.e., not alone. It can provide boys with a sense of identity, community, connection to others, challenge, and fun. But the Pack can also limit boys' experiences.

How? Like any social group, the Pack has both stated and unstated norms. The Pack Rules are distorted masculine norms that can glue boys together. Early in their lives boys learn that these are the norms against which boys learn to judge others, and against which they learn to judge themselves. In his groundbreaking book about boys' emotions, *Real Boys*, William Pollack (1998) refers to a similar phenomenon as the "boy code," while Kindlon and

Thompson (2000) in the book, *Raising Cain*, call it the "culture of cruelty." These are all different names for essentially the same process. I don't think what we call it matters, as long as everyone keeps talking about it.

Although the Pack Rules may be the glue that binds the Pack together, a boy doesn't have to be a member of a Pack to know and follow the Pack Rules. In or out of a Pack, boys follow these rules because they know the cost of not following them . . . they fear that they won't be real boys, they won't be *masculine*, they won't become real men.

Isn't it amazing how everyone knows what the Pack Rules are without ever reading a single "rule" book? This is what culture does. It hands down information from generation to generation, from group to group without ever needing formal embodiment in a book. Boys' experiences with other boys appear to convey the Pack Rules on masculinity very well. Although some of these rules may be fun or appropriate at times, when followed rigidly, they aren't healthy for boys.

This is why the Pack Rules are referenced throughout this book; they can shape boys' emotions in a harmful way, especially the expression of their emotions. So, what exactly are these rules? Here are some that I've either observed or learned about from boys and men:

★ **Younger boys:** *Don't cry when you hurt; boys play with boys; girls are yucky; boys are tough; being strong and powerful makes you a real boy; winning is good, losing is bad.*

★ **Early teens:** *Don't cry when you hurt; don't show excitement unless you score a field goal; don't talk about your feelings to other guys; don't show other guys your fear or uncertainty; nothing bothers you; don't get too close to boys because everyone will think you are gay (and being gay is bad); avoid anything feminine; girls are sexy; boys are tough; being an athlete makes you a real boy; winning is good, losing is bad; it's okay to be aggressive; make fun of others, especially if they're weak or you're uncomfortable; laugh when you feel uncomfortable; mask your real feelings.*

★ **Middle teens:** *Don't cry when you hurt; don't show excitement; don't talk about your feelings to other guys; don't show other guys your fear or uncertainty; nothing bothers you; don't get too close to boys because everyone will think you are gay (and gay is still bad); avoid anything feminine; girls and women are really sexy; tell sexual jokes and stories; being an athlete makes you a real boy; winning is good, losing is bad; boys rule; it's okay to be aggressive; make fun of others, especially if they're weak or you're* *uncomfortable; laugh when you feel uncomfortable; look cool at all times; use one-word answers ("Huh?" "Yeah" "Dunno" (I don't know); mask your real feelings.*

★ **Older teens:** *Don't cry when you hurt; don't show excitement; don't talk about your feelings to other guys; don't show other guys your fear or uncertainty; nothing bothers you; avoid anything feminine; don't get to close to other guys because everyone will think you're gay (it's still bad); telling sexual jokes and stories and having sex makes you a real man; girls and women are sexy; being an athlete makes you a real man; winning is good, losing is bad; it's a man's world; go out into the world and make a name for yourself on your own; drinking is cool; it's okay to be aggressive; make fun of others, especially if they're weak or you're uncomfortable; laugh when you feel uncomfortable; look cool at all times; be stoic; mask your real feelings.*

★ **All ages:** *Don't talk about the Pack Rules.*

There are more rules and variations of these rules, to be sure. But these are some of the ones that rigidly define masculinity for many boys in the United States today. These same rules can profoundly affect boys' emotional and relational lives. Even when boys or men profess that they don't follow this narrow prescription of masculinity, at some level they are still affected because the Pack echoes inside boys' and men's heads. And the rules build on one another. They may shift slightly, but they remain true to the same underlying principle: Boys must act and be more like machines than real people.

When the Pack Rules Boys' Heads and Hearts

Unfortunately, boys believe that the dangerous aspect of these rules lies in breaking them rather than in breaking away from them. The cost of being rejected, called a wimp, sissy, or a *girl*, strikes deep fear at the core of boys' identities. But I ask you to think about how the real danger may lie in what happens to boys' heads and hearts when they *do* follow all of these rules.

When boys internalize the Pack Rules, they don't follow the rules only when they're with the Pack. *They follow the rules all the time.* When boys believe they shouldn't share their confused or excited feelings with other boys, they also stop sharing such feelings with everyone, including their family. It would be one thing if boys hid their feelings from each other only within the Pack. But it appears that the Pack Rules echo in boys' minds all the time. And if boys listen to these rules and subsequently turn off their feelings as a way of hiding them from view, this isn't healthy. It is the beginning of how boys make their feelings *disappear*.

Regardless of temperament or age, the boy who learns from the Pack that only sissies cry when they are hurt, and only *girls* talk about their parents' divorce, also will learn not to talk about his feelings with anyone. And without any education in emotional intelligence skills or intervention by concerned adults, that boy will follow these rules into his adulthood. This restriction of boys' emotional expression is perhaps the most harmful example of how the Pack rules boys' lives.

Boys Lose Out

Terrence Real (1997) describes a two-step process of how boys are socialized in our culture: First we hollow them out, we strip boys of their emotions; then we stuff them with male privilege. I think this description is particularly powerful because it comes from a man, someone who has "been there" and who is willing to talk about it. This method of dehumanizing boys has such potentially dangerous outcomes. If you think about stripping anyone of their feelings and then empowering them with special privileges, you know that this is a recipe for danger. But rather than thinking of such boys as dangerous, I choose to consider them as people who have had invaluable parts of their humanity stolen from them.

In our culture, the ways in which boys cannot and do not display or easily share their emotions may be one of the greatest mental health risks that boys face. It contributes to a range of psychological and physical health problems. Research with adults indicates that restricted emotional expression is associated with depression, poor physical health, unsatisfactory relationships, and substance abuse (Pennebaker 1995). It has been argued that many men and boys' behavioral problems may be linked to the way they mask their emotions.

Just Watch

At the movies. One way to understand how boys lose touch with what they are feeling is just to watch them. You can observe boys anywhere, anytime. For me, two telling incidents took place over the course of a single weekend. One observation occurred at a Saturday matinee showing of *Simon Birch*, a movie based on John Irving's, *A Prayer for Owen Meany*. This is a story about a physically handicapped boy who is born prematurely and who remains abnormally small throughout his life. He's three feet tall in early adolescence; the plot concerns his painful plight during an already difficult age for boys.

For the first fifteen minutes of the matinee, four sixteen-year-old boys (a Pack), forced themselves to laugh loudly each time the physically deformed Simon came on the screen. The boys' deep voices filled the theater in a powerful and odd way. Maybe that was because they looked like boys, but had men's voices? They seemed to be using their newly discovered power in a false and rehearsed way, sounding very much like the laugh track of a TV sitcom. Or perhaps the falsity was just the result of the many rehearsals that these boys must have had for this very situation: *When you feel uncomfortable (sad, vulnerable, horrified) pretend you don't feel it. Hide it. Mask it. Laugh about it. Pack Rules.*

I did some reality checking with my husband, John. He verified my impressions. Yes, the boys were acting inappropriately. He was also annoyed for similar reasons. The entire audience was being pulled into the way these boys were defending themselves from feeling their discomfort. We had to work hard to have our own experience of Simon, a frightening and engaging character. Later, I had the sense that this must be what it's like to live by the Pack Rules. You're sucked into ignoring your true feelings to belong to the group, the Pack.

If I hadn't been the farthest from the aisle in the thick of the boys' laughter drills, I would have gone for the manager. I didn't want the boys to dictate my family's experience of Simon. Sitting there, minute by minute, I fantasized approaching one of the boys and whispering into his ear to stop the silliness, the same way a good classroom teacher does, to avoid a power play and still succeed in silencing the class bully.

I'm so glad that neither the manager nor I had to approach the boys. As it turned out, they did what was needed on their own. During the second hour of the movie they quieted down and watched the movie. When the mother of Simon's best friend died, they didn't laugh. When Simon stood alone near the sea and feebly screamed, "Sorry," into the night sky, because he felt responsible for the death, again, they did not laugh. Since the audience was no longer distracted by the boys' laughter, we could all feel sad and helpless, which were appropriate responses to this movie.

In a church. There was a need for "appropriate responses" in the second situation, too. I attended a religious event for sixteen-year-olds. The gathering involved several girls, two boys, and two adult women. The ritual and activities required the teens to think and feel as they explored their faith. It was a serious and intimate gathering designed to elicit deep, positive emotions. I observed how the girls seemed comfortable with the experience, while the boys did not. It was all the boys could do to keep from laughing. The hysterical kind of laughter that you can't keep a lid on no matter how hard you try.

If the room had been larger or more crowded, the boys might have succeeded in carrying out their efforts to distract themselves—and us—from their discomfort. Sometimes, the bigger the Pack, the more powerful it is. But in this small group, the two boys had no power, just inappropriate reactions. And there were no male role models present to teach these boys that the Pack Rules didn't work here. I wish I could say that the two boys came around by the end of the worship experience. I can't. As we held hands in a circle during the closing prayer, they were unable to control their laughter. Even if they had wanted to, I sensed that the boys had had too much practice for moments like this. When you feel uncomfortable, mask your real feelings. (Pack Rules.)

By now the connection between the two events is probably clear to you. Both situations involved boys who were faced with experiencing and expressing intimate emotional moments in a social group. Talking with the church leader afterwards, I learned that the boys' behavior had been problematic all year. Driving home, I felt sad not only for them but also for all of us. We all lose out when our culture accepts boys' emotional masks as if they were destiny. *Boys will be boys.* I imagined a culture that allows boys to be scared as well as competitive, gentle as well as tough, spiritual as well as worldly. Then I recalled how boys under the age of seven eagerly take part in the children's liturgy at our church, exploring their feelings and spirituality in public, in front of other boys. Hmmm . . . .

So, what happens to boys between childhood and adolescence? How do we lose these boys and how do they lose the ability to feel or show what they feel? What would prevent adolescent boys from turning to drugs or to the Pack Rules to manage uncomfortable feelings, such as those aroused by a spiritual meeting or a poignant movie, without having to resort to laughter?

Peter Pan and the Other Lost Boys

For many years now, psychologists and educators have been asking the same questions. And we've been getting some answers from researchers and writers (Gurian 1996; 1999; Kindlon and Thompson 2000; Pollack 1998). But I believe a first and critical step is for *parents* to ask, and then answer, these same questions for themselves. To loosen the iron grip that the Pack Rules have on young boys, parents must examine how they contribute to the Pack Rules and ask how they can prevent their sons from internalizing these rules. Otherwise, we'll continue to raise a culture of lost boys.

In James Barrie's classic novel and movie, Peter Pan and the Lost Boys live in Never-Never Land without their parents. We don't know why the boys aren't with their parents; we just know that in some way they're lost. The boys fill their days with excitement, leaping from one adventure to another as they blindly follow their leader, Peter Pan. Their bravado is evident in their fearless escapades and narrow escapes from danger.

But the boys still long for one hallmark of a childhood with parents: having bedtime stories read to them. As the plot unfolds, we learn that it's not the entertainment aspect of listening to stories that they miss. It's what the experience represents to them. Under the blustering moxie of their outlaw manners, the Lost Boys long to be *physically comforted and emotionally nurtured.* (Bedtime stories may be one of the universal symbols that encapsulate both.) Indeed, this is the very reason that the determined Peter Pan flies away every night to stand on the ledge outside the nursery window: he listens while Wendy reads stories to her little brothers. This is also how Peter loses his shadow one night. He leaves the nursery too quickly, before he's caught. From a psychological perspective, perhaps Peter's shadow contains the emotional needs that his bravado alone cannot satisfy.

Carrying Wendy off to Never-Never Land seemed like the perfect solution to the Lost Boys. Then, they could play all day and still have their bedtime stories at night . . . a life filled with independence, but with a twist of comfort on the side. But when Wendy and her brothers admit they're homesick in Never-Never Land and start crying because they miss their mother, the Lost Boys also begin to cry.

During this scene in the movie, all the boys weep together as Wendy describes, in great detail, the nurturing and comfort that she and her brothers long for. We see how Wendy *names* the boys' sadness *for* them. She makes the link between their wonderful feelings of comfort and their loss. Perhaps this is what most of our sons lose far too early, that link to their emotions. Thus, the "Lost Boys" is an apt name for the characters in the story because the boys *are* lost without their feelings and real parenting. It is my belief that Barrie's emotionally Lost Boys aren't all that different from many boys in our culture today.

Parents' Role in Finding Lost Boys

In an effort to encourage the idea that men can provide the same emotional nurturing that women do, I believe the "mother" that Wendy and the Lost Boys longed for can be embodied in a man; a "male mother," if you will (Dinnerstein 1976). But for this to occur, our culture must change with regard to *men* (not just boys) who display sensitivity and nurturing behaviors. It's entirely possible for a man to "do mothering." Sound impossible? It's not only possible, it's essential. Especially if boys learn best from role models, and it appears that they do.

When I was in graduate school and my attention was consumed by books, papers, and research, my husband, John, "mothered" our new baby, Morgan. Unlike our first child, whom I cared for while John finished graduate school and juggled a job, Morgan was bonded to her "male mother." The bond between them was evident to everyone. But no one knew how much it meant to Morgan until she was four years old. One day when Morgan and I were looking through a baby album, Morgan saw a picture of herself as a newborn. She was cradled across her dad's chest; head nestled in the crook of his elbow. Gazing at this photo, Morgan asked , "Oh . . . is that when I came out of Daddy's tummy?"

Morgan's experience of men's nurturing abilities is probably different from other children's experiences with men in our society. Throughout history, most literature and religious scripture typically associated the characteristics of emotional comfort and nurturing with mothers, not fathers. This is true across cultures. It is certainly still true in most contemporary media (commercials especially).

It is significant to note here that in some cultures where men are involved with child care ("male mothering"), there is less evidence of violence (Coltrane 1998). I hope you'll understand and appreciate why I purposefully substituted the word "parent" for "mother" throughout this book.

In closing this section, I need to say that it's wonderful when a boy can crack a good joke to relieve tension, or to entertain his buddies over pizza. It's also wonderful for boys to be independent, confident, and competitive. Indeed, it's an empowering human experience to be strong when strength is needed. But problems arise when being strong is all that boys and men are permitted to be. And that's what the Pack Rules dictate.

Stripping Boys of Their Emotions

Think about these words: "Boys don't cry," "mama's boy," "wimp," and "sissy." You know that these words often refer to a boy who shows emotion. When a boy doesn't conform to the traditional gender script, social psychologists call this "out-role" behavior. Out-role behavior for a boy essentially means disobeying the Pack Rules. Girls also perform out-role behaviors, but in a patriarchal (male dominant) culture, there's more punishment for boys who step outside of masculine gender roles. Naturally, boys don't want to engage in out-role behavior because they'll be punished. Thus, boys are effectively rewarded for following the Pack Rules.

Learning Fearlessness Early

What happens to boys when they can't feel their emotions? Chapter 1 suggested that there are physiological consequences. Here the focus is on how stripping boys of their emotions can make them less human. Both the Pack Rules and the sanctions of the larger culture contribute to the ways that boys are stripped of their emotions and some of their humanity is taken away.

From the very first time a crying boy who feels scared or hurt is told, "Big boys don't cry," the disconnection from his feelings begins. He learns to dissociate his real feelings from his experience. When this disconnect is reinforced countless times throughout his life by others who follow the Pack Rules, he learns to not feel vulnerable. And when humans deny their vulnerability over and over and over, they can become . . . fear-less. (Manufacturers really knew what they were doing when they marketed that "No Fear" logo to boys . . .).

By the time the typical troubled adolescent boy seeks counseling, he has already lost many connections to his emotions. Family, schools, media, and the entire culture have been socializing his emotions since birth. To convey the power of this socialization, consider the "Baby X" studies (Stern and Karraker 1989) that described how the same infant, dressed in yellow, was presented first as a baby boy to one group of research participants and then as a baby girl to another group. The participants were asked to describe the baby. Group responses followed stereotypical lines: The baby "girl" elicited descriptors like "sweet," "pretty," and "delicate," while the baby "boy" was given descriptors like "strong" and "determined." Studies like this demonstrate the power of gender roles and stereotypes to name, and to shape, how determined or delicate any of us might become.

Cultural Messages to Boys:
Mask Your Emotions

Socializing messages are everywhere. Wherever they go boys are sent messages about their expected behavior. And what's expected lies in the eyes of the beholder. How many people think it's normal ... okay ... for a boy to be scared? Sad? Nervous? By comparison, how many people think it is okay for a boy to be angry? Tough? Confident? Through the socialization process, mainstream culture teaches boys to be tough when they feel tender, to be stoic when they need to cry, to be aggressive rather than diplomatic, and to mask their emotions rather than express them. In early childhood boys learn to reject any semblance of stereotypic "femininity," particularly emotional expressiveness. Not surprisingly, these cultural norms contribute to the absence of stereotypical feminine traits, such as nurturing and emotional expressiveness.

Boys' Silence Can Be Heard

The magnitude of how culture strips boys of their emotions got my attention in a surprising way. I stumbled upon it when I was looking for something else during my dissertation research (Polce-Lynch 1996). Originally interested in whether girls' self-esteem drops across adolescence (my sample indicated that it does not), I became interested in boys' experiences because my results showed a dramatic decrease in boys' ability to express emotions (positive or negative) from late childhood to late adolescence. The reverse situation was found for girls. That is, both sexes had similar levels of emotional expressiveness in late childhood, but by the middle and end of adolescence, girls reported better ability in expressing their emotions than boys. (See chapter 4 for more information on this research.)

It should come as no surprise then, that many adolescent boys become silent when asked a question like, "How did you feel when your girlfriend broke up with you?" Or that they may just shrug their shoulders when asked, "How do you feel when your parents get drunk and fight every weekend?" Many people don't recognize this emotional silence as a problem for boys. It is so familiar that it appears to be normal ... it's the way it's supposed to be. After all, silencing boys' access to their own emotions has allowed great wars to be fought and distant lands to be conquered.

How Masculine Stereotypes Affect Boys' Lives

There are many positive aspects of masculinity. Yet the perpetuation of masculine *stereotypes* can play a powerful role in restricting boys' emotional expression. Masculine stereotypes are rigid beliefs and attitudes considered appropriate for boys and men, constructed from that culture's definition of masculinity. The Pack Rules are rigid and narrow manifestations of these mandates. You don't have to look very hard to see how boys learn the Rule about emotional expressiveness from masculine stereotypes found in real life and in popular culture.

Indeed, it's rare to see boys or men who challenge these stereotypes either in real life or in popular culture. Yet once in a while, a stereotype "buster" comes along. Although the movie *Jerry McGuire* upheld traditional feminine stereotypes, Cuba Gooding, Jr.'s character challenged traditional masculine stereotypes. A professional football player who plays with his heart? An athlete, who cries when interviewed on television, screaming, "I love my wife!" And then to top it off, in real life, Cuba Gooding, Jr. does the same thing when he accepted his Academy Award. He cried, he thanked his God, and said that he loves his wife. (He broke the Pack Rules and got an award for it. We need more male role models like this.)

Another stereotype buster I learned about was a six-year-old boy whose parents decided to nurture, rather than toughen up, their "sensitive" son. Interviewed on the *Oprah Winfrey Show* (April 5, 2001), this boy described how upset he was that people in Rwanda didn't have clean water, and that he did. So, he worked extra chores for four months to save seventy dollars to buy a well for one village. As it later turned out, he eventually garnered an outpouring of support and, to date, he has helped raise money to dig fifty wells in Rwanda. Had his parents followed the Pack Rules or observed other narrow masculine stereotypes to raise their son, this could never have happened.

Context and Situation Matter

It's important to state that discussions about boys' emotions and gender stereotypes must be context-specific. For example, Cuba Gooding received lots of kudos, perhaps even additional movie deals, for breaking away from the Pack in the entertainment venue. And one particular six-year-old boy wound up on Oprah's show. But many boys who express themselves emotionally in day-to-day life get a double whammy: they are rejected for breaking the Pack Rules, and they don't get the parental or societal support they need. For emotional expressiveness to be helpful to boys, those who listen to them must validate and accept boys' messages. This may sound like common sense, but if you're a boy in this culture, it's a very unlikely occurrence.

Shame Masks Boys' Emotions

Consider this situation: James comes face-to-face with the dreaded school bully who is twice his size. The bully makes strangling gestures aiming at James' neck. They're alone in the locker room. James is terrified and outruns the bully, making it safely to science class. James tells a classmate, Haim, what just happened. He describes how scared he was and how fast he ran to get away. If Haim says, "I'd be scared, too. I'm glad you got away," such a response would affect James positively. He'd feel reassured and he'd be more likely to talk about the emotional experience of fear with someone he trusts in the future.

But if Haim says to James, "You wuss. I'd have stayed and fought that @#*%! Now he knows you're *scared*," then James learns: (1) It's not okay to disclose fear; (2) Being scared and running away isn't manly; (3) It's better to wear a mask and pretend the whole thing never happened; (4) Next time, just stay and get hurt. Shame can be very powerful indeed in silencing boys' emotions.

Less traumatic but still telling is this brief incident in a fifth-grade math class. Will's fingers are on the edge of his desk. The student sitting in front of Will accidentally pinches Will's fingers by pushing the chair back against Will's desk, and his fingers. Will's eyes quickly fill with tears *because it hurts*. Immediately, the first words from the boys sitting nearby are, "Oh, man . . . don't cry . . . don't be a *girl*." So Will doesn't cry. He hides his vulnerability under the watchful eye of the Pack. He is ashamed of his feelings. In that instant, Will and everyone who watches, gets the connection: *If a boy shows how he really feels, he isn't masculine.* When boys get hurt, *it's not okay to feel hurt or to cry.* To be sure, many people (including girls) don't like to cry in public. But boys are specifically instructed not to cry in public and they are shamed if they do.

The Socialization of Boys' Sexuality

Sexuality is a powerful force that catapults boys into manhood. In the United States, boys' sexuality appears to be largely mediated by a sexually saturated culture. If you think about it, the familiar "boys will be boys" axiom about boys' sexual activity is extremely rigid and unfair. It gives boys the permission to have sex, but not to have the experience of intimacy or emotional responses. The well-known system of "scoring" used by boys who've had sex to describe their sexual "conquests" is but one example of the rigidity surrounding boys' sexuality. Sex can't be about intimacy, it has to be about winning. This kind of sexual socialization encourages boys to equate and limit their sexuality to being a "stud."

Indeed, boys are denied many different emotions and behaviors in the service of achieving a narrow definition of masculinity. Although I believe that this process often denies boys the opportunity to become whole human beings, Christina Hoff Sommers (2000) and others may disagree, arguing that boys need to be socialized differently than girls, particularly when it comes to their emotions and sexuality. This essentialist (biological) perspective often reinforces traditional masculine roles and behaviors.

Biological views of male sexuality also appear to affect boys' sexual feelings and actions. I can't count the number of times I've heard of boys' (or men's) "uncontrollable" male sexual desire as being responsible for criminal male sexual behavior, like date rape. Such thinking makes sense if you consider how boys' sexuality usually starts and continues through the complicated emotional terrain of sexual intimacy without any kind of map to guide them—other than the rules of the Pack. Boys (girls, too) clearly need more mentoring to develop healthy sexuality.

The Beginning of Boys' Sexual Socialization

Many examples abound regarding how innocently boys and girls are inducted into their sexuality. I recall a friend describing how her eight-year-old daughter, Sabrina, was publicly introduced to her sexuality (à la the Pack Rules). It happened at a swim meet. As Sabrina walked past two boys she had known since preschool, she heard their stage whispers, "She's sexy!" Sabrina didn't say anything to them. (What can a young girl say? "No I'm not!" or "What do you mean?") Indeed, Sabrina later told her mother that she had felt uncomfortable when the boys said this. And that she didn't know what "sexy" meant. One has to wonder if even the boys *really* knew. (The Pack Rules don't provide definitions, just rules.)

These boys had known Sabrina as smart, a good swimmer, and a stellar soccer player. But sitting there on the bench together, the only aspect of her that *they felt free* to comment upon was her sexiness. What is most ironic about this, and serves to emphasize the Pack Rule's grip on boys, is that Sabrina was prepubescent! She had not even a *hint* of secondary sex characteristics. Yet the boys felt limited in what they could say about her. They couldn't say, "She's really smart".... or a "fast swimmer" ... or a "great soccer player." Instead they remained loyal to the Pack Rule: *Girls are sexy*. Without other rules, boys follow these.

How Boys' Sexual Socialization Progresses

Boys' sexual socialization often leads to "hypersexuality," a term that refers to excessive sexuality as expressed in multiple sex partners and sexual dominance (i.e., keeping score of "sexual conquests") or less extreme but still harmful behaviors, such as sexual harassment. Although sexual harassment is often aimed at girls and women, boys also experience sexual harassment from other boys.

Students in my psychology of gender classes invariably describe how they have witnessed *a lot* of guy-to-guy sexual harassment in their lives. This harassment takes the form of sexual put-downs, those hurtful, emasculating words many of us have heard. Often these words insult a boy for not being "man enough" in terms of sexual activity or physical size. Almost in a circular way then, hypersexuality becomes self-perpetuating as boys continually raise the bar for each other via guy-to-guy harassment, dictating just how sexually active or dominant they must be.

Another aspect of hypersexuality manifests itself in the way that boys receive technical knowledge about sexual behavior, often before they are ready and without the context of an intimate relationship. This can take the form of pornography or other sexually explicit material aimed at adults. Different theories exist to explain men's sexual activity (including evolutionary theory, which emphasizes the biology and propagation of the species), but I argue that when a young boy discovers a stack of *Playboy* magazines in the closet, he wasn't biologically primed or prepared to do so.

In therapy sessions, I have listened to far too many men reflect back upon this very experience with much regret because they *didn't talk with anyone* about their mixed feelings of shock, excitement, and confusion. They kept it all inside and followed the Pack Rules instead. Some of these men later became secretly addicted to pornography as a result of the way they crashed into premature sexual knowledge. This is an example not only of hypersexuality (in the form of pornography), but of its potentially harmful effects upon boys' and men's own sexuality.

Without intervention or education, boys are sent into adulthood with the Pack Rules' version of sexuality. When you look at contemporary culture, it makes sense that boys would identify themselves with hypersexuality. *Playboy* magazines have been augmented by twenty-four-hour, seven-day-a-week Internet access to pornography. But boys receive these sexual mandates without even needing to sneak online. Watch almost any sitcom, TV commercial, music video, or movie. Hypersexuality pervades popular culture and is everywhere boys look.

Another interesting linchpin of boys' hypersexuality involves homophobia, or fear of being gay. This not only appears to put tremendous pressure upon boys to prove their manhood via heterosexual activity, it also limits the degree of closeness boys are permitted to have in relationships with other boys. I watched two college women walk across campus on a spring day, arm in arm. One woman seemed to be distressed and the other appeared to be comforting her. It looked so natural and supportive. I thought how unlikely it would be to see two college men doing the same thing: for fear of breaking the Pack Rules and being labeled gay. For me, being gay is another expression of being human. But for most heterosexual boys, it represents a terrifying taboo.

Given the cultural and social pressures exerted on boys to prove they're not gay, it makes sense that they would use heterosexual activity to convey their "straightness" to others. One can't help but wonder how much safer everyone else would feel if boys didn't feel so pressured to follow the Pack Rules. (Heterosexual dating would probably be much less stressful for parents.) Unfortunately, by now, you've undoubtedly heard true accounts of boys who have raped girls, believing that the rape was okay because "she really wanted it." How can these crimes be understood without considering boys' sexual socialization—their own victimization—by the Pack Rules?

Sometimes we find answers in real life, sometimes in stories. I found one answer in Wally Lamb's (1998) best-selling novel, *I Know This Much Is True*. At one point, the main character, Dominic, reflects on his boyhood experience of sexuality. He observes how sexual intimacy "tethers" boys to someone else, if only for a few moments. At first glance, his testament seems to say more about boys' emotional isolation than their sexuality, yet I think the two are frequently inseparable for boys.

One of the goals of this section is to provide an emotional anatomy of how boys' sexual feelings are socialized. An understanding of what happens when boys' expressions of emotions are straitjacketed within their families and the larger culture will hopefully lead to boys receiving more sexual guidance from parents and other adults.

Lucas

One way to explore boys' sexual socialization is by acquainting yourself with case studies. Consider the following case. Lucas was an "all American boy." His parents, Gerri and Michael, were two people who could be your friends, your neighbors . . . you, yourself. Lucas was loved and well treated by his parents from the moment he was born. His grandparents loved him, too. So, if Lucas had such a loving family in his background, you might be wondering, what's his problem? As it turns out, even very loving families can raise sons who get lost in our hypersexualized culture . . . and the Pack Rules.

At the age of eighteen, while at a party, Lucas put the drug rohypnol (known as "ruffi") into Janie's drink. He had met Janie, also age eighteen, through a mutual friend. He had asked her out a couple of times, but she'd always turned him down. He wasn't sure why. He was confused, because she always seemed very friendly. Lucas figured that Janie was playing some kind of hard-to-get game. After all, if you have cable television, and watch enough MTV, VH1, and BET, the girls and women in the music videos all want to have sex ... all the time. (And when they say "no," they really mean "yes," according to the story lines of the videos). So when Lucas heard that Janie was coming to the party, he decided to "help things along" by "slipping a ruffi" into her drink so he could "have sex" with her. His friends, whom he had known since kindergarten, all agreed it would be a good way to have sex with Janie.

Date Rape

That was the problem. Lucas really believed that he would just be "having sex" with Janie. It never occurred to him that he would be raping her. Neither did the thought that putting this drug into her body without her knowledge or consent was a crime. Lucas was focused on having sex and he never thought about Janie's feelings at all. In fact, he didn't even think of Janie as a person. After all, Lucas' friends had sex regularly and none of them ever talked about their relationships with the young women. All they talked about was the sex. Since Lucas had "had sex" only twice, he felt as if he didn't fit in with the guys (the Pack). Like he wasn't a real guy. And no one told Lucas otherwise.

Some of you might be thinking that Lucas was just being like the other boys, trying to score (this is true). After all, they were at a party and Janie was drinking and flirting (this is true). So, he didn't really "rape" her (this is *not* true.) By definition, many state laws stipulate that when a person is mentally incapacitated (being under the influence of drugs or alcohol counts as being incapacitated), then one cannot give consent to sexual intercourse. Therefore, any sexual intercourse that takes place is rape, i.e., a crime.

Incidents of date rape happen more often than anyone knows. The statistics are unreliable because young women are afraid to report sexual assaults. Furthermore, when the drug rohypnol is involved, victims usually cannot remember the details of the sexual assault because this drug totally erases memory. Apparently, rohypnol doesn't cause victims to pass out. Rather, it short-circuits the brain's memory. So, if a woman is drinking alcohol at a party, she may not even notice when the drug kicks in. She may not look any different to her friends or to the guy who plans to "have sex" with her.

Boys' Cultural Victimization

Perhaps controversially, I don't think that girls and women are the only victims. I see boys and men as victims, too. Although it is clear that Lucas didn't feel any empathy for Janie, much less any sympathy, it's important to put his lack of feeling into the larger cultural context.

Lucas was never taught to view girls and women as people rather than sex objects. He's been tricked in the sense that he's been cut off from the possibility of fully experiencing his own sexuality. Think about it. If a boy believes that intercourse with an incapacitated girl is healthy or satisfying sex, then that boy develops not only a distorted view of his sexual partner, but also of himself, which can lead to sexual and intimacy problems later on.

Boys' sexual socialization needs our serious attention in our culture. This is clearly demonstrated by the fact that, initially, Lucas believed that what he did was not wrong. Or, in his words, "Guys have sex with girls all the time when the girl doesn't really want to. That's the way it is." Tragically, this mind-set teaches that the person with whom one has sex is a mere object of gratification rather than a person with feelings and needs of her own. The boys and men who buy into this mind-set not only do terrible damage to the girls and women in their lives, they also do terrible damage to themselves.

As you know, Lucas' situation is not an isolated one. The type of rape he performed takes place in high schools and on college campuses everywhere. In 1993, there were eight arrests and more than seventeen felony counts of rape and unlawful intercourse in Lakewood, California, just for this specific crime (Smolowe 1993). Many "popular" high school boys were members of the Spur Posse, a pack of boys who kept score on all the girls they had "had sex" with, whether the girls had wanted to or not. When seven of the girls who had been raped decided to press charges, the father of one of the defendants said, "*Nothing my boy did was anything any red-blooded American boy wouldn't do at this age.*" (Sometimes, the Pack still rules adult men's lives.)

Boys' Sexual Dilemma in Context

Where did this father go wrong? Where did Lucas' parents go wrong? What direct and indirect role does culture play? The answers to such questions are complicated. Parents, too, are socialized by the same culture that splashes flamboyant casual sex across TV as if it were the only activity worth doing. In addition, parents are secretly sworn to obey the Pack Rules out of fear (see chapter 1). These two factors are probably the main causes of hypersexuality becoming so common in young boys. Then, add to this the well-known fact that individuals change their behaviors when they are in a group. A boy might not commit the same crime alone that he would commit as part of a group. When boys have internalized the Pack rules in their minds, that combined with youthful hormonal "rushes" can produce tragically painful outcomes such as date rape.

Untangling the causes that led to the rape and finding the reason for Lucas' lack of empathy for Janie requires us to look hard at several different social and individual factors. To be sure, his parents, Gerri and Michael, raised him the way many boys are raised in the United States today: Little League, drum lessons, family vacations, lots of TV and video games, and so forth. But not all boys rape. However, many boys do have a distorted view of sexual behavior and what constitutes consent.

Another way to identify what went wrong might be to consider what was missing in Lucas' life. Two things stand out. One is Lucas' statement about needing to have sex . . . "because all the other guys were." I wonder if the outcome would have been different if Lucas had been able to talk with someone about his sexual feelings. In other words, what if Lucas had been able to talk to his dad (or another adult male) about the pressure he was feeling to be sexually active? And what if his dad had listened and been able to offer good advice? Perhaps Lucas would have learned other ways to handle his sexual feelings in spite of the Pack Rules.

The other fact that stands out is how Lucas viewed girls. Janie simply wasn't a person to him. She was a sex object. What if his parents had been able to talk to him about how girls like to get to know the boys they date before having sex? What if they had helped Lucas to deconstruct (i.e., to question the reality or validity of) the countless cultural messages in the media about girls as sex objects? Lucas might have had a better chance at seeing Janie as a whole person with feelings of her own.

The sexual dilemma for boys is this: How can they be true to their real feelings and thoughts without becoming sexually dominant, and still be seen as a "real" boy or man, by their peers? When you consider how boys typically are socialized in our culture, it isn't hard to see why the restrictions on most forms of emotional expression and the culturally implicit permission to be sexual aggressive interact to produce criminal sexual behaviors at worst and insensitive harassment at best. Unless boys are taught differently, why would they think, feel, or behave differently?

Boys' and Girls' Psychological Needs

I believe that many of boys' sexual and social dilemmas stem from the incorrect assumption that boys' psychological needs are different from girls'. In fact, the opposite is true: boys' and girls' psychological needs are similar. It is true, of course, that boys and girls don't have the exact same hormones, muscle mass, or bone structure. They often don't receive the same educational and athletic opportunities. But I think they do have the same *basic psychological needs.*

These needs include, but are not limited to: the need for safety; the need to think and feel for themselves; the need to express these thoughts and feelings when necessary; the need to love and be loved; the need to master control of anger; the need to be proud of who they are; the need to be responsible for their own actions; the need to trust and be trusted; the need to ... the list could go on and on. Boys' and mens' psychological needs are simply the same human needs that girls and women have.

Boys also have the same emotions as girls. How could they not? But for centuries now, we've been raising and treating boys as if they didn't. Another way to think about this is to ask yourself this question, "If boys don't cry (or are not allowed to be who they are), what can they do? I remember once, back in 1970, I baby-sat for a six-year- old boy named Richard, who loved necklaces. Of course, this didn't go over very well with his father (who had only the best of intentions, and didn't want his son to be rejected by the other kids). One day, when I wore a beaded necklace, Richard said something I never forgot. At the wise age of six, he touched my necklace and said, "It must be nice to be able to like what you want to like." I was only twelve myself back then, but I understood what he meant. I understand even more now that I have "gender glasses" that allow me to see how gender stereotypes and roles can restrict us all. Richard needed to have his thoughts and feelings mirrored back to him. He needed someone to see into him and reflect back *who he really was.*

Mirroring Boys' Real Selves

Mirroring refers to the process of reflecting a person's thoughts, feelings, and behaviors back to that person. Mirroring helps boys see who they really are. As you can imagine, it's a very important form of socialization. The term originates from the attachment research of Mary Ainsworth (1973; 1978) and John Bowlby (1969). In everyday life, mirroring is what parents do with their infants. "Oh, how happy you are," mirrors the parent as the baby drools, grinning from ear to ear. "Yes, I see you're angry now, but it's not okay to hit me," or "Tommy was mean to you; I bet your feelings were hurt," are examples of mirroring with older children. There are endless opportunities for children to have their inner, emotional worlds mirrored back to them. Or not.

Why Mirroring Is So Important

If children's inner worlds aren't accurately mirrored or reflected back to them, it's more difficult for them to think their own thoughts and to feel their own emotions. Their true identities can become distorted. Especially when adults constantly tell them to think or feel a different way than they are actually thinking or feeling.

In its simplest form, mirroring is a matter of teaching boys about themselves. It helps them to form their identities. (Remember, identity is one of the major reasons that emotions matter.) In the complexity of psychological life, mirroring is also a building block of empathy. Boys must be able to identify their own thoughts and feelings before they can empathize with others. It all begins by looking into the "mirror" of their parents or caregivers. Between the ages two to four is an especially important time to teach boys about their feelings and the feelings of others. Unfortunately, this is also the age when little boys are usually taught to "be a big boy" (i.e., to ignore their feelings of fear and pain). When you think about it, this is almost like military training without the consent of those being militarized.

Many boys' inner psychological needs are never mirrored back to them. Take Lucas for example. He was love, fed, clothed, and played in the Little League. But some of his psychological needs were not mirrored. (If they had been, he would have had more empathy for Janie.) The worst part is what boys do with their feelings when they're not accurately mirrored: *Boys learn to make their feelings "disappear." But they don't really disappear, they come out sideways as unhealthy behaviors.*

Mirroring includes reflecting thoughts and behaviors, as well as emotions. When Richard said it must be nice to be able to "like what you like," a mirroring comment that would have reflected his inner world back to him could have been, "You really notice beautiful things . . . like necklaces." A mirroring comment about his feelings could have been, "You really feel sad that you can't enjoy the things you like . . ." A mirroring statement about his behavior could have been, "You really want to have beautiful things." Instead, what Richard got from his dad was, "Don't be silly . . . necklaces are for girls . . . you can't like those!"

Simply put, the act of mirroring means that a person has really been seen and heard. This simple act appears to be an emotional cornerstone for the development of healthy psychological functioning, identity development, and ability to connect to others.

Boys' Temperaments

As explained in chapter 1, the environment affects children and children affect their environments, and this transactional process continues throughout life span development. Temperament is discussed throughout this book because of the interactive role it plays in development in general, and emotional development in particular.

Temperament can be considered the tendency or pull toward a certain way of feeling or behaving; it shapes much of our personality. Some boys are naturally more outgoing than others ("extroverted") and some are quieter and more withdrawn ("introverted"). Related personality traits include being agreeable, open to experiences, emotional/sensitive, and worrisome. There are other personality characteristics, but these are referred to as the "big five" by personality theorists.

Why Temperament Is So Important and What to Do with It

It's important for parents and other adults to know about different temperaments, because boys' temperaments elicit different responses from the adults around them. That is, different temperaments will elicit different mirroring behaviors and socialization practices. For example, some boys find it very, very easy to cry. Parents of these boys will tend to react differently than parents of boys who are silent and stoical when they're hurt. The same is true for timid boys. The seven-year-old who wants to ski down the mountain after his first day of lessons will receive different responses from his parents than the same age boy who wants to stay tucked, "pizza wedged," between his dad's legs going down the bunny slopes. How either boy's feelings are mirrored back to him is the real issue.

Some boys find it very easy to tell their feelings to people while other boys act as if they're having a tooth pulled when they have to talk about their feelings. It makes sense that adults' reactions vary according to the ease with which boys identify and express emotions. But since biology is *not* destiny, no matter what a boy's temperament is, he can learn to "stretch," so that he can feel and expresses his emotions in healthy ways when needed.

Boys' temperaments are involved with mirroring and the Pack Rules. How? If a boy has a temperament that doesn't readily lend itself to emotional expression, it becomes too easy for his parents and other adults to conclude that he doesn't *have* feelings, or that his feelings aren't important. In contrast, a boy who is capable of intense emotional expression may elicit the "ignore it to toughen him up" response from his parents and other adults.

Regardless of boys' individual temperaments, it's a given that because boys are human, they have feelings; these feelings need to be both honored and mirrored. The challenge, then, becomes finding ways to honor a boy's temperament, respect his feelings, and figure out how he can learn to express them in healthy ways . . . all in the face of the Pack Rules.

Social Forces That Shape Boys' Emotions

Relationships and social situations are important elements in shaping boys' emotional development. And the cost of stepping outside of narrow masculine roles (i.e., the Pack Rules) in relationships and social situations also appears to be an important element in shaping boys' development. Expressing emotions is a central part of any relationship, whether we are talking about relationships with other boys, girls, parents, siblings, teammates, teachers, co-workers . . . anyone at all. This should be self-evident. Yet the importance of expressing emotions often gets buried under the weight of other issues, especially for boys. For example, the boy who has trouble "getting along with others" is often considered as just having behavioral problems. People rarely stop to wonder if he may be feeling upset about something at home or school.

By the same token, in a more positive way, the popular boy who relates well to adults and peers is considered just to be a "nice boy." He's rarely thought of as emotionally healthy or as someone who is able to identify and regulate his feelings well in social situations. This boy obviously identifies and regulates his emotions better than the other. Yet the emotional aspect of his social development is totally eclipsed.

Social-Emotional Experiences

Social cues, or feedback, from others either can help boys learn healthy emotional expression or help them hide their feelings. Based on these cues, boys develop social skills, or clusters of behaviors that help us all to know what to do or say, and what not to do or say, in certain social situations. Boys are always receiving specific social cues about their behaviors. But what's often missing is information about the importance of expressing emotions in social interactions.

So it's not surprising that some boys' social-emotional skills may be lacking. For example, a whining boy receives many negative social cues about his emotions: he is ignored, socially isolated, called names, and/or told to stop whining. But until he (or his parents) learns what's underneath the whining (fear, sadness, anger?), he probably won't stop. Or, he will stop, without having his emotional need addressed. Teaching a whining boy how to express his feelings directly so they don't "bleed out" everywhere actually is easy to do and has an effective outcome. It requires an intervention that shows him how to blend his thinking together with his emotions to be more assertive about his needs. Teaching this social-emotional skill requires support from a parent, teacher, or counselor.

Often, when boys' strong feelings aren't expressed directly or aren't heard, they come out sideways in behaviors like whining. "Sideways emotions" (see chapter 4) usually result in behaviors that don't endear boys to anyone. They also don't help boys to get their emotional needs met. Whining is one type of sideways emotion, but there are others: aggression, bragging, and bullying, to name a few. All of these behaviors can often be traced back to an underlying emotion. Furthermore, all of these behaviors can shape the social relationships that in turn shape boys' emotional development.

Aggression. This is a sideways emotion that causes social problems for boys in school and on the playing field. The ten-year-old who is frustrated by a bad play comes back to the bench and kicks over all the water bottles. His anger (fear?) is being expressed sideways. Anger control is a social skill that can be taught. This boy needs to learn how to regulate his emotions better. If his teammates reject him in response to his outbursts, such feedback can help him learn to control his behavior and emotions, if he has an adult "coaching" him. Another outcome could be that if everyone simply ignores his outbursts and no one teaches him what else to do, he won't learn how to control his anger.

Bragging. The boy who constantly brags about his baseball or basketball triumphs is also likely to receive negative feedback from his teammates or peers. If he's paying attention or if an adult explains it to him, he'll "get it" and stop. This requires the social-emotional skills of understanding how the other boys are feeling and how he is feeling within himself. Every interpersonal interaction is charged with some kind of emotional energy. These energies need to be recognized and understood as the powerful forces they are. That's another major reason why boys need to be coached about what to do with their emotions other than ignoring them.

Bullying. A common explanation for a bully's behavior is that it is an expression of the need for attention, power, or revenge, or that it reflects feelings of inferiority. I think that the boy who bullies is really no different than anyone else. He wants to feel better. But he goes about meeting and expressing this emotional need in ways that hurt others. Many schools across the country have developed bully prevention programs (Olweus, Limber, and Mihalic 1999), in part due to recent school tragedies that have been associated with bullying. Although school intervention efforts are important, we won't begin to see real changes until parents and adults can respond directly to boys' needs and emotions (rather than to "sideways" expressions such as bullying). Boys must first be supported in expressing their feelings and needs so we can respond.

It is also very important to recognize the effects of bullying behavior. Victims of bullying must also be able to express their feelings to others so these experiences don't fester or become internalized (i.e., "Maybe I really *am* a loser"). One of the inherent reasons that bullying "works" is that the younger we are, the more likely it is that we will believe what others say to us about ourselves. Although talking about a negative experience like being bullied is common sense, for boys it involves breaking the Pack Rules (*If you feel uncomfortable, mask your real feelings*). The intervention for bully victims is the same as it is for bullies: Boys must be able to express their feelings and needs directly to parents and other trustworthy adults.

Athletics and Competition

Team and/or competitive sports relationships are a huge part of boys' socialization process. Whether boys play sports or not, it still affects them, because identification with an athlete or a team is one of the Pack Rules. Boys who play sports and those who do not are all being measured by the same yardstick. Some measure up and some do not—enter the *Win at all costs* Pack Rule.

I think that the phrase "win or lose" needs to become "win *and* lose." Competition can help develop character but it can also have a dark side. Part of the darkness is the "win/lose" dichotomy. When sports and athleticism are solely wrapped up in competition with an opponent, then the only outcome can be a winner or a loser. If you think about this, it's an untenable place to live: to be on top *or* on the bottom. Such "either/or" thinking doesn't leave room for being like everyone else. I think that both winners and losers actually are often dehumanized. One for being more than human (superhero) and one for being less than human.

If the essence of one's identity is tied up with winning, it will require formidable psychological defenses, perhaps constant aggression and hypervigilance, to defend against the fear of losing. This constant focus on winning takes its toll on emotional development. Winning at all costs, all the time, certainly doesn't leave much room for empathy.

Fortunately, the experience of competition is also a positive one. Team sports are good exercise for many emotions: frustration, anger, joy, pride, embarrassment, determination, and so forth. When playing sports, there are endless opportunities for emotional expression and emotional regulation. Anyone who has ever played tennis, golf, or basketball is aware that these opportunities come repeatedly throughout a game or match. (A friend once described golf as a game that makes you want to throw yourself in front of a train after a bad swing or jump for joy after a good one.) Indeed, when boys use competition to build an identity based on hard work, perseverance, and always doing one's best—regardless of the outcome—then competition via sports can be wonderful exercise for healthy emotional development.

Friendship

The ability to be intimate is at the core of most deep friendships and long-term relationships. Intimacy involves many different experiences and skills. One is the ability to trust. Another is the ability to empathize with one's self and others. Yet many boys are socialized to build their friendships on doing activities together (Maccoby 1990). This doesn't necessarily lend itself to the more "interior" aspects of a friendship, such as intimate talking and listening. Indeed, most boys build friendships upon sports, video games, more sports and more video games. I remember watching two seven-year-old girls watching a video. They were slumped together on a couch, one resting her head on the other's shoulder. How unusual this would be for boys of that age. The social and biological reasons for these differences continue to be debated. Here, I just want to suggest that like girls, boys also need to be able to build friendships based on closeness, trust, and empathy. Why wouldn't they?

When boys have a friend they can trust and talk to, this friendship serves as a mental health buffer. It provides a neutral space in which they can relax when other events in their lives may be causing emotional difficulties. When I see children and teens in my practice, invariably the ones having the toughest time are those who don't have close friends. Yet, finding a friend is not an easy task and keeping the relationship going takes a lot of time, attention, and social-emotional skills.

Perhaps what's most relevant to boys' expressing their emotions is that boys need to have people to whom they can "tell all." When boys don't know to whom they can talk about their inner emotions or "important stuff," several things can happen. One result can be that the boys will keep their emotions locked up inside, and these emotions will come out sideways through negative behaviors (whining, bullying, etc.) or, possibly, through physical health symptoms.

Another possible result is that the boys may not discriminate properly about with whom it is safe to talk. They may pick someone who cannot be trusted to respect their inner selves. The consequence of choosing someone who cannot be trusted can be devastating. Especially to a boy who breaks the Pack Rules in order to talk to someone. A bad experience after sharing vulnerability can make the Pack Rules more attractive.

So, boys need to practice the basic skills of friendship. Unless they have practice with talking intimately to someone whom they can trust, they either will spill out to unsafe people or learn to silence their emotions. If boys have "activities only" friendships that adhere strictly to the Pack Rules, this is not the same thing as an intimate friendship. It almost seems as if boys need to be coached into how to make and keep a "best friend." The experience of having a best friend in childhood is essentially skills practice for relationships later in life: talking, listening, attaching, supporting, confronting, forgiving . . . and all the emotions associated with these, ranging from fear to love.

Out-Role Behaviors

Any discussion of boys' socialization practices and their relationships must consider "out-role" behavior. This refers to any behavior that differs from traditionally prescribed gender roles. Out-role behaviors for boys are those actions that are not considered stereotypically masculine, behaviors that break the Pack Rules.

The punishment for boys who step outside of masculine stereotypes and roles occurs far too early in life, is far too harsh, and lasts far too long for boys (Lynch and Kilmartin 1999). The same is not true for girls. A high school girl can participate in athletics like softball and track and receive less out-role punishment than the high school boy who studies ballet and takes jazz classes, or the boy who loves poetry.

The wimp/sissy factor and fear of being called a girl are anathema to boys' masculine identity development. I think that fear of punishment for out-role behavior probably does the most damage to boys' abilities to express their emotions. At some point in their lives, everyone gets rejected and made fun of for being different from the norm. But the shame and punishment boys receive for out-role behavior probably contributes significantly to how and why boys' emotions "disappear." They rob themselves of their own emotions for fear of being punished.

Conclusion

Emotions are often perceived as just the negative feelings of anger, sadness, and fear. In our culture, "Don't get so emotional" is a pejorative statement. This tells us that the positive emotions of joy and pride often aren't valued much either. If you're a boy, having and expressing positive or negative emotions often continues to be a stigma—a mark of shame. Nevertheless, emotions are just part of being human. And boys are people, too. The ability to feel happiness and sadness, pride and fear, is about being fully human. I believe that permission to have and to express emotions is everyone's birthright, including boys.

As you think about boys' socialization and the punishment they receive for stepping outside of narrowly defined masculine roles, such as the Pack Rules, it's important to constantly observe what's missing in the process of socializing boys. Then, provide it. If boys don't learn how to be fully human in their homes, schools, or neighborhoods, where will they learn?

Having pointed out the negative effects of the Pack Rules, I think it's important to clarify a few points. I'm not saying that boys shouldn't enjoy their pack of friends or that at times some of the Pack Rules don't come in handy. Some life experiences require a mask, a "win at all costs" attitude, and extreme toughness. I am suggesting, though, that if the Pack Rules are the *only* rules, then boys' emotional development will likely suffer. At the very least, boys need some alternatives to these rules.

CHAPTER
3

Developing Boys and Their Emotions

Boys' emotions become endangered somewhere between birth and adolescence: Our goal is to prevent these emotions from becoming extinct.

Jimmy was the kind of boy everyone liked. Even though reading was hard for him in elementary school, he succeeded on the soccer field, and he was naturally funny. You couldn't look at him and not smile. But when Jimmy entered high school, his winning ways quickly vanished. He traded his soccer ball for a skateboard and grew his hair longer than his parents liked. Soon after he got his driver's license, he was often seen careening around corners with **No Fear** stenciled across the front windshield of his new car. The logo on his windshield seemed to fit the image he was projecting. Ironically, though, about the same time Jimmy was driving around town proclaiming his lack of fear, his father was terminally ill.

This chapter discusses boys' emotional development by focusing on real issues like "What do boys feel?" and "How do we help boys to develop in healthy ways?" The No Fear logo that adorned Jimmy's windshield (and many other boys' T-shirts) suggests that boys don't feel fear. Seeing this logo on cars and clothing seems natural on boys, but if girls wore No Fear T-shirts, it wouldn't seem as natural. Why not? One explanation might be that our culture permits girls to feel afraid while denying the same permission to boys. The

No Fear logo fits the culture's "natural" stereotype of masculinity, but it is far from natural in the human sense. As long as a person is alive, on occasion, that person will feel fear.

I believe that the No Fear logo is a symbol of boys' contemporary socialization. Furthermore, it's a psychological oxymoron that summarizes concisely the dilemma of boys' emotional development: boys are not allowed to feel fear, but at the same time, they must feel their fear . . . or any other emotion, if they are to remain psychologically healthy and alive.

The Role Of Temperament In Emotional Development

Temperament, introduced in the previous chapter, can also be described as a style or predisposition toward general patterns of emotional responses and reactions, changes in mood, or sensitivities to particular stimulations (Dworetzky 1996). Like emotions, temperament involves both physiological and psychological components. Most theorists and researchers recognize there is a strong genetic predisposition toward particular temperaments. Some believe that 50 percent of temperament is genetically determined (Carey 1999). Indeed, there is some evidence that some children may even inherit a physiological tendency to experience specific fear states (Robinson, Kagan, Reznick, and Corley 1992).

Types of Temperament

An important function of temperament is the way it regulates emotional development. One example of this involves children's reactivity levels. Children who have what Werner (1993) refers to as an "easy" temperament appear to have less sympathetic nervous system reactivity (raised blood pressure, faster heart rate) to threatening events. They also show fewer behavioral signs of distress. From a scientific perspective, this suggests that this type of temperament blunts or inhibits the limbic system's physiological reaction in some way. From a day-to-day perspective, a boy who has this type of temperament may not experience or show signs of distress when scared the way a "sensitive" boy would. He's also much less likely to become an adult with an anxiety or phobic disorder, especially when compared to a boy with a shy or anxious temperament.

Children's temperament has been studied for several decades. Thomas, Chess, and Birch (1970) are pioneer temperament researchers who examined the stability of temperament over time. Jerome Kagan (1978) is a child psychologist who has researched the "bold-timid" continuum of temperament (Kagan, Reznick, and Gibbons. 1989; Kagan and Snidman 1991). More recently, researchers have written books about children's temperament for lay readers (Carey 1999; Greenspan and Salmon 1996; Neville, Johnson, and Cameron 1997). I do not present information about temperament here so that you can try to change boys' temperaments. Rather, I believe it's important for parents and other adults to be aware of temperamental differences because this awareness can be a useful tool to cope with the different styles that boys use to interact with their world. Ultimately, parents will also want to help boys to understand and cope with their own temperaments.

Results from a pioneering study by Thomas, Chess, and Birch (1970) categorized children into three broad categories (Easy Child, Slow-to-Warm-up Child, and Difficult Child) and rated five temperamental qualities. These included: *rhythmicity* (eating and sleeping patterns), *approach/withdrawal* patterns (ease when separating from parents, trying new activities), *adaptability* (to changes in environment), *intensity of reactions* (to small or big experiences), and *quality of mood* (affect range: sad when something sad happens, happy with happy events).

William Carey (1999) conducted more recent research on temperament, and recognized additional aspects of temperament such as: activity level, distractibility, initial reaction, persistence and attention span, regularity, and sensitivity. Consistent with other estimates, he also concludes that temperament is about 50 percent genetically determined. Although earlier categories for temperament like "easy" and "difficult" may still be used for research, there has been a shift in popular culture to use phrases like "the spirited child" and "the strong-willed child." The phrase "challenging child" has even been categorized into five different types (Greenspan and Salmon 1996). You probably know children who easily fit into these categories.

Researchers and theorists typically consider emotional skills like affect regulation (the ability to control one's emotions) and emotional openness to be aspects of temperament. Indeed, emotions are intimately related to temperament on many levels. A boy's temperament may shape how much or how little he expresses his emotions. And his parents' reactions to his emotional expressiveness will, in turn, shape that emotional expressiveness.

Now, let's see how these theories apply to little Raul who has an "easy" temperament. Not much ever seems to bother him. He didn't fuss much as an infant, his responses to his environment were easygoing throughout his early childhood, his quality of mood was positive, and he adapted well to changes (including going off to overnight camp at age ten without a tear). Raul's parents observed this easygoing nature and concluded that the emotional aspects of his life didn't need much support. This is a common parental response to an easygoing child. He seems okay, so there's no need to bring up the subject of emotions (or "problems" as they're euphemistically called). This attitude is summed up in the popular saying: Why fix something that isn't broken? However, this is precisely where the baby (boy's emotions) are often thrown out with the bathwater.

Linking Emotions to Temperament

When parents assume that nothing ever bothers their son, often they also ignore the boy's negative *and* positive emotions. As a result, he doesn't get much "practice" thinking or talking about his own, or anyone else's emotions. He doesn't learn important emotional intelligence skills such as analyzing and perceiving emotions in himself and others. So, even when a boy has an easy temperament, if his emotions aren't mirrored back to him, he will be less likely to develop the ability to recognize, express, and respond to emotions in healthy ways. This applies to *all* boys regardless of temperament. Boys with difficult (aggressive, impulsive) and slow-to-warm-up (anxious or shy) temperaments are just more likely to get their parents' attention. How parents respond to boys' different temperaments and their emotions depends on factors like the parents' knowledge about temperament and how much they are aware of and/or are influenced by the Pack Rules.

Perhaps what's most interesting about the link between boys' emotions and temperament is that by the end of adolescence most boys' emotional expression looks the same. Extroverted and shy boys alike follow the same display rules. The direct expression of emotions is usually limited to stoicism, aggression, or an occasional friendly slap on the back. Athletic triumphs provide one of the few arenas where boys can freely express joy and affection. This restricted range of emotional expression can be prevented by encouraging boys to talk about their feelings when they are learning to talk, and continuing to encourage them to talk about their feelings when they are adolescents. (See chapter 4.)

As you read through the rest of this chapter, it's important to remember that regardless of boys' different temperamental qualities (attention spans, activity level, sensitivity, moods, etc.), all boys need emotional intelligence skills. The way these emotional skills "look" will vary depending on the boy's age and his temperament. But I think you'll be surprised to see in the next section just how young children are—at birth—when they can feel their emotions.

Developmental Timeline

The following sections describe the development and socialization of boys' emotions in five different age groups. Various emotional skills are presented, but the focus is on the skill of emotional expression because it is an essential part of shaping healthy emotional development in boys for a lifetime. *You're strongly encouraged to read about all age groups for a full perspective on where boys have been, where they are now, and where they're headed.*

Birth to Age Three

The years between birth and age three are so important because so much happens in these few years. There was a time when people, including psychologists and pediatricians, believed that babies didn't feel anything except hunger and arousal. Despite the challenges of measuring emotions in infants (Izard 1982), psychologists have come a long way from thinking that babies and children can't feel emotions. Current developmental researchers conclude that several common emotions develop under the age of three.

Zero-to-Three Emotions
(and Observable Behaviors)

The emotions and related behaviors from age zero-to-three include: *Newborns:* **Anger** (crying writhing); **Fear** (startle response); **Disgust** (facial grimaces or tongue thrusts at bitter tastes); **Happiness** (smiling); **Contentment** (absence of fussing) ✴ *Three Months:* **Joy** (in response to happy expressions in others); **Distress** (in response to sadness or angry expressions in others; may be a precursor to empathy) ✴ *Two and One-Half to Six Months:* **Sadness** (facial expressions): **Surprise** (facial expressions); **Fear** (facial expressions) ✴ *Eight to Ten Months:* **Social Anxiety** (checks with caregivers to see if this emotion is okay; this may be a precursor to emotional regulation); **Fear of strangers** (cries and refuses to talk to or look at new people) ✴ *One to Two Years:* **Elation** (squeals of delight); **Determination** (temper tantrums); **Embarrassment** (eyes turned away, chin tucked in, may blush); **Shame** (eyes turned away, chin tucked in, may blush); **Guilt** (eyes turned away, chin tucked in, may blush); **Pride** (smiling or clapping after an accomplishment); **Rage** (more temper tantrums!) ✴ *Three Years:* **Empathy** (responds and "feels" others' sadness, hurt, joy, etc.); **Emotional regulation** (conceals some feelings based on cultural display rules, e.g., boys may *not* cry when hurt because they are being taught that "big boys don't cry"). (Sources: Dworetzky 1996; Greenspan 1985; Izard 1982; Shaffer 1999).

It appears that babies and toddlers not only *have* feelings, such as the ability to recognize or perceive emotions in others and to regulate their own emotions, they also *understand* other peoples' emotions. This is a central tenet of the "discrete emotions theory" in developmental psychology, which holds that basic emotions and emotional skills are present and functional at, or shortly after, birth. If this is true, then the importance of the way that parents and caregivers respond to boys' emotions really begins *at the very beginning of life.*

How Boys Are Socialized
From Birth to Age Three

Boys under the age of three probably receive more nurturing than at any other time in their lives. This is when they are cuddled, coddled, and mirrored. They're kissed, caressed, and cared for. It's also the time in a boy's life when he seeks this type of affection without feeling fear or shame. It's not surprising that boys are also more likely to *be* affectionate during this time of their development. Think about it. Babies, toddlers, and early preschool boys are frequently observed throwing their arms around parents and other adults, and planting kisses (often sticky) without restraint. Shouting to a mom or dad, "I love you" is not uncommon with younger boys. Neither is admitting to feeling sad or crying spontaneously when upset.

Showing affection and crying are forms of emotional expression. Our culture is more tolerant of boys' emotional expression during this age than it is when boys are older. Or perhaps it's more accurate to say that our culture is more *comfortable* because the fear that "boys are not masculine" when they show their feelings isn't in full force yet. This is not to say that Pack Rules don't influence parents' and other caregivers' reactions to boys at this early age. Indeed the Baby X studies (discussed in previous chapter) showed how the sex of a baby elicits gender stereotyping at *birth.*

Working with Boys' Temperaments
From Birth to Age Three

Even at this young age, different temperamental qualities can be observed. Many of these characteristics influence a boy's emotional expression and, thus, how others respond to him. For example, the baby who is "sensitive" either will elicit comfort from parents and caregivers or the "toughen him up" response. Some adults allow boy infants and toddlers to cry as a way of preparing them for preschool, "real life," or manhood, while others give the baby comfort that provides the necessary sense of safety. Many parents fear that if they pay attention to a boy's sensitivity, he'll be a "sissy" all his life.

Importance of attachment. Ironically, the opposite appears to be true: comforting a sensitive boy validates his feelings; it doesn't reinforce them. This is a difficult concept—and difficult set of behaviors for parents of sensitive boys to embrace. No matter what adults do, many temperamental traits remain essentially the same. So trying to toughen up a sensitive boy will not "cure" him of his sensitivity. The most therapeutic and healthiest response to a sensitive boy of any age is the countercultural response: *Pay attention to his hurt feelings, provide comfort,* and then teach him how to handle his strong feelings.

Indeed, results from longitudinal attachment studies by Ainsworth, Blehar, Waters, and Wall (1978) indicated that when infants' crying is comforted rather than ignored during the first year of life, these same infants cry less—not more—at the end of their first year. They also appear to be more secure, independent, and have a more harmonious relationship with their caregiver. Other studies have reported the same results (Sroufe 1983). This classic research on attachment has helped to shift the earlier belief that allowing infants to cry helped them learn how to comfort themselves. In fact, providing comfort to infants when needed is part of the important mirroring process, while the toughen-up approach appears to foster (among many other outcomes) the disappearance of boys' emotions. And when emotions disappear at this very early age, it takes a lot of work to find them again.

What to do. I chose sensitivity as an initial example of temperament because it is the trait that often causes parents of boys the most concern . . . in the face of the Pack Rules. Sensitivity may underlie the approach-withdrawal behavior of "slow-to-warm-up" and "difficult" boys; while the emotions of the "easygoing" child are easier to miss (at this and every other age) because of the absence of intense behaviors that call attention to feelings. It is easy to see how the temperamental qualities of "difficult" or "slow-to-warm-up" boys are connected to their emotional expression. Intense behaviors like fussing and crying, shyness, aggression, and other oppositional behaviors are the squeaky wheels, while the boy who doesn't show what he's feeling by his behaviors is less likely to elicit his caregiver's attention.

There are two main approaches when considering how to respond to the different temperamental qualities in boys during the zero-to-three stage:

★ **Trust your intuition instead of the Pack Rules.** Most parents would say that when their baby boy, toddler, or preschooler is crying because he's hurt, they want to comfort him (*yes, go* *ahead!*). But when he's tantrumming, they don't want to comfort him (*right, he needs space to cool off, followed by limit setting*).

★ **Accommodate temperamental qualities first,** *then* **work toward** *"stretching"* **in the opposite direction.** This is a tedious process and it takes a lot of time for both parent and child. Some might argue it takes a lifetime. Think of a shy adult whom you know. He may be a successful public speaker because he "stretched" in that direction. That kind of stretching involved a great deal of energy because he has a shy personality base. In developmental terms, he may have had a slow-to-warm-up temperament. As a toddler or preschooler, boys like this initially tend to withdraw when faced with new situations, with a mildly negative mood and emotional reactions. Parents of a boy with this type of temperament can expose him to the situations and people he withdraws from in a gentle way, rather than accommodating his withdrawal with more withdrawal. Similarly, the "difficult" (impulsive or inattentive) child will need to be stretched toward slowing down, being more positive in mood, and less intense in reactions. Stretching boys' temperaments in the opposite direction takes lots of coaching.

How Parents Can Improve Boys' Emotional Development From Birth to Age Three

Mirroring. One of the most important interventions for helping boys' emotions develop properly at this early age is "mirroring." Introduced in chapter 2, mirroring is a type of attunement that refers to the specific behaviors a parent performs to reflect what a child is feeling, thinking, or doing. It can be done with or without words. When a baby is elated and smiles and the parent smiles back with equal elation, this is mirroring. When a child is sad and the caregiver reflects a similarly sad facial expression, this is also mirroring. Saying sentences like, "You're so happy," or "You look so sad," is mirroring with words. Parents naturally use facial expressions to mirror babies. Then, as children grow, this is augmented and eventually replaced by words.

Parents can mirror at the same time they set limits with their child. For example, if a toddler is angry and throws a block, parents can both mirror and set limits by saying, "You can feel mad, but it's not okay to throw things." The next step in teaching anger control is then to tell him what he can do when he's mad: "You can tell me that you're mad with words," or "You can go to your room and cool off—and then come back and tell me with words." Both ways, boys learn to use words rather than physical aggression. But to do this, first they must know the names of those emotions and understand how they feel when they are experiencing them.

Naming emotions. A boy is never too young (or too old) to hear the names of feelings. The earlier this vocabulary is developed, the better. It can be as simple as naming a feeling while a boy is experiencing it (this is mirroring, too). Or in the absence of emotional expression, parents may need to suggest the emotions that their son is feeling. For example, if Roberto watches a favorite Blues Clues puzzle break apart as the dreaded cousin slowly (and intentionally) slides it off the desk, it's normal to feel angry. If Roberto doesn't say or do anything, his parent might say, "Oh, Roberto, I'm so sorry your puzzle was ruined by Meesha . . . I'd be very sad or mad if that happened to me. How do you feel?" Even if Roberto says, "I don't know," you've begun important emotional skill practice by modeling the appropriate emotions and naming them.

Modeling. The modeling of emotions is another form of naming. It involves naming with your behavior as well as with your words. Modeling can (and should) occur at every age for boys, from birth through adolescence. This naming of emotions may be the simplest and most profound way of encouraging boys' emotional development. Why? Because it does two things at once. (1) It helps to develop the emotional competence skill of identifying emotions because it allows boys to observe others doing the same thing. (2) It normalizes emotions for boys. For example, parents can share stories of when they felt a similar way. If Roberto can hear his dad's voice whispering in his mind, "It's okay to feel mad . . . I remember when my cousin smashed my Lego blocks. I was so angry," then Roberto has permission not only to feel, but also to talk about what he feels.

How Adults Can Influence Communities From Birth to Age Three

I think it's possible for families to influence their communities with regard to boys' emotional development during this age. At every age, really. Because many of the norms of masculinity are largely constructed and upheld by men, much of the adult influence in the community must come from men who can model the importance—and acceptance—of boys' emotional development. Emotions and related behaviors don't take place in a vacuum. In fact, emotional expression by boys and men commands a lot of attention and response from home, school or other public forums.

Men's Unique Role. Picture this: a neighborhood meeting with approximately fifteen families gathered to hear a speaker. During the middle of the talk, Mikey goes to the center of the room, directly in front of the speaker. He plops down on the floor and begins to play with some action figures. It looks like a comfortable arrangement for everyone. Then, suddenly, Mikey bursts into tears. Without hesitation, Mikey's father goes to him, picks him up, and starts patting him on the back. He whispers soothing words into Mikey's ear. After a few seconds, Mikey stops crying and asks to be put down. Then he goes back to the same spot and resumes playing. Happily.

What Mikey needed (and got) is known as "refueling" in attachment theory. A toddler, usually between twelve to eighteen months old, suddenly realizes he's alone. He feels terrified. He needs to touch a secure base (parent, caregiver) to get his psychological "supplies." In this case, it was Dad who provided the supplies. Three decades ago in the United States (and still in many other cultures today), mothers were the only parents who provided these psychological supplies.

Public displays of emotional comfort by fathers like Mikey's have helped to change the norm for the father's role in promoting healthy emotional development in boys. Programs that promote a nurturing role for fathers are more likely to encourage tolerance and acceptance of boys' emotions. Indeed, prevention programs (such as Nurturing Fathers, see Resources) and cross-cultural studies have suggested that when fathers are regularly involved with the care of their children, those communities and countries are less violent.

Fathers can provide support for their babies' and toddlers' emotional development. Their influence shapes the way a community responds to boys. And when norms change, individuals notice. If there is a shift toward valuing boys' emotions in the larger community, individuals are more likely to do the same. The main point is that boys' emotions need the same mirroring and facilitative responses that girls' emotions receive during the infancy and toddler years. Individuals and communities can both help to establish that norm.

Ages Four to Seven

Developmentally speaking, these are the years when children are on top of the world. Stanley Greenspan (1993) refers to this stage of children's growth as, "The world is my oyster!" They survived their toddler years unscathed (no small feat), they have newly discovered independence (foraying into preschool and play dates without parents nearby), they have playmates who introduce them to the larger world, and they don't have to worry about acne or designer clothes (yet). Although social status rules do apply at this age, all children generally have an equal shot at being King or Queen of the Playground.

Piaget's (1952) cognitive theory places children of this age in the later stage of pre-operational thinking, also referred to as the intuitive stage. This refers to the way children rely on what they *sense* to be, rather than on logic. For example, if children watch water poured from a tall and narrow glass into a short and wide dish, they believe that there is "less" water in the dish because it *looks like less* water. Also, during this stage of cognitive development, children still have islands of "magical thinking" floating around in their minds . . . little Robert knows scary dreams aren't real, but he shuts the closet door, leaves the hall light on, and squirts go-away-bad-dream spray before going to sleep—*just in case.*

What does this information about cognition have to do with emotional development? First, it's always important to consider cognitive development side by side with emotional development (a concept highlighted throughout this book). All the emotions evident in boys' earlier years are still here, but the psychological connections are different. They can *think* more about their feelings now. So, it becomes important for parents to provide plenty of emotional guidelines during this stage, while keeping the earlier emotions alive and well.

As boys become aware of what the Pack Rules dictate for boys' expression of their emotions, what their parents say to support or refute these rules is noticed and it *registers* in a different way now. For example, when Allen is not invited to Calvin's much-awaited six-year-old birthday party, he feels hurt. He mopes around at home the day he finds out he has not been invited. How Calvin's parents respond to his behavior (he is expressing his emotions sideways by moping) teaches Allen a lot about how to handle his hurt feelings, his vulnerability, in the future. Boys need very clear emotional guidance at this stage because they're watching, learning, and remembering *everything* their parents say and do about their sons' feelings

Between birth and age three, much learning takes place at a sensory-motor level, as neural connections are laid down in the brain and preverbal experiences may be stored somatically (in the body). In contrast, between four and seven, boys can think about their feelings and remember what they learn about those feelings in ways that use distinct forms of cognition. When told, "Be a big boy . . . don't cry," boys at this age can conclude that feeling sad is bad behavior and that sadness should be hidden. They don't understand display rules (or the Pack Rules for that matter) yet, but they can begin to think there's something wrong with feeling the way they do feel. So, they learn to hide it. Often, this is the beginning of the process whereby boys' emotions "disappear."

Although the world may be their oyster, children's own imperfect sense of their power may frighten them at this age. For example, when little Luke was angry because he could not get his way, he screamed to his mom and dad, "I wish you'd get into a car crash!" and then he stomped off to his room. But once he got there, he began to feel extremely frightened, because *it could happen*. After all, he's King of the Playground and the world is his oyster.

This awful experience actually happened to a ten-year-old boy whom I counseled. His mother did get into a car accident a few days after her son screamed exactly those words at her. It was extremely difficult for this ten-year-old to learn to understand that he had not caused the accident with his powerful emotions. But under stress, children (and adults) regress. So it wasn't surprising that the boy slipped back into an earlier cognitive level (more like a six-year-old) in his cause-effect thinking. To summarize, parents must keep in mind just how powerful little boys' emotions are, especially in light of their intuitive cognitive style at this age.

How Four-to-Seven-Year-Old Boys Are Socialized

From four to seven years of age, gender roles are more flexible and Pack Rules are less powerful than they will be later. But "emotional seeds" are planted in preschool and the first years of elementary school that can grow into narrowly defined gender roles of masculinity. Beyond the family, educational experiences, team sports, and clubs have a hand in shaping and molding boys' range of emotional expression at this age. Yet, there are common threads in these influences that link these different experiences to boys' abilities to express their emotions. One common thread is the presence of girls in the world.

Fear of Femininity Starts Early

How are girls connected to the disappearance of boys' emotional expressions? It is through an indirect connection. Girls *per se* don't make boys' emotions disappear. Rather, it's the content of what mainstream culture communicates *about* girls to boys at this age: The Pack Rules explicitly state that girls aren't "cool." Thus, being like a girl is bad. Maybe even worse, since a boy is *not* a girl, and if he acts like one, not only is he not cool, he is uncool in the worst possible way. At this stage of cognitive and social development, girls represent symbols of vulnerability, weakness, and all that "emotional stuff." Although boys aren't friendly with girls at this age, it's more okay for a girl to act like a boy in stereotypical masculine ways (being athletic, playing in the woods, knowing the rosters of professional sports teams) than it is for a boy to act like a girl in stereotypical feminine ways (playing house/dolls, dressing up, crying). This contrast, by itself, highlights how much social approbation and permission girls receive to practice relational and emotional development skills, when compared to what boys receive.

At this age, the socialization of boys seems to be a downward extension of the more rigid gender stereotypes and roles that are just around the corner. The Pack Rules have a lot to do with this. And mainstream culture is both the arbiter and the conveyor of these values.

Working with Boys' Temperaments Between Ages Four and Seven

A timid six-year-old boy who lives in a rural setting and whose parents are both introverted and somewhat taciturn may feel uncomfortable talking, especially about private matters like his emotions. Thus, he doesn't get much "practice" talking. It should follow that another shy boy, who has had some practice talking about his emotions, will feel more comfortable in social settings. But talking about their emotions is never the norm for boys. A shy boy can learn to talk about football scores, but this doesn't necessarily transfer to telling someone about his fear of thunder and lightning. Talking about feelings is intimate conversation that requires trust, a skilled listener, and practice.

Emotional expression practice. Practice in expressing emotions needs to take place in day-to-day life at every age. From four to seven, much of this practice happens simply by watching adults. If a son sees his father hiding his emotions, the son learns to do the same. Modeling emotional expression in healthy ways is a powerful teaching method because it not only names feelings for boys, it also shows boys what to do with them. For example, if a dad says to his son, "I'm worried that Mommy isn't home yet . . . but I think she's okay . . . she's probably just stuck in traffic," this modeling does three specific things: (1) it names (rather than hides) his feeling; (2) it describes his thoughts; and (3) it models a coping skill in how to deal with worry or fear. Not incidentally, it also engages another person in an intimate relationship. All of these ingredients are powerful, and simple, ways to teach boys about emotions and how to handle them.

I began this discussion of temperament by focusing on temperamental qualities closely aligned with timidity, because parents of shy or sensitive boys too often cope with their sons' vulnerability by denying, rather than validating it. Button's (1969) book, *The Authentic Child*, includes a vignette I haven't forgotten even after eighteen years. I think it stayed with me because it captures, in one brief story, how the most common way we reassure children can totally miss a child's real need!

In this vignette, a five-year-old boy is worried because his mom hasn't come home on time. He starts to cry at bedtime because he misses her. Dad tells him there's nothing to be afraid of and that she'll be home soon. Hearing this, the boy cries louder (because his feelings haven't been heard). Although his dad speaks words that he thinks will comfort his scared son, the truth is, there is something to fear. So, this little boy can either "make his feelings disappear" or he can continue to cry until his father validates his fear. Such validation could be to say: "Yes, it's scary when Mommy doesn't come home on time. It's hard to fall asleep." Once the fear is validated, *then* the coping strategies follow.

Feelings must be mirrored to validate boys' inner worlds, their *authenticity*. Without emotional validation by a caregiver, boys cannot take the next steps of learning what to do with their emotions (other than make them disappear). Often boys are left with only half of their experience validated. They receive reassuring thoughts, but they don't learn about their feelings.

Paying daily attention to boys' feelings. In addition to modeling and mirroring, practice with expressing emotions at this age must take the form of directly naming the boys' emotions and helping them to name their feelings by themselves. Daily practice helps boys to become familiar, perhaps even comfortable, with the language of emotions. For example: A teacher notices that Joey is frustrated about his handwriting. He holds the pencil with an awkward grip and his letters never look quite right. Joey doesn't talk about any of this trouble he is having. He probably doesn't understand any of it. He just constantly whines about having to do written homework and tries his best to get out of doing it. Emotional expression practice in this situation would be as simple as, "Joey . . . it makes sense that you feel frustrated about your handwriting. I would, too. How can I help?" Depending on the particular boy's temperament, parents and teachers will get a variety of answers ranging from, "Nothing . . ." to a boy who bursts into tears from the weight of his frustration. The main idea here is for the feeling to be named. I believe that when adults practice the naming of emotions with boys, it doesn't really matter how the boys respond after the feeling is named in that moment. If an emotion is named, then that goal has been accomplished.

At this age, adults can do a lot to shape boys' emotional responses and behaviors *regardless of the boys' temperaments.* Whether boys are "easygoing," "slow-to-warm up," or "difficult," they all need practice naming and expressing their emotions. A "difficult child" may deflect any type of intrusion into his inner emotional world. Parents of difficult children often may feel like giving up on practicing emotional expression. The same is true for a very active boy who won't sit still in the classroom, much less talk about something like *feelings.* But both boys still need the practice of naming emotions and understanding what those emotions feel like.

How Parents Can Improve Boys' Emotional Development from Ages Four to Seven

Although at this age children venture away from home more often, their lives are still primarily family centered. This is so important for parents to keep in mind. They haven't lost their sons to the Pack Rules (yet). However, boys *are* becoming more aware of what the Pack Rules say about expressing emotions. And boys notice keenly what their parents say to support or refute these rules. This is why, at this age, I recommend that parents provide practice, especially with the identification of feelings, on a daily basis.

Talk about feelings. This practice is like a vaccine against the Pack Rules. It can involve modeling or a direct reflection of boys' feelings. At this age, a general conversation about emotions is also appropriate. Without guidance from parents, boys (and girls) may not get the message that their feelings matter, because mainstream culture still devalues and often ignores expressions of emotion, except in horror movies.

I recently tested a seven-year-old boy for intellectual giftedness. He had a superior IQ, but he was unable to define "anger" in one of the subtests (the correct answer is simply that anger is a feeling or emotion). I thought how odd it was that a smart child didn't have verbal knowledge about such a common emotion. Teaching boys the names of feelings is a need that cannot be stressed enough. In addition to "old-fashioned" conversations, there are commercially produced board and card games designed to teach children this age about emotions and how to handle them. Many games are designed for the whole family. (Childswork Childsplay is a catalogue that offers such games. See the Resource section.)

Don't forget to model positive emotions. Parents and other family members must always keep in mind that *both* positive and negative emotional expression are important to boys' emotional development. It's extremely important for parents to validate and name the entire range of emotions. As discussed throughout, the presence of positive emotions is not only normal and healthy, it's also serves as a mental health buffer. So, when boys are feeling proud, excited, happy, etc., parents would do well to name and reflect these emotions back to their sons as often as they recognize and mirror the negative emotions (which usually get parents' attention more often through problem behaviors).

After boys have learned the names of feelings, which should be well established by the end of this age period, the easiest and most effective way to practice emotional expression with boys is simply to ask, "And how did you feel about that?" to whatever the experience or event is. The practice of asking this laser-like question can be started at this age (earlier, actually) and continue throughout adolescence. It's the emotional equivalent of, "What do you think?" which is also a very validating question in terms of identity development.

How Adults Can Influence Communities for Four- to Seven-Year-Old Boys

As boys move away more from the family and head toward the ball field, the classroom, and church, mosque, or temple activities, their community becomes larger. Each of these settings readily lends itself either to changing or to reinforcing the rules about boys' expressions of their emotions. It's important to remember that anywhere there is a gathering of boys, that place is usually covertly governed by Pack Rules. So, anytime adults can challenge or provide different norms for boys' emotional expressions in community settings, that helps foster healthy emotional development.

Changing the Pack Rules' norm. Adults who are active community leaders are in key positions to facilitate "re-norming" boys' emotional expressions. This includes teachers, coaches, youth ministers, church leaders, or anyone with whom boys spend time. Coaches have a unique role to play in boys' lives. They serve as gatekeepers to the Pack Rule about being an athlete and winning. It's especially important that coaches who use "get tough" or "ignore the pain" approaches also teach boys to distinguish between being tough on the field and being sensible in other settings.

If coaches don't help boys learn how to separate the competitive ethos of sports from all other social interactions, then parents must. Unless boys hear respected adults make this distinction, the "get tough" way of thinking spills over into nonathletic and noncompetitive life. I once counseled a highschool football player who had been playing football since the age of seven. By the time he was in high school, he had effectively turned off all of his emotions. He had to cut on his arm with a knife, frequently, in order to feel the emotional pain he was experiencing. He had gotten very tough indeed.

Adults who are not coaches are less likely to *intentionally* force boys' softer emotions underground. Many coaches have specific goals in mind (like winning) when they tell boys to ignore their pain or fear. Other adults are usually just caught up in the cultural resistance to boys' emotional expressions when denying boys' vulnerable feelings. Nonetheless, when adults interact with boys between the ages of four and seven, it serves the boys well when these adults acknowledge boys' emotions rather than ignoring them. Most elite coaches know this. Not only do they *emphasize* the role of emotions in sports, they teach athletes to *use* their emotions. Rather than ignoring pain or fear, these coaches teach athletes to acknowledge these emotions and transform them to enhance performance.

Education. Another way that communities can promote boys' emotional development is through "affective" education in the schools. Affective education refers to a curriculum that teaches the "whole" student (including feelings, coping skills, communication skills, etc.) as opposed to teaching only academic subjects. Guidance counseling programs in the schools are common examples of affective education.

Such efforts can help "undo" the Pack Rules and may immunize boys from negative influences on their emotional development. In his popular book, *Emotional Intelligence*, Daniel Goleman (1995) lists many affective school programs that have been implemented to address the emotional needs of students in K-12 schools.

Ages Eight to Eleven

As with younger ages, emotions that emerged in earlier years are still present (or should be). What may be new at this age is the ability to "blend" emotions. Blending refers to the ability to mix a thought with an emotion, or to mix two different emotions together regarding the same person, experience, or object. For example, a boy can feel both anger and love for his sister at the same time; and if he's aware of *both* feelings, he is much less likely to hit her when he's angry. Researchers have noted the ability to blend positive and negative feelings for the same person during this eight-to-eleven age period (Harter and Whitesell 1989). But I've found that some children as young as five can learn how to blend their emotions.

Blending is considered a mature and healthy skill that helps regulate emotions. Therefore knowing how to blend thoughts with feelings is relevant to mental health. Consider the boy who feels scared but who knows how to blend a reassuring thought with his scared feeling. The result is that his fear doesn't interfere with his functioning. Unlike the inhuman "No Fear" approach to life, when a boy learns to blend his thoughts and feelings, he discovers that he can feel his fear and cope with it.

In fact, one effective form of psychotherapy, which I developed in my clinical practice, is based on this type of blending. It's called Cognitive-Emotional-Behavioral Therapy (CEB-T). As the name indicates, it involves intervening at all three levels: thinking, feeling, and acting. I've found that children and adults benefit from identifying and processing the underlying emotions connected to inner thoughts and outward behaviors. This is very helpful in resolving problems and developing emotional intelligence skills. Techniques based on CEB-T can be adapted and used at home or in the classroom.

Boys are better equipped to blend their thoughts and feelings between eight and eleven years old because they have "grown" new cognitive skills. They no longer need to rely just on their senses or intuitions. They can observe, deduce, and conclude. They can see and understand that the water poured from a tall, thin glass into a short, wide dish is still the same amount of water. Given these more accurate observations of life around them, boys naturally start looking for clues about what to do with their emotions. And without different information from parents, they will rely upon the Pack Rules.

How Eight- to Eleven-Year-Old Boys Are Socialized

After the age of seven, boys have more frequent contact with friends, peers, and others outside the family. It's probably a time of continued involvement in team sports. At this stage boys may gravitate toward all-boy teams rather than the co-ed teams of earlier years. Also, they may be developing serious hobbies (art, music, collections) for the first time. They're beginning to figure out who they are and what they do and do not like. It's also the time when the Pack can begin to rule.

Growing influence of the Pack Rules. Why would the Pack rule more at this stage than earlier? It may be because of the increased contact with others outside of the family who follow these rules, particularly other boys. Depending on the activities and hobbies boys are involved with, as well as the friends they select, some boys will be more influenced by the Pack Rules than others. For example, the boy who rigidly identifies with masculine stereotypes will follow the Pack Rules because it is clearly the best way to become a "real" man. He'll avoid ballet classes (even if he is interested in dance). He'll play baseball, football, hockey, or any other "real" man's sport (even if he doesn't really like them). In short, if he's looking for acceptance in mainstream culture, then in some way or another, he will follow the Pack more so than the boy who has discovered flexible alternatives.

Alternatives to Pack Rules are needed. There aren't many (any?) acceptable alternatives to the Pack Rules in mainstream culture. But, every once in a while, a brave boy comes along who discovers other options. Even when no other options seem available to him.

I remember an eleven-year-old African-American boy, Jeremiah, who had just transferred to a new middle school. He was one of the few nonwhite boys there. It was a difficult time for him in many ways. Middle school is tough enough without being the new kid or being a member of a minority group. He wanted so much to be accepted and liked by his teachers and classmates. He figured playing sports would help. So Jeremiah decided to play on a community football team in sixth-grade to get football experience for a year, and then to play for the school team the following year. He thought that surely he would make friends and gain respect this way. After all, he would be following the Pack Rules.

Well, after his first football game, Jeremiah realized that he didn't like football at all. In his own words, "It's terrifying . . . and it hurts . . . so I quit." What was so interesting about Jeremiah's decision was that he wasn't ashamed about it. He didn't hide his vulnerable emotions. He openly told his parents and grandparents that he didn't like it because it was scary and it hurt. At that point, I knew that Jeremiah would eventually be okay, based on the way he handled this situation. He remained true to his real self and didn't adhere to the Pack Rules once he figured out that he had a choice, and that, in this situation, they weren't safe for him to follow.

Working with Boys' Temperaments Between Ages Eight and Eleven

Much of what has been said about the stage between ages four to seven also applies to boys between eight and eleven. Briefly summarized, it's important to continue to name feelings and to ask boys how they feel about things on a daily basis, regardless of their temperaments. The main difference at this stage is in how the influence of peers may interact with boys' temperaments and their ability to express their emotions. Or, more accurately, how the influence of the Pack Rules interacts with temperament.

More tools for "stretching." Most temperamental traits continue throughout childhood and adolescence, the functional and not-so-functional ones. But this is not to say that these personal characteristics cannot be moderated in some ways. The older a boy becomes, the more skills he has to compensate or "stretch" in the opposite direction than his own temperament would lead him. When very young, shy or sensitive boys have fewer cognitive skills to help them through social situations. The same is true for impulsive boys who have demonstrated aggressive or irritable characteristics. When younger, their feelings and biological urges are "bigger and stronger" than their cognitive abilities.

I once worked with a boy who had a "difficult" temperament. But once he reached the age of twelve, he found that he could "talk himself down" (his words) when he was upset. He had learned how to stop hitting and throwing things by the age of nine, and by twelve he was telling his parents how to calm down when *they* were upset!

Overall, the presence of new cognitive skills in this age period provides for the possibility of self-talk to soothe the shy boy and to calm the excitable or irritable boy. At this age, parents can and must tap into these new and continually developing cognitive skills to help their sons regulate their temperamental qualities.

How Parents Can Improve Boys' Emotional Development Between Ages Eight and Eleven

Once boys have the foundation of knowing how to name their own feelings, they need to learn how to identify and understand others' feelings. Of course, practicing this skill can, and should, begin at earlier ages. But during the eight to eleven stage, boys have access to higher cognitive abilities than in earlier years, and can do more abstract thinking at the upper end of this age range. This allows them to see the perspective of others better.

Keep in mind that if boys cannot identify or name different feelings easily at this age, then more practice is needed with this basic emotional skill. (In fact, ongoing practice with this is always recommended.) Indeed, parents can begin to help boys understand the complexity of their emotions, including how to analyze complex emotions, and how to respond to the feelings of others.

A helpful tool. One way to teach boys how to perceive and analyze emotions is a technique I call "processing with distance." This refers to the technique of using a third person to help explore boys' feelings or reactions. It can be as simple as asking how so-and-so might feel if such-and-such happened. This query provides practice with several emotional competence skills at once. It teaches the names of feelings, the anticipation of emotions, how to analyze complex emotions, and how to empathize with others.

One reason this technique works well with boys this age is that it creates safety by putting some distance between the boy and his own emotions. For example, if a mother asks her son how he feels about his report card, and he says, "I don't know," if she were using this technique, she would then say, "How do you think (name a peer) would feel about a report card like this?"

He doesn't know or doesn't *feel*? It's important for parents to be able to distinguish whether a boy doesn't *want* to say how he feels or whether he really doesn't know how he feels. This distinction matters because the parents' response should differ. If the boy really doesn't know, then he needs concentrated practice on identifying his feelings. If he does know, but doesn't want to say, then it's either a privacy issue and he wants his boundaries to be respected, or he's just following the Pack Rules. Parents need to know which is which. The difference between stoicism and privacy is usually distinguished by the amount of energy in the response. As a rule, more *energy* is expended on demanding privacy.

Continue to immunize boys from the Pack Rules. If parents provide daily skills practice in naming emotions and allowing their expression at this age, then boys just might become immunized to the negative effects that the Pack Rules have on emotional expression. Because many boys will balk at playing board games about emotions (some girls, too), the practice can be as simple as listening intently when he talks about something that happened at school. Anything. And then asking in a matter-of-fact way, "And how did you feel about that?" If parents get too many "I-don't-knows," then, again, it's time to work on identifying emotions, perhaps using the "processing with distance" technique. After a while, when talking about feelings has become a staple of conversation in the home, boys' responses will become more natural, too.

How Adults Can Influence Communities for Eight- to Eleven-Year-Old Boys

Small but significant steps. There are daily opportunities to model the natural presence of boys' expressions of their emotions to other adults. When a boy tells of his triumph at school or on the basketball court, and an adult responds with, "You look so proud," in front of other adults, that gives tacit permission to other adults to do the same. Here's another example, but this time with the expression of a negative emotion: Johnny went trick-or-treating with a group of boys and their parents. Unfortunately, at one of the houses, Johnny was first in line when the *headless man* jumped out from the bushes and screamed, "Aaaaaaah ... Where's my head ... did *you* take it?" (his arms reaching for Johnny). Johnny's dad saw his son's natural fear reaction and said, "Wow! That was scary! You must have been terrified, Johnny ... is your heart racing?!" This breaks the Pack Rules in front of other boys and other parents. It models a normal and healthy expression of emotion.

The power of labels. Consider how one mistake influenced an entire school community. There was a very difficult (badly behaved) fifth-grade class that went through three different teachers in one school year. The first teacher took early retirement, the second developed a stress-related medical condition, and the third stayed. By the end of the school year the last teacher who stayed had a successful and well-behaved class. How? It turned out that this teacher had misinterpreted the students' "locker numbers" taped inside the teacher's desk drawer to be the students' IQ scores (140, 142, 144, etc.). This teacher had treated the students as if they were very intelligent children. And they responded to being respectfully treated with good behavior and learned accordingly. This amazing story expresses the power that resides in "the eye of the beholder." It is possible for single individuals to shape and change the expectations about who children are and what they're "made of." It's my hope that more individuals within many communities will help this happen with boys' emotional development.

Ages Twelve to Fifteen

As at earlier ages, there are no new primary emotions (i.e., mad, sad, scared, happy). But due to continued cognitive development, now boys may be able to feel and describe more complex emotions such as: indignant, humiliated, elated, and peaceful. Unlike the primary emotions, these have more of a cognitive element. These emotions are thought about. Yet I have often found that these more cognitive emotions can usually be simmered down to one primary emotion. It's possible to take complex cognitive emotions like jealousy and peel away the layers to identify the underlying primary emotion.

Anger and fear are frequently at the root of many complex negative emotions, while happiness is at the root of positive ones.

At this age, with the advent of abstract reasoning skills (the ability to "think about thinking"), boys also have more awareness of their emotions and can regulate them better. Social cues are especially important in shaping boys' emotional expressions at this age. The Pack Rules encourage boys to monitor and negate their softer emotions and restrict expressions of tenderness or compassion, and any public displays of empathy or affection.

And, as stated in chapters 1 and 2, when boys begin to ignore these feelings over and over *within* themselves, then it is no longer merely a matter of masking their emotions in public. It can become a matter of not feeling them at all. This type of dissociation, or splitting off the experience from consciousness, serves to help humans survive traumatic experiences. But when boys don't feel their emotions on a daily basis, this puts their mental health at risk.

Boys can, and do, ignore their emotions before age twelve. But in early to middle adolescence, gender roles become unmercifully rigid. There's even *more* cultural pressure to be stereotypically masculine and to hide the pain. During adolescence, boys' emotions appear to become endangered. Our goal is to keep these emotions from becoming extinct.

How Twelve- to Fifteen-Year-Old Boys Are Socialized

Being a boy at this age means strict adherence to the Pack Rules. Any rule that proves a boy is not a wimp is the kind of rule that boys will find and follow. And the Pack Rules offer clear guidelines about how *not* to be a wimp. Aggression, sexual power, and winning exert a powerful grip on boys at this age. Cooperative behavior isn't highly prized. For example, many middle schools and high schools offer peer mediation programs to allow peers to resolve their interpersonal conflicts by themselves without adult intervention (or very little) using co-counseling methods. But these programs attract only small numbers of students. It's precisely during this stage that boys look to the Pack Rules as the compass that will lead them through the land of adolescence. So it is precisely at this stage that parents and other adults must try even harder to immunize boys from the Pack Rules. They must vigorously promote alternatives like peer mediation—or just *talking* about what's bothering them—to prevent boys from relying solely on the Pack Rules to solve their relationship and other social problems.

Sexuality as a Dominant Social Force

The main socializing agents during this time continue to be family, peers, and activities. However, at this age, sexual and romantic interests begin to capture some of boys' attention. Girls aren't exactly yucky anymore . . . but they're not exactly cool, either. Why not? In early adolescence, it's not okay for boys to be "feminine" *in any way*. According to the Pack Rules, the value girls have lies exclusively in their sexiness, and part of the power of being "masculine" involves having access to sexual knowledge and activity.

Boys need to learn alternative ways to look at and relate to girls. Their preoccupation with the size of girls' breasts and "butts" at this age isn't fair either to the boys themselves or to the girls. Relating to girls in broader and healthier ways is possible. However, during this age, boys need a lot of sexual coaching. So be sure to ask them what's going on with sexual issues for themselves and with their peers. (Remember how much peer pressure Lucas felt to have sex.) What questions do boys have, what concerns do they have, what *feelings* do they have? Ask them.

Initially, boys may try to prevent their parents (or other adults) from discussing sex with them. They will make rude noises and comic faces to defend themselves from such "intimate" talk. But if the adult is willing to persevere, sooner or later, the boy will calm down and be able to discuss some of what he is experiencing. Keep trying, because without some adult coaching, the Pack will rule on this essential issue. Remember, you want to know what the boy is feeling, but you don't want to pry. This is a fine line to walk, but it is worth doing.

Interpersonal Relations and Communication

In general, there appears to be little serious interpersonal communication between boys at this age. In contrast, girls are jockeying in and out of relationships while they somehow also manage to remain loyal to their "BFF" (best friend, forever). Boys don't have secret codes like this to express affection or attachment to each other. Rather, boys seem to meet their need for intimacy by "hanging out" with "the guys." As in earlier stages of childhood and documented in empirical studies, boys' relationships with other boys at this age still focus on *doing something* together rather than on *being with* each other (Maccoby 1990).

This indirect style of interaction and communication between boys is often used to engage boys in therapy. William Pollack (1998) says that often the way he works with boys in counseling initially involves playing a game. This puts an activity between them as they talk. Many other therapists begin this way, too, mainly because it's

more comfortable and familiar to boys. Another common way to talk easily with boys (as you may have discovered) is while driving in the car. The most intimate conversations between boys and other people often take place as both sit or stand side by side while looking forward, rather than toward, each other.

Family "Versus" Peers?

It's not clear exactly how much influence families have with their children in general, and adolescents, in particular. Ron Taffel (2001) and Judy Harris (1998) assert that peers influence teens' lives more than parents. Others have challenged these perspectives (Borkowski and Ramey, In press). It is indeed true that peers will influence teens' decisions about what clothing to wear, which social events to attend, and whether or not to smoke tobacco, or try marijuana, but parents appear to have a stronger influence with regard to deeper and longer lasting issues. Parents of teens also seem to still have a lot of influence regarding whether a new haircut or piercing really looks good because translated the haircut or piercing really means, *"Do you still know me . . . Will you still love me . . . no matter how I look?"*

The activities that boys participate in at this age tend to be those sanctioned by the Pack. But if a fourteen-year-old boy has received enough immunization and has a strong enough sense of who he is, he can decide that jazz dancing is important to him. Or he can decide it's not okay to pull girls' bra straps at school . . . and *actually say so* to the boys that do. Breaking the Pack Rules at this age requires a strong sense of self, apart from the Pack. I believe that such a strong sense of self can be encouraged through emotionally supportive relationships with peers, family, and other adult caregivers, if those relationships mirror and validate his experiences from childhood through adolescence.

Working with Boys' Temperament Between Ages Twelve to Fifteen

The shy, impulsive, perfectionist, or easygoing twelve- to fifteen-year-old boy may display the same basic temperamental traits he had as a toddler. But now, he has more "cognitive power" to cope with his temperamental tendencies. So working with boys' temperaments gets easier for parents as boys grow older. Between twelve and fifteen, boys' cognitive abilities are approaching adult thought. At this age, the best way to interact with boys' temperamental characteristics is to be a coach. Help them to identify personality quirks that need "socialization" practice. Be sure, also, to reinforce their strengths. Boys are much more likely to succeed at understanding and stretching their temperaments with adult assistance, especially when it is built upon boys' strengths.

Keep mirroring and "stretching". In addition to the general principles discussed throughout this chapter, the following issues may emerge during this age: *Shy boys* need (and want) to learn how to be more socially adept, especially in regard to dating. They may start to demonstrate anxiety symptoms secondary to their shyness. They don't know what to do socially, or how to cope on their own, so they need someone, preferably an adult with a large fund of common sense, to explain to them how to handle the social stuff. *Impulsive boys* need to learn to delay their gratification and to cope with boredom. They're more mobile now and learning how to drive. An impulsive boy driving a car creates a dangerous combination that requires close monitoring. *Perfectionist boys* must learn, if they haven't yet, how to be more flexible. School and grades are the perfect place to practice not being perfect (it's impossible to get everything right). The emotional skill that typically needs attention for perfectionist boys is regulation, usually in the form of anger and frustration management.

The emotional needs of "easy" or "all-boy" boys may still be hard to see. It may seem as if such boys do not *have* emotions because they either look and act okay, or they mask their feelings behind gender-role stereotypes. Adults must bear in mind that when boys don't get practice expressing their emotions, then the Pack Rules will become their reference point. This is true regardless of temperament.

How Parents Can Improve Boys' Emotional Development Between Ages Twelve and Fifteen

Boys in mid-adolescence are steeped in very rigid gender roles. Thus, one of the biggest challenges for parents is to find a successful way to give boys permission to question the prevailing cultural norms and go "counterculture" (doing the opposite of mainstream culture). Going counterculture for boys at this age mainly involves not being macho and stoic all the time . . . and breaking some of the Pack Rules.

Deconstruct the influence of the media. Watching TV shows and movies with boys is a great way to teach them how to think in a countercultural way. It also allows you to see what's influencing them. Because TV sitcoms, music videos, and most magazines present the world of gender relationships in such distorted, aggressive, and sexualized ways, it's important to help boys "deconstruct" media messages. This involves challenging and questioning boys about what they see and what they *think* about what they see. Deconstructing media can take the form of reality-testing (i.e., "Do you think most guys *really* look like that in *real* life?") or putting media information into a broader context (i.e., "Do you agree with the message in that movie or commercial?).

Most of the time, media messages are so subtle and fast they escape challenge. Once I tried to deconstruct a TV commercial with an eight- and a twelve-year-old, and by the time we had finished, four other commercials had flashed before us. The onslaught of "information" was so relentless that it resembled a form of brainwashing. The vast majority of media messages about gender are extremely stereotyped and very loyal to the Pack Rules.

The way that men always run the meetings seated at the head of the table, and the way that they constantly rescue women from danger (usually at the hands of other men), are familiar and not-so-subtle messages in everything from car commercials, to movie scripts and music video story lines. Find out how boys think and feel about this just by asking them. Get a discussion going as to the meaning of these messages. It may not be easy, but it will be well worth trying.

Disappearing emotions. Regardless of all the good work a parent may have done with their son's emotional development up to this point, at this stage, boys' emotional expression seems to disappear. I'm not saying that boys' emotions *really* disappear at this age (really disappearing means that the boys can no longer feel their emotions). But from twelve to fifteen, even boys with a good emotional foundation typically hide their feelings from others, not from themselves. However, if boys do not feel their emotions anymore, then they need more intensive attention, perhaps psychotherapy.

How Adults Can Influence Communities for Twelve- to Fifteen-Year-Old Boys

Community influence is broad at this age. Music, sports, peers, media messages, and Internet usage are major socializing agents. It's extremely important for parents to monitor these social forces. In the boy's preschool days, parents could pick the children with whom he played, the books he read, and the TV shows he watched. To a large extent, in mid-adolescence *this is still true*. But the community and larger social forces now lure him out of the family home. In response, parents' influence must also grow rather than diminish. And, given how rapidly culture changes due to technology, parents need to learn how to be just as fast.

The music industry. Song lyrics usually deal with emotions; sometimes they even challenge the Pack Rules. The band, U2, won a Grammy for their song, "It's a Beautiful Day," not your typical male rock 'n' roll tune. The same is true for Hootie and the Blowfish, the all-male band whose hit song of the late 1990s has the refrain: "I'm such a baby, yeah, the dolphins make me cry ..." Listening to a male African-American vocalist sing this in a deep, sonorous voice is certainly an alternative to the Pack Rules. These are just two examples of how male musicians can break the Pack Rules, provide counter-cultural role models for boys, and still make fortunes as rock stars.

Talking about boys. Another way that parents and other adults can influence communities is to talk about boys in *empathic*, rather than competitive, ways. This can take place in a simple conversation between two adults. When one adult says to another, "You must be so proud of Robert's scholastic honors ... how does *he feel* about it?" or "That must have been so hard for Billy when he was suspended from school last week, how did *he feel* about it?" This models empathy to other parents, while also reminding them about their son's emotions. Often, small seeds like these, seeds that run counter to the Pack Rules, can take root in a community of friends.

Ages Sixteen to Eighteen

When boys are this age, their parents tend to think of them as mini-adults. In many respects, they are. The development of the frontal cortex (involved with higher reasoning) is closer to completion now. This part of the brain is important in emotional development because, in addition to continued integration (or blending) of feelings and thoughts, these new cognitive skills allow boys to analyze, infer, and "think through" complex emotions. By the end of adolescence, boys should have the necessary tools to both feel and express their emotions, to blend, to analyze, to regulate, and to empathize. But as you know, there are many social forces that act to either sharpen or blunt these tools.

Despite the presence of these new cognitive and emotional skills, I've observed that many boys do not express their emotions in late adolescence. Such absence of emotional expression can occur at any age, but the general pattern indicates that in late adolescence, boys tend to decrease the expression of their emotions. It is not yet clear whether these boys are *just not expressing* their emotions or whether they're actually *not feeling* their emotions.

This distinction between experiencing and expressing emotions is significant with regard to mental health. As described in chapter 1, when a person cannot feel his/her emotions, that person has a condition known as *alexithymia* (this means literally "without words for feelings"). It refers to the inability to feel emotions. When alexithymia is present in boys and men who have no history of head trauma, it probably has been caused by social forces that blunted their innate ability to feel.

How Sixteen- to Eighteen-Year-Old Boys Are Socialized

The Pack Rules lay down some very clear mandates for this age: it's the time to "score" with girls (i.e., have lots of sex), drive a car, play sports, and be more independent. In most communities, it is rare for a boy between the ages of sixteen and eighteen *not* to be driving and having sex with girls (or obsessing about these two activities). Boys who are not part of this mainstream subculture are likely to have chosen to go counterculture; they are the boys who have found alternatives to the Pack Rules and who feel secure in their identities. But there are also the boys who loyally follow the Pack Rules, and who still don't quite fit in with the Pack. These boys may be ridiculed, rejected, or labeled "gay." They are often lonely and miserable because, despite their best efforts, they don't fit in. Ironically, boys who do fit in may also be lonely and miserable following the Pack Rules, but they don't have to deal with the added misery of scorn and social rejection.

Milestones. Poised on the edge of adulthood, most boys continue to rely on the familiar Pack Rules to get through. *Don't be scared* (*No Fear*) and *Be independent* are the two main rudders to set sail for the seas of manhood. However, another new edict arrives at this age: *Be somebody when you go out into the world . . . Make a name for yourself.*

Boys feel this pressure in a palpable way now. Although they may have felt it previously, now they have to deliver. Unfortunately, unrealistic pressure to *be somebody* and *make a name for yourself* is an expectation that, by any yardstick, usually leads to a chronic sense of failure and of "not measuring up." This type of unsuccessful launch into adulthood can haunt a man throughout his life like a ghost, especially when it's left unnamed.

Yet with adulthood looming ahead of them (in addition to going to college, they can join the armed services; they can vote; in many states they can purchase liquor and get into nightclubs; they can marry; etc.), it's often difficult to see whether these boys are even thinking about what it means to be an adult, much less feeling anything about the concept of adulthood. Indeed, if boys have been following the Pack Rules throughout their adolescence, by now they've mastered some form of stoicism: their positive and negative emotions are masked, mitigated, and muted. They restrict all expressions of their emotions, even with those whom they most trust.

The typical exception to restricted emotional expression at this age involves girlfriends. The role that girls play in boys' lives can shift to a positive, life-affirming force, as boys discover the benefits of exchanging confidences and exploring intimacy. However, since it is rare for a teenage romance to last beyond high school, when the romance ends, the relationship with a "best friend" also ends. After the breakup, boys are left without anyone with whom to discuss their inner lives. Not surprisingly, this is the period when boys often initiate counseling for the first time. Although counseling can be very helpful, at this age, the Pack Rules suggest other activities for dealing with the loss of a relationship. Drinking, drugs, and other dangerous behaviors may be considered more acceptable "coping skills" to deal with the anxieties of growing up. Our culture needs to reconnect the experience of fear and courage for boys and teach them other coping skills.

Working with Boys' Temperaments Between Ages Sixteen and Eighteen

As boys move closer to adulthood, the temperamental qualities that they display now likely will stay with them throughout their lives. In fact, the word used to describe temperament after age eighteen is "personality." This isn't to say that the "easygoing" boy won't have bad days or that the shy teen will become a social outcast. It just means that temperamental tendencies still present will probably continue well into adulthood. The different experiences boys have had along the way can result in different behavioral outcomes, even if their temperaments remain the same. For example, the shy boy who has been working on his social skills and the impulsive boy who has been coached on how to delay gratification will both function differently from boys who have these temperamental qualities but who did not stretch in the opposite directions.

Listen for and talk about emotions. Since this is a time of transition in boys' lives, it's also an important time to monitor their emotions. It is normal for a boy, regardless of temperament, to feel excited about driving, proms, college, enlisting in the services . . . and to feel scared or sad about these very same things, especially if he is turned down for a prom date, or his first choice of colleges. The same approach described for earlier ages is probably still the best approach now: Validate his temperamental style and help him to build upon his strengths to stretch in the opposite direction. Then, invite discussion about his feelings and the feelings of others.

The life decisions that boys are making at this age probably will be connected to their temperaments. Because parents influence major life decisions, their knowledge of how their sons' temperaments interact with career and post–high school plans is very important. More specifically, as boys begin to make career and college decisions, parents can help their sons by *not* pushing them into jobs/careers, colleges, or majors that aren't a "good fit" with their temperaments. For extreme examples, the shy boy would probably not be comfortable in sales or as a trial lawyer, and the impulsive boy would not do well as a surgeon. The best parents can do now is to look at their son's temperament realistically, and guide him toward life decisions that would be a good match. In this way, parents can contribute to their sons' emotional development in adulthood.

How Parents Can Improve Boys' Emotional Development Between Ages Sixteen and Eighteen

Given the rapid social changes taking place today, it's clearly a time when boys need to talk about their emotions. He's driving, and in some states, he's inching toward the legal drinking age. He has one foot at home and one out the door, headed toward more independence.

Drinking. Parents of boys must be very aware of how the Pack Rules lure boys into thinking that drinking, and in some subcultures, drugs, are really okay. It's part of the "boys will be boys" mentality. Getting "wasted" or "trashed" is an American "rite of passage" for many boys at this age, especially during their first year of college. Although drinking and drug use may begin earlier, it is at this age that our culture tacitly sanctions substance abuse for boys.

While a separate book is needed to do justice to this topic, the most important message to parents is this: Even if you think your son is not drinking (or doing drugs), you're probably wrong. I've found this to be true again and again in my clinical practice. Boys rarely admit that they're drinking and, when they do admit it, they minimize how much. It's almost as if they know it's really not okay (so they hide it), but they still do it because it's totally acceptable in many parts of our culture. Parents and other adults must be involved in changing the Pack Rules about drinking.

Talking is *still* important. Social milestones are accompanied by emotions that need to be named and processed. It doesn't have to be an elaborate or overly serious conversation. As always, it can be as simple as asking, "How do you feel?" after he passes (or fails) his driver's test or gets into his first choice of college. Another quick and effective way to promote healthy emotional development in boys at this age is just to "keep the lines of communication open." When boys know that they can talk to their parents about anything at anytime, this is not trivial in any way. Something as simple as setting time aside (even a few minutes) each day to be with boys, without a scheduled activity or distraction, is valuable because it allows talking to take place naturally.

Driving. One of the biggest dangers that boys face at this age is car accidents. In this regard, parents and other adults would do well to treat boys more like they treat girls. Thus, a good rule of thumb is this: Ask yourself if you'd allow your sixteen-year-old *daughter* to drive to school daily or to late night, out-of-town concerts, immediately after she gets her driver's license. Perhaps protecting our boys more when it comes to driving may help them to learn that they aren't indestructible machines after all. In the case of driving, it's fear of breaking the Pack Rules that seems to prevent parents from protecting their sons.

The same Pack Rules also cause boys to refrain from adopting a commonsense approach to driving. So many teenage boys (and other people) die because of driving recklessly (too fast, too many people in the car, under the influence). Boys need to know that driving isn't about being tough or cool. Adults can help to shift the accepted norm in this regard, so that we can stop burying so many young men.

Sexual activity. Although boys may be sexually active before they reach this age, I chose to discuss sexual activity here since I believe that it is healthier for boys to be mature (i.e., older), before becoming sexually intimate with another person. I assume that parents already have been talking to their son about his sexuality (masturbation, sexual orientation, sexual activity). Furthermore, I assume that parents have discussed how our sexually saturated culture promotes hypersexuality in boys (pornography, erotica, mixed with violence and power). But, at this stage of his life, it is critical to talk about how he feels about sexual activity with others. And I don't mean just in regard to "safe sex" practices. Rather, I encourage parents to talk with boys about how they feel about this intimate and powerful experience . . . and all the consequences associated with it. Usually, boys only have the influence of the Pack Rules to guide them through the many questions they may have about sex.

I have a relative whose almost eighteen-year-old son wanted to spend a Saturday night with his girlfriend at her brother's college.

Although both mother and son agreed that he could have sex with his girlfriend anywhere, anytime (i.e., he didn't have to go off to a nearby college to do so), the son's response became more reflective when his mother asked, "Steven, are you *really* ready to become a parent?" (In previous discussions, she had asked if he really *wanted* to have a baby; there was something about becoming *ready to be a "parent"* that made this time different.) His demands to spend the night with his girlfriend stopped. Despite the ready availability of contraception, a critical issue associated with sexual activity involves parenthood, and boys need to talk realistically about this aspect of sexual activity.

Graduation. With regard to launching boys into post–high school plans, probably the most important idea to keep in mind is that boys need as much social and emotional support as girls do. But they may not express this need in words. For example, it would be rare for an eighteen-year-old boy to come right out and say, "I'm really scared about graduating from high school." Yet, his feelings may come out sideways through increased drinking that summer, sleeping late, or playing ball all the time. These distractions can mask strong feelings even to the most discerning eye.

How Adults Can Influence Communities For Sixteen- to Eighteen-Year-Old Boys

When boys are at the edge of adulthood, cultural forces often create and reinforce certain rigid traits associated with masculinity (*Only be independent; Only be tough*). Some of these traits are also reinforced for girls, but the critical difference is that girls may receive more emotional support, when launched into the world of adult driving and post–high school plans, than boys do. Boys this age really need to talk about their feelings about all of this, too.

Role models. Families can help influence communities by modeling more emotional support for boys during this age, rather than by reinforcing the stoicism so often associated with masculinity. Independence is important, but so is *interdependence*. Being tough is important, but so is being *nurturing*. Parents can reinforce or reestablish new emotional norms whenever there is a community gathering.

For example, when a seventeen-year-old boy taunts younger boys at the local pool, it's important not to tolerate this and just look away because "boys will be boys." Saying something to the seventeen-year-old like, "Hey, stop that!" Or, "How would you feel if I did that to you?" teaches empathy on the spot if spoken in a concerned rather than shaming way. It also challenges the Pack Rules norms.

Another way to achieve the same end is to compliment older boys on nurturing behaviors that they may display in public places. I once praised a seventeen-year-old boy for how well he cared for his baby sister at a community gathering . . . in front of his friends. He beamed. These may seem like small drops, but it's one way to start filling an empty bucket.

Guns. Boys in middle school and high school have committed almost every school shooting that has been reported in the media. This topic is beyond the scope of this book. However, it's important for all of us to be thinking about how we can educate and reprogram boys about their access to, possession of, and use of guns. And, of course, how they feel about gun use.

Alcohol and drugs. Like carrying and using guns, alcohol and drug use can begin at a much earlier age. However, this is the age for which both the larger culture and the Pack Rules overtly sanction experimentation with and use of alcohol and drugs, especially for boys. There are many ways that adults such as teachers, administrators, health professionals, coaches, and neighbors can help to change these norms. These include: (1) Don't look at boys' drinking and drug use as merely "boys will be boys"; (2) Consider alcohol and drug use as poor coping skills that make problems go away (temporarily), aid socializing (temporarily), and anesthetize feelings (temporarily); (3) Don't look the other way when you see boys drinking or doing drugs: Tell them it's not okay, and then tell their parents; and, (4) Don't sanction underage drinking by allowing boys to drink at your house or at parties.

Now that colleges and universities have become aware of the dangers associated with drinking, there's been a trend in discouraging age-old traditions such as binge drinking at fraternity parties or football tailgating parties. Now, promoting nonalcohol events at football games and other college-sponsored events is becoming a norm. When norms change, boys can see alternatives to some of the narrow, stereotyped rules of masculinity. As boys learn to choose these alternatives, it's important not to shame them for rejecting the Pack Rules. It is also important to remember to help them process their experience when others do shame them. This is important to do at every age, really.

CHAPTER
4

Boys and Emotional Expression

*Boys often tell us their feelings by doing,
not by saying.*

—Patti Atkins Noel, elementary school
guidance counselor

After three-year-old JC finished watching the movie The Lion
King, *he crawled around the house roaring like a lion for days. His
father couldn't get him to stop. At least not until JC's dad figured
out, after the two of them watched the movie together for the second time, that JC had been frightened by Scarr and Mufasa's fight,
and by Mufasa's death.*

*Michael ended second grade with daily tummy aches. He was
extremely shy and his classroom was very noisy and unpredictable.
It apparently got worse with the end-of-the-year frenzy, and finally
overloaded his threshold. He felt anxious and worried, but was
unable to verbalize these feelings. So his tummy did it for him.*

*Ten-year-old Jacob missed the soccer goal that would have resulted
in a tournament win. He showed no one how awful he really felt.
But he picked fights with his younger sister for the entire week
after the game.*

*David's girlfriend broke up with him in December of his junior
year. They had been dating since their freshman year of high school.
She was his only friend and confidant. This was revealed during the
fifth family therapy session, after David had attempted suicide.*

Each of the preceding (true) vignettes is an example of emotional expression. *Emotional expression* refers to the outward ways a person shows positive or negative feelings. This includes vocal and gestural expressions, as well as behaviors that range from "jumping with joy" to stomping up the stairs, and slamming the door. *Emotional restriction* is a particular form of emotional expression that refers to a narrowing or blunting of this expression. In its extreme form, people who restrict their emotional expression always present themselves to others in the same way, whether they're teetering on the edge of tears or triumph. The adjective *stoical* captures the essence of one type of restricted emotional expression. The word "stoic" itself comes from an ancient school of philosophy which taught that the wise person should live free of all passion, unmoved by joy or grief. In the modern world, we are learning that such emotional restriction may be harmful to one's physical, mental, and spiritual health. Often when boys try to be stoical, their feelings come out "sideways," as with JC, Michael, Jacob, and David.

Focus on Emotional Expression

The words "emotion," "emotional," and "feelings" unfortunately often carry a negative connotation, and not only for boys. As noted previously, the phrase "Don't get so emotional" is usually used pejoratively. I want to offer a different way of thinking about emotions. I believe that *all* emotions are important. None are better or worse than others. As described in chapter 1, emotions are a natural part of human biology. Yet, although emotions aren't problematic, problems can arise based on what people *do* with their emotions. Simply put, it's what people do with emotions that makes the difference.

With this broader view of the value of emotions, it then becomes important to examine the relationship between the positive emotions (e.g., happiness and pride), the negative emotions (e.g., sadness, anger, fear), and boys' conditioning and behavior. One way to do this is to think of balance. If boys have access only to one set of emotions, then those emotions will become most fully developed. For example, if a boy always shows anger and never delight, anger will be a stronger presence for him both in his outer and inner lives. Feeling more anger than joy is like lifting weights with only the left side of your body. Something is out of balance.

Indeed, current theorists and researchers suggest that the presence of positive emotions helps to "broaden and build" thought-action behaviors in a way that may even undo the power of negative emotions (Frederickson 2001).

Boys' "Sideways" Emotions

One way to exercise emotions is through expression. There is a developmental aspect to this emotional skill. Verbal expression is the most expedient and effective way to say how you feel, but young children first need to learn the names of feelings in order to say them. In the absence of words, emotions are expressed as behaviors. But if boys learn along the way that it's not acceptable to express emotions, they'll continue to use such "younger" behavioral patterns to communicate their feelings. Finally, if boys (and others) continue to ignore boys' feelings, their emotions can almost "disappear."

When emotions are not expressed, they are hiding in the psyche and within the body. Emotions don't really disappear, they just come out "sideways," or indirectly, as physical symptoms and behavior problems. Physical symptoms often communicate young boys' emotions in the form of tummy aches and illnesses, while older teens may show their sideways emotions in depression, high-risk behaviors, substance abuse, and sometimes self-mutilation.

The four examples that began this chapter illustrate emotions that were expressed sideways. None of the boys used direct verbal expression, which can be very effective for getting one's needs met. Why didn't these boys just come out and say what was bothering them directly? There are many cultural and developmental factors that contribute to this phenomenon. The Pack Rules are certainly one factor. Boys' language development is another.

Yet, what's important to remember here, is that when underlying emotions are not processed verbally and consciously, the emotional energy does not disappear; it has to go somewhere. When it cannot come out directly, it finds another way. It is like a radiator that relieves pressure by letting steam out sideways through a valve. As noted throughout this book, such sideways expressions of emotion includes behaviors like aggression, depression, tantrums, and self-destructive behaviors, as well as physical symptoms like tummy aches, headaches, and panic attacks. Fortunately, emotional expression skills are very teachable.

Redirecting Sideways Emotions in Younger Boys

If JC had been able to say, "I'm scared," during the movie (or if he had covered his face and said, "I don't want to watch this"), then his father would have known to soothe his son's fears. The benefit of communicating such feelings directly is that JC would have learned that his feelings are real, that they matter, and that scary feelings can go away with some help. This makes the world feel much safer to a three-year-old. When his fear goes, he doesn't have to keep up his protective growling around the house.

Michael's tummy aches were clear communications that he was upset (remember, there are receptors in the stomach that receive emotional messages from the brain). Let's assume that in this situation there was no way to prevent Michael's tummy from hurting. Let's also assume he has the type of arousal system that is easily overwhelmed, which is found in many children with shy temperaments. So, rather than suggesting that Michael can *prevent* a tummy ache just by talking, consider how he might make it *go away by talking to someone about it*. That's exactly what happened. Michael and his parents talked about his feelings. His parents told him he could make his tummy ache better by talking to them about his feelings. Then Michael's parents made a pocket-sized jingle that he carried in his jeans' pocket. It said, *"I'm feeling a little scared, but I'll be okay, tummy ache, tummy ache, you can go away!"*

Michael tucked that torn paper into his pants' pocket every day of school that year. And it worked! The words to the jingle were chosen very carefully, and it's important to explain why. Michael insisted on using the word *"I'll* be okay," rather than the original *"It'll* be okay." He knew he needed a way to soothe his very self. Children are the real experts on feelings.

This intervention also was supported with some behavior management at home in the form of a sticker chart on the refrigerator. Michael's parents gave him a sticker every time he told them about his feelings that day . . . and every time he made his tummy ache go away. The tummy aches stopped after the first week. (Charts like this are usually most effective in the first week or two.) But they kept the sticker chart up for a while to remind everyone to keep talking about feelings in the whole family.

Processing Sideways Emotions in Older Boys

If Jacob had been able to tell his parents and his coach, "I'm really disappointed and embarrassed that I missed the winning goal," he would have begun the necessary process to release the physiological chemicals related to his emotions. Instead, Jacob was processing his emotions sideways physically by tormenting his sister. In psychotherapy and crisis debriefing, *processing* refers to talking about an event that is linked with strong emotions. The event can range from a horrific trauma to an everyday happening. Emotional processing often needs to take place more than once and over time, especially if it was a traumatic experience. Usually, both children and adults benefit from talking immediately after an emotionally charged event. And they'll continue talking about it until it's been thoroughly processed.

As always, the first goal for boys is to experience or *feel* their emotions. The second goal is to handle the emotion by talking about it, rather than acting out or making it disappear. If Jacob had talked about his disappointment in missing the soccer goal, he might have prevented it from splitting off from his awareness and coming out sideways in hurtful behaviors toward his sister. Jacob hid his feelings so well that it was hard for his parents to see his feeling of intense disappointment underlying his aggressive behavior. The end result was that Jacob did not learn how to cope with losing—not winning—and the feeling of disappointment in a healthy way. For many boys, this pattern of burying their disappointment, not processing it, turns into shame. Carrying shame around isn't healthy for anyone.

The fourth vignette provides an extreme example of emotion expressed sideways in a suicide attempt. David was older and his family had never talked much about feelings, so he had had plenty of experience learning to ignore his emotions. During a family therapy session, David revealed that he had also wanted to hurt his ex-girlfriend. He wasn't quite able to explain why he had not hurt her. He also could not promise that he wouldn't try to hurt himself again (which is why he was still hospitalized). His therapy progressed very slowly while he was in the hospital. He was unable to remember ever feeling any emotions. But with ongoing individual and family therapy, David's family began the slow and tedious work of "undoing" the lessons David had learned about not feeling his emotions.

"Exercising" Boys' Emotional Expression

When boys' emotions are ignored, then those boys may lose the ability to experience or feel emotions at all. One solution is to prevent this problem from ever happening. Another solution would be to intervene and exercise boys' emotional expression on a regular basis. This exercise varies in different situations. In general, emotional exercise involves helping boys to develop and maintain a range of emotional skills.

Blending: An Important Skill

Emotions can be transformed through a skill I call blending. Blending occurs when one emotion is "mixed together" with thinking or with another emotion. Blending is especially helpful when trying to regulate strong emotions like rage and fear. Unfortunately, our culture places more value on thinking and being *rational* than on feeling and being emotional. Yet it's probably impossible to have a thought without an accompanying feeling, a concept referenced throughout this book. Indeed several theorists (Powers, Welsh, and Wright 1994; Salovey and Sluyter 1997) suggest that for every emotion, an integrated thought co-exists. This means that thoughts and emotions are naturally intertwined in an inseparable way.

Try this short exercise. Stop reading and think about the following words and phrases. Take your time and really think about them. As you do this, notice which emotions you attach to them: death . . . money . . . Christmas . . . Hanukkah . . . Ramadan . . . money . . . marriage . . . exercise . . . chocolate . . . divorce . . . winning the lottery. The emotion is naturally there if we take the time to notice it, and *feel* it.

Blending emotions with thinking. When blending is applied to boys' emotional development, it means that boys, and the adults who care for them, need to pay attention to the emotional aspects of boys' thinking. The end result of blending emotion with thinking is control and mastery. The simple act of verbalizing an emotion is the most common form of blending feelings with thinking. This way, the emotions are no longer just a chemical sensation in the body. A good example of this transformation from biochemical response to blended thinking and feeling was the note that Michael's parents gave him (*"I'm feeling scared, but I'll be OK"*). Such blending allowed Michael to "listen" to his tummy ache and helped him to regulate some strong feelings.

Other ways to blend emotions with thinking include: (1) verbally identifying and expressing feelings to trusted others; (2) engaging in self-talk (talking to yourself in your own mind); and; (3) writing or "journaling" about your feelings on a regular basis. Perhaps the most important benefit of this type of emotional skill is that it provides boys with the opportunity to transform a sensory experience into a feeling and thought that makes sense.

Blending emotions with other emotions. Blending doesn't just involve thoughts. Emotions can be blended with other emotions. Negative emotions can be blended with positive emotions. Indeed this may be what makes life tolerable most of the time . . . being comforted while grieving, or reassured when scared are two examples. The outcome of a positive emotion blended with a negative emotion is that boys can cope with and regulate their emotions better. Think of it as a balancing act. Too much grief and not enough comfort, or too much anger and not enough hope, are unbalanced emotional experiences. When negative emotions are unbalanced, it's possible for stoicism and depression to become engrained patterns. Thus, blending positive with negative emotions can help to balance emotional experiences.

It's also important to point out that when negative emotions are blended with other negative emotions, the end result is a "layered" negativity. When emotions aren't processed, they can just keep adding up, layer upon layer. For example, when Jacob kept his disappointment to himself about not making the winning goal, his disappointment blended with anger, and later with shame. Talking about his feelings might have prevented Jacob's layered negative emotions.

Positive Emotions

Boys' positive emotions also need to be exercised. Positive psychology is not a new science, but it's been gaining more attention recently. Martin Seligman is a pioneer in this area. He is a psychologist who studied and researched "learned helplessness" in his earlier career, and "learned optimism" in his later career. Positive psychology includes the study of how characteristics like wisdom and persistence, and positive emotions like joy, hope, happiness, and love can affect children and adults (Seligman 1998; Seligman, Reivich, Jaycox, and Gillham 1996). When applied to boys' emotions, it seems that boys who are able to feel positive emotions in their everyday lives may be more resilient and healthier than boys who don't.

You may be wondering which boys would not experience positive emotions like these? Any boy, really. All it takes is an environment that restricts his experience and expression of joy, hope, pride . . . love. This includes boys who live in countries devastated by war, boys who live in neighborhoods terrorized by drive-by shootings, or boys who are chronically abused and neglected. I believe, along with other recent writers and researchers, that the "all-American boy" is also at risk because he has learned to restrict the experience and expression of his emotions.

An absence of positive emotions in boys' lives is significant for several reasons. The most obvious is that these boys have been denied access to the full breadth of experiences that life has to offer. Then, as you consider the interdependent role that positive emotions play in blending, positive emotions are also needed for balance. If boys don't have access to these positive emotions, then they're left with only the negative half of their experiences . . . fear without comfort, anger without being understood, disappointment without optimism, and despair without hope.

Benefits of Emotional Expression for Boys

A summary of the benefits of identifying and expressing ("exercising") boys' positive and negative emotions includes: (1) the release of physiological tension to prevent *physical* symptoms; (2) the release of psychological tension to prevent *psychological* struggles such as alexithymia (without words to express feelings), depression, anxiety, and conduct disorders; (3) the opportunities to blend thoughts and other emotions; (4) the opportunities to balance positive and negative emotions; and (5) the opportunities to prevent boys' emotions from disappearing and going underground—only to reappear later in another form.

The "Nerve" of Emotional Expression

What do thumb sucking, crying, rocking back and forth, physical exercise, and talking have in common? Answer: They're all forms of emotional expression because, in some way, they're all attempts to "feel better." This is one of those important areas in which the physical and the psychological are undeniably related.

The Physiology and Feeling of Emotions: Revisited

Thumb sucking and rocking are connected by at least one common physiological thread: the vagus nerve. When vagus nerve receptors are stimulated by either of these behaviors, blood pressure and heart rate decrease. This physiological response is called "vagal tone" (Katz and Gottman 1995). Vagus nerve receptors carry messages from the brain to the heart, lungs, pancreas, kidneys, and large intestine. Quite a track record! The vagus is one of the few nerves in the body that is connected to so many organs. It also coordinates communication between the adrenal glands and the amygdala (in the brain), helping to make the decision to stop pumping adrenaline to various body organs, which, in turn, helps to restore calm to the body. Interestingly, the vagus nerve is also receiving recent experimental attention as a focus of treatment for mood disorders, specifically for depression.

Self-Soothing

Boys need to learn self-soothing skills, and stimulating vagal tone is at least one way they use to calm themselves. One end of the vagus nerve can be stimulated by sucking at the back roof of the mouth. Thus, thumb sucking appears to enhance vagal tone. (That's probably why children like to suck even after bottle-feeding ends). Rocking may also enhance vagal tone. It's no surprise then that parents frequently sway back and forth while holding their little ones, or that children like to rock.

Similarly, the emotional expression of crying is a self-soothing behavior that can lessen reactivity in the body and promote calm by decreasing the amount of steroid stress hormones that prime the stress response. Thus crying may help to lower cortisol levels. Seen in this way, crying actually might keep some children from having more intense and out-of-control behaviors. But since boys learn not to cry early in life, they have less access to this emotional coping skill.

Physical Exercise and Talking

Physical exercise and talking are two of the most socially acceptable forms of emotional expression. They are healthy ways to regulate emotions and to self-soothe. You may not think of exercise as being related to your emotions, but physical exercise and sports, too, appear to have a physiologically calming effect. It's no wonder that boys are drawn to athletics and sports. But physical outlets are not always available when needed.

Talking is the most accessible, portable, and socially acceptable way to express emotions. It allows you to relieve tension, process grief, dissipate anger, and recover from a disappointment or any other unpleasant emotional experience. That is, unless you're a boy. Talking about feelings violates the Pack Rules.

Most boys participate in different forms of emotional expression, depending on their age: crying, thumb sucking, rocking, hitting/kicking, playing sports, or talking. Boys need access to these different forms of emotional expression and coping at different ages and indifferent situations. Chapters 5 and 6 discuss the role of empathy and the socialization of aggression as factors that influence which form of emotional expression boys will use. Another factor involves emotional regulation.

Emotional Regulation

The term *emotional regulation* refers to the ability to organize and complete the necessary tasks at hand in the face of strong negative or positive emotions (Gross and Levenson 1997). Simply put, it means "dealing with it." For a boy, this might mean calming down and doing long division after a fast-paced game of tag during recess, or getting on the school bus even though he just remembered that he forgot to do his homework. Children who function successfully despite the presence of strong emotions are regulating their emotions well.

The two accounts below describe how two boys learned how to regulate their emotions in healthy ways. It goes without saying that this doesn't mean they kept their positive and negative feelings inside or made their emotions disappear. Rather, they learned how to feel their emotions, handle them, and still complete the social and academic tasks at hand.

Charles

At the age of thirteen, Charles still sucked his thumb when he was upset. Going into middle school he had never learned another way to calm himself. (After reading the previous section, you know the physiological reason for this behavior of his: Sucking engages the vagus nerve and this relaxes a tense body.) Charles was an anxious boy by temperament, but there was also a lot of chaos in his life. His biological father had abandoned him and there was chronic domestic violence in his stepfamily. Although his mother did the best she knew how to do, she never taught Charles how to calm himself down when he was a young boy. So he taught himself.

Other ways to relax. Charles didn't know that there were other ways to calm himself down: ways like self-talk, deep breathing, challenging irrational thoughts, or talking to someone. No one had ever taken him to a counselor to help him deal with the chronic trauma in his life. So he did the best he could and calmed himself down by sucking his thumb. The main problem with this was that thumb sucking is socially unacceptable when you're sixteen. Also, he couldn't suck his thumb in school when he needed to. So when Charles felt anxious anywhere but home, he had no way to calm himself. As a result, he frequently got into fights at school and had difficulty concentrating in class. His feelings were definitely coming out sideways.

Getting help. Charles was finally ordered into therapy by the juvenile court system. His behavior problems had escalated into sexual acting out (indecent exposure) and shoplifting. When parents don't bring their children to therapy, the court is the next best chance for boys to get treatment. But Charles didn't tell me about his thumb sucking. His mother did. She was both embarrassed and concerned. When I told Charles that I understood how thumb sucking helped him to calm himself, he looked more relieved than embarrassed. I taught him about vagal tone and many of the other physiological reactions the body experiences as a result of feeling emotions. Then, I told him that I knew of many other ways he could calm himself without sucking his thumb. He understood that these would take lots of practice and that he would still be tempted to use his thumb (it was such a quick fix). But he agreed to try because he knew it was way past the time for him to learn new ways to regulate his emotions.

The intervention that seemed to help Charles regulate his emotion best was self-talk. This makes sense, because he had more cognitive development now (compared to age eight) and he saw how easily his thoughts could influence his feelings and behaviors. The tool of blending also was useful to him. He used a chart to track when he sucked his thumb and what triggered it. This gave us a map for knowing which situations were most challenging, as well as measuring his progress.

Charles' behavior problems improved within the first month of therapy. He still had more work to do in terms of recovering from the traumas he had witnessed and experienced as a younger boy. But at least now he had a new and more "grown-up" way to calm himself. I credit his mother for being brave enough to tell me about Charles' thumb sucking. He would have wasted a lot of time in therapy if he had continued with his thumb instead of learning other ways to soothe himself.

Billy

Billy wasn't your typical eight-year-old, either. What made him unique was how quickly he caught on to using healthy ways to control, or regulate, his anger. He'd been in trouble at day care and at school for as long as his mother could remember. Most of Billy's problems involved physically aggressive behaviors toward his younger brother and other children at school and day care. Billy on top of somebody, throwing punch after punch, was a frequent sight. Whenever he was sent out of the room for a time-out, he always gave a logical explanation that involved perceived victimization. "Jill said she didn't like me," or "Bobby tripped me on purpose," were typical. Whether these precipitants actually happened or not, Billy's aggression was always out of proportion compared to the insult.

Billy met the criteria for a diagnosis of Attention Deficit/ Hyperactivity Disorder. To improve his anger control, he benefited from a combination of medication and Cognitive-Emotional-Behavioral Therapy (CEB-T). The medication helped Billy to delay his impulses, but that was only part of the solution. It was his newfound ability to identify feelings and *think* about different ways to cope with them that really seemed to make the difference, according to his parents.

I would describe a new coping skill for him to try when he felt mad or scared, and Billy would go home and try it out right away. I'd show him how *not* to throw a punch and use words instead to say that he was mad, and he'd go home and practice that, too. I had never worked with a boy so cooperative and so eager to change. I give credit to Billy's parents for seeking therapy early and for monitoring and reinforcing his CEB-T progress at home.

Both Charles and Billy had difficulty regulating their emotions. What they had in common were the ways that their emotions got too big for them to handle and that they needed help in finding socially acceptable, and effective, ways to express and regulate their feelings. There are many other types of emotions that need to be regulated, ranging from excitement to loneliness. Here, you see *how* emotions can be regulated; and that boys often need assistance in learning how to do this.

Restriction of Emotional Expression in Boys

One common and unhealthy pattern of emotional regulation in boys is to restrict (to blunt or to make less) the expression of their emotions. Emotional restriction occurs when people don't show their positive or negative feelings; that is, they hide their feelings from others and even from themselves. Their feelings do not "disappear," however; they just move deeper into the psyche. They go underground, as it were, and may no longer be consciously felt.

Overall, boys display more emotional restriction than girls do. In a seemingly intangible way, kindergarten boys learn that it's not okay to cry at school (or anywhere, really). The same is not true for girls. Although no one wants to be a "crybaby," there are different rules about showing one's vulnerability in public for boys and girls. These rules are more tolerant of girls' vulnerability than boys.' How does this come about?

There are many different theories that explain the development of human behavior, including these: social learning theory, gender schema theory, cognitive-developmental theory, psychodynamic theory, evolutionary theory . . . to name but a few. A review of these theories is best left to a textbook about developmental psychology. The bottom line appears to be that both social and biological theories together explain how and why boys express their emotions. My years of clinical practice tell me that social and cultural influences account for much of boys' (and men's) emotional restriction.

Perhaps boys learn not to cry or show vulnerable feelings because the other kids and adults in their lives tell them not to—with and without words. This explanation seems both more plausible and more hopeful to me than any other theoretical construct. It suggests that we all have a hand in turning off boys' tears, and that we also can have a hand in changing this situation.

Emotional Expression Research

Theories don't actually prove anything. Scientific research doesn't always, either. But both provide systematic ways to observe and describe all kinds of phenomena, including human behaviors such as emotional expression. One theory or research study alone cannot fully account for all of the observed phenomena. Such is the case with the development of boys' restriction of their emotional expression. Here, I present the results of research that provides some idea of what's happening with the study of boys' emotions.

In two different studies I conducted, I observed how boys' emotional expression became more restricted as they moved from childhood through adolescence. The quantitative study (using numerical data) used a cross-sectional design of different age groups to examine age and gender patterns in self-esteem and to explore how emotional expression and contemporary social influences relate to self-esteem (Polce-Lynch, Myers, Kliewer, and Kilmartin 2001). The sample consisted of ninety-three boys and 116 girls in grades 5, 8, and 12 who attended private religious schools in the southeastern United States. The following social predictors (correlations) of self-esteem were measured: media influence, sexual harassment, body image, family and peer relationships, and emotional expression.

This set of predictors accounted for a significant portion of the variance in self-esteem, suggesting that this model is a good "fit" for exploring self-esteem. Girls reported lower self-esteem than boys did in early adolescence, but there was no gender difference in late adolescence.

Unexpectedly, in late adolescence, boys reported lower self-esteem than younger boys did. Most significantly for the thesis of this book, was the fact that *large gender differences were present for emotional expression,* with boys' emotional restriction becoming even more restrictive across adolescence. (See figure 4.1 for this comparison.)

The qualitative study (using words and narratives) found a similar pattern (Polce-Lynch, Myers, Kilmartin, Forssmann-Falk, and Kliewer 1998). Boys and girls in grades 5, 8, and 12 were asked to respond to several questions in writing. The question that focused on emotional expression was: "Is it easy or hard to tell your feelings to others? Tell why." Responses included a steady decline in boys' emotional expression, while girls' emotional expression increased.

What is also interesting about these results is that the actual *number* of words written by boys was much fewer than for girls. Another indicator of the differences in emotional expression is reflected in the fact that thirty-nine boys and only twelve girls chose to pass (not answer) this question.

These two studies combine to suggest that boys restrict the expression of their emotions and girls increase their expression as they move across adolescence. Although this was a relatively small sample, the results are generally consistent with other recent research and clinical observations.

What Unhealthy Emotional Expression Looks Like

Unfortunately it is fairly easy to provide examples of what unhealthy emotional expression looks like in boys: It happens each time boys express their feelings sideways through problem behaviors (atypical for them) rather than talking to someone about their feelings. Consider how these boys expressed their emotions:

★ Jeremiah "tells" his parents he's hurt about not making the cut for the basketball team by stomping to his room, slamming the door, and punching a hole in the wall.

★ Two months after Seth's parents divorce, this ten-year-old boy, who has been "taking it all so well," starts playing with matches in the barn ... near the dry haystacks.

★ One week after Sean's dog dies, this twelve-year-old boy becomes irritable and has trouble concentrating in school. He has not yet shed one tear over losing his beloved dog.

Jeremiah and Seth acted similarly to Jacob (who missed the winning goal in soccer, and communicated his anger and shame *indirectly* by bullying his sister). Each boy restricted the direct expression of his emotions, only to have his feelings come out sideways through aggressive behaviors. Other boys, like Sean who didn't grieve over his dog, may show anxiety and depression symptoms, or stoicism. These are also considered unhealthy expressions of emotions.

Aggression. You may think that Jeremiah, Seth, and Jacob's behavior is "typical" of boy behavior generally. Although it may be typical in the normative sense (i.e., lots of boys do the same things), it's still aggression and it's still unhealthy. Aggression is never a healthy experience for the aggressor, the victim, or the witnesses. The rules for expressing anger hold that: it must not hurt you,

Comparison of mean score of emotional expression

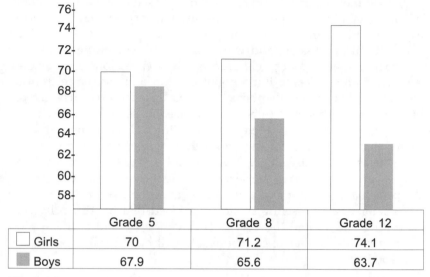

	Grade 5	Grade 8	Grade 12
☐ Girls	70	71.2	74.1
■ Boys	67.9	65.6	63.7

Figure 4.1

anyone else, or property. Of the boys who expressed their feelings via aggression, Jeremiah was the only one who hurt property. Seth might have, given the dryness of the barn. And Jacob did hurt someone else—his sister.

So often parents don't "count" sibling fighting as aggression. This is unfortunate because events like these present opportunities to teach boys how to control their anger and feel empathy. Chapter 6 talks at length about the difference between anger and aggression. Here, it's important to see how aggression is a form of unhealthy emotional expression for boys, and how it is all too commonly accepted as "boys will be boys."

Anxiety and depression symptoms. Everyone experiences "the blues" at some time in life and everyone feels anxious occasionally. Both psychological reactions are normal, especially in response to sad or frightening events. But when depression symptoms (depressed mood, irritability, aggression, low self-esteem, etc.) and anxiety symptoms (difficulty concentrating, inability to relax, irritability, etc.) continue for more than a couple of weeks, a mental health problem may exist and professional help may be needed. But before you seek professional help, keep in mind that parents can do a lot to help cure their son's blues or soothe his supercharged sympathetic nervous system.

Most children bounce back from life's challenges and losses if they can talk with an adult who listens and teaches them how to cope with their feelings. You could probably see how Sean's irritability and inability to concentrate resulted from the way he hadn't expressed his sadness about the death of his dog. Sadness by itself isn't clinical depression, and worrying doesn't constitute an anxiety disorder. Indeed, many children show depression and anxiety symptoms after a death. But without comfort and assistance from an adult, Sean, like many other boys, followed the Pack Rules. He masked his feelings and his grief came out disguised as something else. When this happens, adults are then left correcting a "discipline" problem rather than helping boys cope with their underlying emotions.

I learned this lesson early as a school psychologist intern. I still remember Barry, then a third-grade student, who had been sent to the principal for "not paying attention" at school. When I saw him a week later in a counseling session, I learned that his difficulty concentrating had started the very next day after he had witnessed his father beat his mother unconscious. He still hadn't talked with anyone about it.

Stoicism. This is another face of unhealthy (restricted) emotional expression. You've seen it. The tight-jawed teen who doesn't smile, doesn't frown, hardly even moves his lips when he's talking to you. There's very little eye contact, either. When doing an examination to evaluate someone's mental status, psychologists observe that person's range of affect. Healthy, or broad, affect includes appropriate verbal and facial expressions: sadness when describing a sad experience, or happiness when describing a happy event. When a person exhibits a narrow affect range (a monotone of emotion), this is diagnostically remarkable and that person will be labeled as having either narrow, blunt, or restricted affect. In other words, stoicism is not seen as good mental health.

Today, there seems to be a lot of restricted affect in both boys *and* girls. If the prevailing emotion among young people in the late 1960s and early 1970s was anger, the face of the new millenium is stoicism. The first time I noticed this was at a high school graduation in 1999. The teens and graduates were somber at best. But what's most telling is the fact that stoicism in girls is interpreted as depression, while for boys, it's seen as masculine . . . normal.

What Healthy Emotional Expression Looks Like

Healthy emotional expression is seen in the four-year-old boy who may not want to give his mom a good-bye kiss at day care, but gives her the special (and secret) three-fast-eye-blinks, which is code for "I love you." It's seen in the six-year-old boy who cries when he is hit in the chin by a fast ball, then receives comfort from his parent, and then goes back to finish the game. The ten-year-old who qualifies for regional swimming champion and beams with pride when he tells his parents is demonstrating healthy emotional expression, as is the thirteen-year-old who loses his temper and screams at the referee on the basketball court, but gets himself under control quickly, and apologizes to the referee (without being forced). It's also seen in the sixteen-year-old who knocks on his parents' door at midnight because his girlfriend just broke up with him and he really needs to talk about it.

Watch a group of girls and/or women when they are talking openly, supporting each other, and showing their feelings. *That's* what healthy emotional expression looks like. Healthy emotional expression exists in the boy who can feel his emotions, share them with an appropriate and trusted person, and regulate them in a given context or situation.

In addition to verbal expression with trusted others, boys' emotional expression can take several other forms. Emotions can be expressed through music, poetry, and the visual arts. Although these forms of expression are indirect in that they aren't "eyeball to eyeball" conversations with another person, they're still very valuable for two reasons. First, they allow boys to know, feel, and keep their emotions (instead of making them disappear to follow the Pack Rules) and secondly, when shared, they can lead to a conversation or to direct communication with another person.

Consequences of Restricted Emotional Expression

One major symptom of restricted emotional expression is the previously mentioned disorder called alexithymia (the inability to feel emotions). This clinical disorder is diagnosed more frequently in men than in women. It can be a result of brain trauma or brain surgery. But it also can be a learned, defensive posture that protects boys and men from punishment for showing emotion. That is, it protects them from breaking the Pack Rules.

Mental Health

It's important to consider what happens to boys when they can't or don't express their emotions, because the consequences may have lasting effects throughout their lifetimes. Current scholarship suggests that men's emotional expression is related to both their physical and mental health. Indeed, an effective treatment for depression involves expressing emotions through writing or talking with others (Pennebaker 1995; 1997). The way that adult men mask their feelings is linked to a type of "masculine depression" (Lynch and Kilmartin 1999). This refers to the way that men can be *clinically* depressed but not *feel* depressed. Instead, they feel only anger and display only aggression, rather than the sadness and hopelessness that their anger masks. It's called *masculine* depression because it looks different than traditional depression. In fact, in many ways, it resembles the Pack Rules.

Boys, girls, and adult women can also develop masculine depression because it's essentially a depression masked by *masculine* gender roles and behaviors. It's not about being a biological male. The book, *The Pain Behind the Mask: Overcoming Masculine Depression* (Lynch and Kilmartin 1999), describes masculine depression in great detail. You may find it well worth reading because it describes a common but often overlooked depression that boys may have, one that adversely affects interpersonal relationships, and mental and physical health.

Clearly, one of the most obvious consequences of restricted emotional expression in boys involves interpersonal relationships. By definition, an interpersonal relationship requires some give-and-take between two people. This process often involves self-disclosure, or revealing inner thoughts and feelings. If boys are not comfortable talking about themselves, they'll have difficulty initiating and maintaining intimate relationships with others. Furthermore, having relationships appears to be a protective factor in mental and physical health. In fact, one of the greatest threats to human development is the loss of such protective factors and systems (Masten 2001).

Physical Health

The evidence that points to a connection between men's physical and psychological distress, interpersonal relationship problems, and the restriction of emotions is persuasive. There also appears to be a link between rigid masculine gender roles and high-risk behaviors such as alcohol abuse, unsafe sexual practices, dangerous sports, tobacco use, physical fights, neglecting nutrition, and physical health, to name just a few (Courtenay 1998).

As Professor Chris Kilmartin (2000) points out, the relatively new field of behavioral medicine is focusing on physical disorders that may be strongly influenced by psychological functioning. Boys' and men's socialization via the Pack Rules may contribute to physical diseases and disorders, such as cardiovascular disorders and peptic ulcers, that are seen predominantly in men.

What Do Other People Say About Boys' Emotional Expression?

In preparation for this book, I wanted to obtain some perspectives outside of my clinical practice and review of empirical studies to learn more about what other adults think about boys' emotions, and in particular, boys' emotional expression. Using an informal survey of forty-five adults, ranging in age from eighteen to sixty-eight years old, in five states in the eastern United States, I obtained answers to the following questions. I have summarized their responses and I use direct quotes to reflect themes.

Do you think that boys' emotions are important? Why or why not?

The answer to this question was unanimous. *Everyone* responded, "Yes, boy's emotions are important." In response to "Why or why not," the answers ranged from, "If boys learn to express emotions at an early age, then they'll know how to do it as an adult" to "Boys are human, that's why." In general, the theme was that it's very obvious that boys' emotions are important.

Do you think that boys need to express their emotions? If so, where and how?

There was a unanimous, "Yes," to the first part of the question from both men and women. But differences emerged for the second part. Women consistently said boys should talk to "safe, trusted others . . . like friends, parents, teachers, coaches." The women seemed to list nearly all of the people they knew, while men identified only a select few as okay for boys to talk to, mainly the boys' families. For example, one man, a forty-nine-year-old professional, and the father of a teenage boy, said, "Being sensitive isn't advantageous to boys" [but that] "in a family setting or [a] group of close friends, males need to be more open with their emotions." His statement was echoed in the majority of men's responses.

One man had a different response. John Serafine is a forty-three-year-old high school guidance counselor and basketball coach in Fairport, New York. He's the father of four (two girls, two boys). He's also a former talented high school and college athlete, listed in his city's sports hall of fame. Despite his own socialization by the Pack

Rules, he has learned to challenge some of these narrow masculine norms. Here's what he had to say about boys' emotional expression:

> Boys most definitely need to express their emotions, anytime and anywhere. The message that we need to send to boys is that their emotions are theirs and they should be free to display them without receiving permission first. They need to know that it is okay to be happy, sad, afraid, nervous, embarrassed, angry, etc. I'd like to see us focus on teaching boys that it's what they do with their emotions that is ultimately important.

A recent study indicated that boys restrict their emotional expression beginning in early adolescence, while girls' emotional expression increases. Why do you think this happens?

All of the answers to this question referenced the socialization process. Most quoted the Pack Rule, "boys don't cry," and the general idea that boys must be strong and that, "for boys to be strong, crying can't be in the equation." Left unsaid was the punishment and shame that boys usually receive for out-role behavior like crying.

Some boys have a shy temperament and keep to themselves, some have an extroverted temperament and freely talk to others, and some fall in between. Describe your son(s)' temperament and how it relates to his emotional expression.

What I learned from the answers to this question is that many parents (who generally lack degrees in psychology, education, or a related field) usually don't focus on their sons' temperament. But when they do, this kind of reflection can become another helpful parenting tool.

Although girls are socialized to express their emotions, they don't turn out to be "wimpy" in middle and high school . . . they're formidable competitors in sports and other venues. Do you think it's possible for young boys to be socialized to keep their emotions without turning into "wimps" when they're older? If so, how? If not, why not?

The responses were primarily, "Yes, it's possible." Those who disagreed with the overall observation said that they think girls *are* still generally considered to be wimpy, i.e., softball is easier than baseball and girls' basketballs are smaller than boys. Perhaps more to the point, was this response, "Emotions are considered a weakness, so boys can't show emotions without being wimps."

Here is a range of responses to the question of how and why boys might be raised to express their emotions without becoming wimps:

"Yes if a man is secure and confident he can show emotions. Ironic, isn't it ... how showing feelings really is a sign of strength" (fifty-year-old Caucasian father of three girls).

"Yes, I believe that if society allows males to express themselves in a way that is more reasonable they'd be less likely to explode" (fifty-five-year-old Caucasian mother of two sons).

"Yes, suppressing emotions is unhealthy for everyone" (sixty-year-old African-American father and grandfather).

"Yes, just treat boys 'normally' and [have them] cultivate everything from sports to talking about feelings" (twenty-one-year-old Caucasian woman).

"Yes, in my mind, the boy who doesn't express his feelings is the *real* wimp" (nineteen-year-old male, African-American, college student).

Responses to this survey describe a confusing world for boys, one that sends them a double message: *Your emotions may be important, but it's still not safe to show them outside of your family.* Unfortunately, there are many boys who can't exhibit their emotions either in public *or* with their families. It's interesting to note that it wasn't only the men who gave voice to the idea that it's not safe for boys to show their vulnerable emotions outside of the family. Women, too, are familiar with the Pack Rules (especially the one that states: *boys don't cry*) and they can see how these rules limit boys' emotional expression. I guess it's hard to miss. Overall, the survey reflects the general belief that boys' emotions *are* important, but we still don't know how to allow them to *be* important.

Conclusion

Changing the norms that boys' emotions are not important and that expressing feelings isn't necessary or appropriate is a daunting task. It goes against the cultural grain. It makes parents and other adults feel anxious because no one wants to set up boys for rejection intentionally. Yet this fear of not being "masculine," of being a wimp, a mama's boy, or a sissy is what fuels the Pack Rules.

At some deep level, though, everyone agrees that boys need to be able to have and express their emotions. It would seem that the next logical step would be to change the cultural norms so that boys will not have to mask their emotions through stoicism and aggression. Fortunately, emotional expression is a very teachable skill. If boys learn to feel and express their emotions, then their emotions won't come out sideways. If they receive no punishment or shame for showing their emotions, boys' physical and mental health will improve, as will the lives of those who are in relationships with boys, which is truly everyone.

Boys' Empathy: A Hallmark
of Emotional Health

"E.T. and Elliot have a special way of communicating,"
Michael whispered.

"You mean they think each other's thoughts?"
asked the scientist.

"No . . . They feel each other's feelings."

> —Dialogue from Steven Spielberg's
> movie, *E.T.*

It's difficult to find anyone who doesn't like Steven Spielberg's
movie, *E.T.* Yet this wonderful movie isn't merely entertaining, it
appears to be a modern myth about boys' emotions. It tells the story
of an extraterrestrial botanist (E.T.) who, when he can't make it back
to his spaceship, develops a special relationship with a boy from
Earth (Elliot). (Eventually, E.T. figures out how to go back to his
home planet.) It's not the plot that is so mythlike, though. It is the
relationship between E.T. and Elliot, and the natural emotions
expressed in that relationship. The snippet of dialogue in the quote
above captures the essence of the importance of empathy in their
friendship. *Each could feel what the other felt.*

Why is empathy a hallmark of emotional health? One reason is the relational dynamic of empathy; it involves other people. Being in relationships with others (family, peers, teammates, co-workers) serves as a protective factor in maintaining good mental health. Good relationships are good for us. However, when someone is without the ability to empathize, that person is essentially cut off from intimate relationships. No one can be in a healthy relationship with another person without being able to understand that person's experience of life and point of view. Empathy is a hallmark of emotional health because the ability to empathize is what separates humans from monsters and machines.

In a book about boys' emotions, empathy is such an important subject it merits an entire chapter. What follows is a discussion about the nature of empathy: how it develops, the role it plays in boys' emotional development, and how it influences interpersonal relationships and mental health. Two case studies are provided as a way of illustrating the dynamics of empathy in boys' lives. My goal is to provide enough information about empathy for you to help the boys in your lives develop, nurture, and employ their capacity to feel empathy in their daily life experiences.

The Root of Boys' Humanity Is Their Empathy

Empathy comes from the Greek word, "empatheia," which translates as "feeling into." Such feeling into requires understanding how another person feels. It also includes "feeling into" other living creatures, like animals and pets. Over two centuries ago, Adam Smith described empathy as "the ability to understand another person's perspective and have a visceral or emotional reaction" (Zahn-Waxler, Cole, Welsh, and Fox 1995, 28).

These descriptions leave unstated what I consider to be the core feature of empathy: to know how another person feels requires you to know what you feel. Put another way, *empathy for the self must come before empathy for others is possible.* From this perspective, many boys are disadvantaged when it comes to empathizing with others. Why? Because if empathy begins with an awareness of one's own feelings, and if boys have been trained not to feel their own emotions, then their ability to *feel into* the feelings of others will be severely limited. It may even be impossible.

Empathy has been described as an antidote for anger (Goleman 1995). I believe that empathy also is an antidote to narcissism (preoccupation with the self). And narcissism appears to be one of the steel

I-beams that upholds the unhealthier aspects of stereotypical masculinity (i.e., win at all costs, dominate, etc.). Thus, to be empathic runs directly counter to the Pack Rules and narcissism. As long as a boy can still "feel into" another person's experience, he is less likely to hurt others. He's also less likely to hurt himself because empathy for the self results in good self-care.

Lack of Empathy

The complete absence of empathy can have a very destructive face. For example, in 1994, a Pack of eight high school boys used a baseball bat to beat Eddie Polec to death outside Philadelphia (Freedman and Knoedelseder 1999). Eddie was a sixteen-year-old boy literally in the wrong place at the wrong time. And the members of this Pack, all later convicted of murder, were also in the wrong place *within themselves*. Fueled by anger and unable to empathize with the helpless boy they were hurting . . . killing . . . each boy took turns beating Eddie. One held his small body as the others struck it over and over, leaving Eddie unrecognizable.

The absence of empathy is most striking when a person continues to inflict pain on another person *who is already hurting*. When the lack of empathy goes as far as it did with Eddie, it has another name, that is, torture. It is ironic that this Pack of boys used a universal symbol of boyhood, a baseball bat, in their act of inhumanity. They had *No Fear* and they had no empathy.

Of course, Eddie Polec's haunting death is an extreme example of how the absence of empathy can affect boys and those around them. A less extreme example is seen in the actions of the thirteen-year-old boy who spread untrue sexual rumors about his ex-girlfriend. She broke up with him and he was angry and hurt. Spreading malicious rumors took care of his need to win or to "save face" (Pack Rules). And, since he did not empathize with how she felt about the rumors he spread, he didn't feel bad. He didn't *feel into* her experience, the very same girl he said he cared for, just two days before. Empathy could have prevented his anger from becoming so hurtful to someone else, and certainly empathy would have prevented Eddie Polec's death.

How Empathy Develops

Knowledge about the origin and development of empathy isn't an exact science. Very little about human development is. Here, I combine a phenomenological approach (an individual person's experience) with developmental psychology to understand how healthy empathy develops. Mentioned previously, both scholarly research and my clinical practice continue to lead me to theorize that empathy for others begins with empathy for the self. Thus, boys won't feel another person's sadness unless they can feel their own sadness, and they won't feel another's joy unless they can feel their own joy.

So why does one boy develop a healthy ability to feel empathy and another boy doesn't? As with any other aspect of human development, there are biological and environmental influences, and both of these interact and affect the other. The simplest explanation is this: It appears that a boy who receives empathy-reinforcing behaviors from his environment is more likely to develop the "emotional circuits" that allow him to feel empathy for himself and others. The opposite also appears to be true. If a boy does not receive the type of stimulation, i.e., empathy-reinforcing behaviors that will help him to develop his own empathic feelings, his ability to feel empathy may be distorted in some way.

Boys' Empathy Begins in the Beginning

The roots of empathy can be traced back to infancy. Some researchers have suggested that the way newborns cry when they hear other newborns cry is a form of empathy. Indeed, an infant's mimicry of another's distress may actually be a precursor to empathy. During infancy and until approximately the end of the first year, it appears that babies respond to others' distress as if it were their own. They demonstrate some type of connection or "feeling into" the distress of others. One explanation for this is that babies haven't quite developed a sense of themselves as being separate from others yet (Mahler, Pine, and Bergman 1975; Masterson 1993).

Between approximately one to two and one-half years old, toddlers begin to develop a sense of themselves as being separate from others. The critical first step in empathy development is to be able to feel your own feelings. Once a boy begins to figure out that he is separate, his feelings become, or need to become, his own. Clearly, the importance of mirroring, understanding, and accepting boys' emotions at this age is essential in the development of the capacity to feel empathy.

How the Environment (Parents and Adults) Influence the Growth of Empathy

The researchers who investigate empathy development pay particular attention to the emotions and prosocial behaviors related to empathy (Eisenberg and Miller 1987). Responsibility appears to be connected to both empathy and guilt, with girls showing more prosocial, empathic responses than boys as early as preschool (Zahn-Waxler and Robinson 1995; Zahn-Waxler, Cole, Welsh, and Fox 1995). Why is there such a wide gender difference at this age?

One explanation holds that the powerful combination of children's temperaments, environmental experiences, and cultural forces come together to create a gender gap this early. As described in chapters 2 and 3, boys' various temperaments *elicit* different responses from parents, and these responses in turn affect boys' learning and behaviors. This doesn't mean that boys' temperaments decide their fate. Rather, it is that a complicated dance (in scientific terms, a transactional process), takes place between parent and child within a culture that rarely supports boys' emotions. And the development of empathy appears to be related to the way the environment responds to boys. Simply put, regardless of temperament, it seems that without teaching directly targeted to their own emotions and the feelings of others, boys will be less likely to develop the ability to empathize.

The most important environmental response to facilitate the development of empathy in boys (in everyone, really) appears to be the knowledge that their inner emotions are known, understood, and accepted. Thus to learn empathy, a boy must first experience someone *empathizing with his feelings.* And this needs to occur on a regular basis beginning and continuing throughout childhood and adolescence. The parent or caregiver must "feel into" boys' experiences. Boys must have the felt experience of being seen and understood *from the inside.*

Although it appears that precursors to the development of empathy are present during infancy, estimates of when empathy behaviors first develop in children range from age two to age four. This may seem like a wide age span for such a critical aspect of human development. It is. But like so many aspects of human behavior, particularly in infants and toddlers, it's difficult to measure and observe what cannot be spoken. Despite this challenge, researchers have found many interesting patterns that facilitate or interfere with empathy development.

Empathy research. In a series of studies conducted under the auspices of the National Institute of Mental Health, researchers examined interactions between parents and their preschool children (Radke-Yarrow and Zahn-Waxler 1984). Based on these observations, the researchers concluded that parents' discipline methods were related to their children's ability to empathize. More specifically, when parents' discipline methods involved helping their children see how their behavior caused other children to feel distress, e.g., "Look at how sad Johnny feels since you hit him," these children appeared to display more empathy than those children whose parents disciplined them only with behavioral correction, e.g., "You were naughty."

Another interesting finding from this research project was that children appeared to learn empathy from both direct teaching and indirect modeling. The direct teaching of empathy is more familiar, as when adults directly tell children how to attend to another child's feelings. Indirect modeling (observing empathy in others) may be less familiar. The parent who says, "Look how sad Charlie is because he couldn't get on the tire swing," and "I'd feel so proud if I drew a picture like Steven's" are both examples of indirect modeling.

Such modeling also occurs when children observe other peers who provide an empathic response to another peer in distress. For example, the boy who witnesses another boy offer Charlie a spot in the sandbox (because Charlie was rejected at the tire swing) is observing indirect modeling. He learns not only how to recognize another boy's pain, but he also sees how comfort can help ease pain. This is a good lesson for boys in many ways. There are endless opportunities for parents and adults to use indirect modeling of empathy as a teaching tool at every age. Taken together, these studies suggest that empathy can be directly taught by reflecting boys' own feelings, by certain discipline techniques, and by direct and indirect modeling.

The environmental response that seems to help boys develop empathy, regardless of their temperament (the boy doesn't have to be a "sensitive" type to feel empathy), is this: Boys need to first feel their own emotions and *to receive empathy* for these emotions from parents, trusted caregivers, and then from their peers. Boys can learn how to empathize with others through teaching, discipline, and modeling. Furthermore, boys who receive empathy are then most able to give it.

How Empathy Is Snuffed Out of Boys

If teaching and learning empathy are so simple, why are boys at such high risk for not developing it? The process of snuffing out boys' empathy involves several steps. But before focusing on boys, it's helpful to think about how empathy does not develop, regardless of gender. Environmental risk factors for the development of empathy appear to be lack of bonding with caregivers, emotional neglect, and any type of child abuse, including physical, emotional, and sexual abuse (Cicchetti and Carlson 1989; Herrenkohl and Herrenkohl 1981). These risks increase with chronicity and severity. In other words, the more frequent and severe the risk factors are, the more likely that children's empathy development will be disturbed (Main and George, 1985; Klimes-Dougan and Kistner 1990). The disturbance can range from a lack of empathy to "hyper" empathy.

Although you are probably familiar with the terms "sociopath" and "antisocial personality" (without empathy or a conscience), the term *hyperempathy* (extremely sensitive to the feelings and moods of others) may be less familiar. Hyperempathic people don't call as much attention to themselves because they don't break social or legal rules in the ways that a person without empathy does. Rather, they tend to be "people pleasers." People pleasing is a psychological defense that serves as a form of self-protection.

The "Window" of Teaching Empathy

The timing of teaching empathy appears to be important in its development. Since empathy development appears to begin in infancy, the earlier a boy receives mirroring and bonding with a caregiver, the better. Developmental psychologists have suggested there is a "critical window" (meaning some skills must be learned at a specific age) for certain aspects of human development (Sroufe 1997). Empathy may be one of these. Yet, much of the human brain remains "plastic," meaning that new skills can be learned and experienced throughout the life span. More is known about when the critical window for empathy opens than when it closes. Thus, although it's known that eliminating risk factors and mirroring boys' emotions when they're very young is important, since the brain is so plastic, it may be possible for older children (even adults) to develop empathy.

Good intentions are sometimes harmful. Most parents don't intentionally set out to ignore their son's feelings. Or to snuff out his ability to empathize. My experience as a psychotherapist has taught me that parents' intentions are usually positive. Although the outward behavior may be harmful to the boy, almost always, his parents' underlying intent is about protecting him in some way. I have worked with parents who honestly believed that beating their son was the best thing they could do to help him behave.

When parents consistently ignore their son's feelings for well-intended reasons, this can also result in negative outcomes. For example, in an effort to prevent their son from getting a "swelled head," some parents may ignore his pride about a school project or a starring role in the school play.

Following the same reasoning, other parents may ignore their son's sadness about not winning a prize in the science contest or not making the final cut for the basketball team. These parents don't want their son to "dwell" on the bad; they don't want him to focus on losing. Unfortunately, this can also result in not talking with him about how he is feeling. Although some researchers have found that going over and over negative events in the mind may contribute to depression in children (Nolen-Hoeksema 1994), focusing on boys' feelings is not the same thing as "dwelling on the bad." To the contrary, talking about negative experiences often stops negative thoughts from reoccurring in one's mind.

Indeed, boys benefit from expressing their positive and negative emotions and having these emotions seen, understood, and accepted by others. And this is *especially* important in regard to empathy development. If boys' emotions aren't validated and understood, then valuable empathy skills won't get practiced. When parents and other adults ignore boys' emotions and uphold the Pack Rules, this can contribute to a distortion of boys' ability to empathize.

What Boys' Empathy Looks Like

Boys may have healthy empathy, too little empathy, or too much empathy. The boy with healthy empathy is often described as "a nice boy." He is genuine and caring, but also stands up for himself. A boy with too little empathy usually violates social or legal rules and he has few (if any) real relationships. He lacks regard for how others feel. This boy can be very charming or very mean. The boy who has too much empathy is the "people pleaser," sensing the moods and needs of others as if they were his own. He puts others' needs before his own, always.

Knowing what it feels like to be in a relationship with each type of boy is also important. Relating to "nice boys" genuinely feels good. There's a healthy give-and-take to the relationship. Relating to the hyperempathic boy feels tenuous, like walking on eggshells for fear of hurting him in some way. Relating to the boy with too little empathy often feels as if you've been used or manipulated, quite often after the fact, and especially so if the boy was charming when he was manipulating you.

It's important to note that young children's intuitive thinking style leads them to believe that "what they see is what they get." In other words, if a boy without empathy is nice to them, then he *is* nice. Eventually though, older children will sense that there's something that they don't like about a boy with little or no empathy. Sometimes they're unable to name what it is, saying something like, "I don't like Donnie . . . I don't want to hang out with him." When queried about why not, the similarly vague answer is likely to be, "I don't know why . . . I just don't."

Jake: Too Little Empathy

Another way to see the healthy and unhealthy aspects of empathy is to look closer into boys' lives. Jake was the kind of boy who didn't have much empathy. He was the mean rather than charming type. When I first met Jake, it was September of his junior year in high school. Because of the many fights he was in, he was getting suspended from school on a regular basis. The assistant principal and the guidance counselor recommended counseling to Jake and his parents. Jake's parents had been given the same recommendation the previous year, but since it hadn't been during the football season, they had no motivation to follow through. This term, Jake's conduct problems put him at risk for being kicked off the football team. Neither parent wanted this to happen. So they sent Jake to counseling. The parents refused to participate, though. Instead, they would drop Jake off at the clinic and leave, or most of the time, they'd have an aunt bring him to the clinic.

This hulk of a boy dwarfed my office chair. He sat in the chair closest to the door, the one most people sit in when they're not sure they want to be there. Jake was polite and forthcoming with answers to my initial questions about school, friends, the fights, and his family. He said that he didn't have many friends and that he got along "okay" at home. When asked why he fought so much at school, he replied that other kids picked on him. (Since Jake was so tall and muscular, I had a hard time imagining anyone who'd mess with him.) He explained that it was simple. Kids made fun of him for not being smart, so he beat them up.

When I began to explore Jake's feelings, he said that he didn't have any. I continued to explore with every clinical tool I had, but he remained stoical. As it turned out, he was right. Not only did he not feel empathy for the kids he had seriously hurt at school, he had little empathy for himself. He told me how he had been secretly cutting himself for a couple of years with razor blades. He rolled up his long-sleeved jersey. There, on top of his boyishly chubby but almost manly arm, were countless thin white scars. I wasn't surprised when Jake showed his scars to me after I had asked him about his feelings. He explained that cutting was the only way he could feel anything.

How he forgot feelings. Jake couldn't remember the last time he had felt sad, scared, or emotionally hurt. He told me that, on the football field, he sometimes didn't even feel the pain of being tackled and dragged for eleven yards. When asked how the other boys felt at school after he slammed their heads against the locker for mocking him, Jake said, "I don't know. I don't care."

How did Jake arrive at the point of not feeling his emotions or the emotions of others? Or in terms of empathy, how could he not empathize with his own pain or the pain of others? Remember, some of the risk factors for not developing empathy include chronic abuse and neglect during childhood. Jake had experienced both of these risk factors. It is very common to find child abuse and/or neglect in an alcoholic home and both of Jake's parents were alcoholic. They weren't neglectful of his physical needs; they fed and clothed him and they gave him shelter. Despite coming from this upper middle class family, Jake's emotional needs were neglected. Alcoholism, child abuse and neglect, and domestic violence cut across all socio-economic class and racial lines.

Jake couldn't remember the last time his father had said anything nice to him. He also couldn't remember a time when his father got angry and didn't hit him. Or one of his siblings. This abuse had been going on for as long as Jake could remember. Jake's mother was emotionally abusive and neglectful, too. She would yell and scream at his brother and sister, insulting them because they were having trouble learning in school (just like Jake). When I asked Jake how his brother and sister felt about his parents, Jake said he didn't know, with a blank look on his face.

Trauma can cause the absence of feeling. When soldiers experience the horror of war and then return home, they may be diagnosed with Acute Stress Disorder. If their symptoms continue, or if the onset of the symptoms is delayed and they become evident only several months (or years) later, the diagnosis is Post-Traumatic Stress Disorder (PTSD). Similarly, when children witness the horror of domestic violence and experience abuse in their homes, they also may have PTSD or Acute Stress Disorder.

Post-Traumatic Stress Disorder includes a variety of symptoms. The most prominent symptom for Jake, and the one that kept getting him into trouble at school, was the numbing or absence of feelings after he was hyperaroused; he would "overreact," and then act without any feelings. Jake had lived through a war during the critical years of his life when his emotions were developing. It was not surprising that Jake no longer was able to feel anything. His emotions had not been mirrored, validated, or understood by his parents or early caregivers. And empathy was never modeled for him. Any mirroring he received from other adults in his life (teachers, coaches, grandparents), apparently wasn't enough to balance out the severe and long-term effects of the abuse and neglect he had endured in his family life.

I don't know whether Jake ever developed empathy for himself or others. Once I learned about the abuse, I had to report it to the Department of Social Services. (By law, therapists must report suspected child abuse to the appropriate child protection agency in their state.) When I told Jake that I would have to do this, he responded with both fear and relief. He thought he would get into more trouble at home, but he knew that something needed to change. I'm not sure what, if anything, changed for Jake and his family. Jake stopped coming to see me after I made the report.

Given the presence of so many risk factors, it isn't surprising that Jake's ability to develop empathy was nonexistent. With so much violence and neglect in the home, it would be surprising if Jake had learned to cope with his anger in a more socially acceptable manner. Clues that boys' empathy has been snuffed out come in many ways: frequent aggression, self-inflicted injurious behavior, or high-risk behaviors (drinking, driving fast) are all red flares. The inability to develop intimate family relationships and solid peer relationships are others. Jake was sending up all of these flares.

Antonio: Healthy Empathy

Probably the best way to describe Antonio is that he's a "nice kid." This description may be one of the best predictors of healthy empathy in boys. Think of someone you consider to be a "nice guy." Typically, he's someone who cares about others. And one of the reasons he cares is because he can empathize. Nice boys don't swing cats by their tails and they don't hurt others. Nice boys aren't "too nice" in the hyperempathic way, or charming as sociopaths can be. Nice guys stand on their own two feet and, although they care about others, they don't sacrifice their own needs, and they don't ignore their own feelings.

This nice kid lived with his grandmother. Antonio had never known his father, and his mother had been in and out of drug rehabilitation ever since he was born. Antonio was a very active two-year-old when he went to live with his "Nanna." She was a hardworking woman who provided for herself and Antonio on a housekeeper's salary. She made sure Antonio knew right from wrong, was proud of himself, and that he cared about others and treated them respectfully. Despite some annoying hyperactive behaviors, Nanna loved her grandson beyond words. The feeling was mutual.

Antonio came for therapy about six months after his grandmother died of a sudden heart attack. He was living with an aunt and uncle in a new town now. His grades had dropped. His relatives knew that Antonio had been an excellent student and that he had always had a nice, sunny disposition. But now the boy who was living with them looked dark. He was frequently irritable and most of the time he didn't seem to care about anything. His aunt and uncle were afraid Antonio might be headed down the wrong path and they wanted to keep him straight. They knew that, in their neighborhood, there were many crooked paths to take.

Healthy empathy can "hurt." Antonio didn't want to go down a wrong path, either. The problem was, naturally, that he was still grieving his Nanna's death. When I first interviewed Antonio, he made good eye contact and he talked openly about his sadness. He seemed relieved that someone finally was talking with him about his feelings. Although his aunt and uncle were good to him, they didn't talk openly about feelings in their home. Antonio had had the sense that they were afraid to talk about Nanna to him for fear that such talk would upset him. Ironically, Antonio had figured out on his own that he'd feel *better* if they would talk about Nanna more often . . . or listen while he talked.

So the focus of Antonio's therapy became grief education for his new family. His aunt and uncle were given the tools they needed to help Antonio get through the difficult first year after losing a loved one. Gradually, his grades began to rise and a year later he seemed like his old self.

How did Antonio become such a nice boy? Why didn't he run with a Pack or participate in behaviors that hurt others? Despite an early start in life that had not met his needs (abandonment and early neglect are risk factors), his environment from the age of two to nine was one that mirrored his inner world. Even with Antonio's "difficult" (very active, very high energy) temperament, he had learned to understand his own feelings and those of others. He had learned to empathize in healthy ways.

Practical Ways to Help Boys Learn and Keep Empathy

Many environmental influences shape the development of boys' empathy. Indeed, despite Antonio's active temperament, Nanna never missed an opportunity to pay attention to Antonio's emotional life. She always mirrored his feelings and freely discussed his and her emotions in their home.

According to current brain-emotion-behavior research, it now appears that the environment *can* shape and change the biological basis of behaviors. For example, a recent study of dental phobia showed that patients who had learned how to calm themselves by using *behavioral* techniques (relaxation exercises and self-talk) demonstrated less anxiety at the dental appointments than the control group (who received no interventions), or the medicated group (who took anti-anxiety medication) (Thom, Sartory, and Johren 2000). Thus, by changing behavior, related emotions can change, too, even with fear of the dentist!

So, how can parents and other adults help boys to develop empathy? Which exercises are as effective in shaping boys' empathy skills as the relaxation exercises were in shaping dental patients' emotions? The main environmental supports for developing empathy skills seem to involve the following behavioral interventions for boys of every age.

★ **Empathize with boys.** This involves genuinely understanding boys' emotions and "feeling into" their experiences. It isn't difficult to do this, but it does fly in the face of the Pack Rules. Adults often feel uncomfortable focusing on boys' feelings because of the fear that it will harm boys in some way. They fear that paying attention to boys' feelings will make boys more "feminine." This is not true. Empathizing with boys' feelings doesn't make them anything but more human.

★ **Validate boys' emotions.** Validation of feelings simply means that once you understand the emotion, you acknowledge and accept it. This can be done with words or with actions. A hand on the shoulder when a boy is discouraged is a form of validation. So are the words, "Feeling _____ makes sense to me." Just listening to a boy talk about his feelings is validating. The opposite of validation is ignoring or shaming boys for how they feel (this is also the opposite of empathy).

★ **Teach empathy.** This can be done in simple ways. The more empathy becomes a part of the family's way of thinking (and feeling), the more it will be a skill that boys learn, almost unconsciously, like riding a bike. It becomes effortless after a while. The simplest way to teach empathy is to frequently *talk about how other people feel*. For younger children, characters in storybooks can be used, as well as playmates and family members. For older children and adolescents, it can be just as casual, focusing on siblings, extended family members, TV shows, movies, characters in novels, friends, teammates, teachers, and so forth. It doesn't have to be about major life issues; teaching empathy is just about acknowledging that other people have needs and feelings. After this is understood, the next connection to make is to focus on how other people feel in response to boys' behavior: "And how did Jamie feel when you said that?" If the answer is "I don't know," then encourage the boy to take a guess. If he still doesn't know, describe possible emotions. This will establish the connection between the boy and another person's feelings.

★ **Teach boundaries.** When children and adolescents feel another person's feelings, it is important that they learn to establish a psychological boundary between themselves and the other person. Without a boundary line between the self and another, a state of symbiosis (psychological merging) takes place, creating confusion about whose needs and feelings belong to whom. Symbiosis is considered a natural stage of psychological development under age two and is eventually replaced by individuation (solid identity). Healthy psychological boundaries reflect this individuation and define the difference between *caring about another person* versus *taking on that person's problems*. When boys empathize with others, it's important that they learn to care without giving up their own needs, thoughts, and feelings in the service of caring for another person. Psychological boundaries help establish and maintain identity.

★ **Model empathy directly.** Modeling empathy *directly* can take place in the daily conversations that you have with boys. It's as simple as "thinking out loud" so that boys can hear adults say things like: "I feel so badly for the family whose house burned down . . . they must be shocked and desperate." Or, "I feel so helpless about the children in Guatemala who search through trash heaps eight hours a day to feed their families." And don't forget to model the positives, as in, "How thrilled the football team must be for making it to the state championship." Note that all of these statements directly model empathy by describing another person's emotions.

★ **Model empathy indirectly.** *Indirect* forms of empathy can involve observing when others display empathy and positively commenting on this. It might occur when a brother empathizes with someone in the family and you remark, "Samuel was really kind to Joshua." In later childhood and adolescence, there are plenty of examples of boys who display empathy about which you can comment. All it takes is an adult to observe and say something. Reinforcing boys' empathy in a positive way is what makes the difference between being a "wimp" and being a "nice guy." Too often, boys show empathy to other boys and it's either ignored or not perceived as a good thing. Teach boys that empathy is good.

Conclusions

The biological basis of empathy must also be recognized. Some theorists have suggested that there is a "criminal gene" as well as differences in brain functioning that prevent some people from experiencing empathy or having a conscience (Brothers 1989; Patrick, Cuthbert, and Lang 1994). There is ongoing debate about this theory and research. Here, I want just to acknowledge the possible genetic aspects of empathy development.

The discussion of boys' empathy in this chapter focused on the environmental aspects of developing empathy because this is the part that can be shaped. Clearly, parents have more control over how they raise their sons than they do over the genes their sons inherit. Environmental responses to boys' emotions can affect the development of empathy in both positive and negative ways.

Is it possible for boys with too little or too much empathy to develop healthy empathy? I cannot answer that with certainty for every boy, but I will say that teaching boys about their own feelings and the feelings of others—at every age—appears to enhance empathy skills and behaviors. Consistent with my stance on boys' emotional expression, I contend that boys can be taught the emotional skill of empathy for themselves and for others. It's a necessary skill for boys' emotional health.

CHAPTER 6

Boys' Anger: Alternatives to Aggression

"What was I supposed to do . . . just stand there and let him get away with it?"

> —David, age 15, after slamming his younger brother into a wall for teasing him

Anger is one of the few emotions that our culture allows boys to have. Boys can be mad but not be scared; they can be mad but not be hurt; they can be mad but not be embarrassed. So it makes sense that anger is a frequently experienced and expressed emotion for boys. It also makes sense that boys' anger is most often expressed as active aggression. Why? Because aggression is not only widely accepted in the Pack Rules, it is also encoded in the popular phrase that so often defines masculinity: *boys will be boys.*

Much of boys' aggressive behavior first takes place within the home—between siblings. An older or bigger brother will pick on his younger brother or sister. If that is allowed to continue, boys may become aggressive with peers and property at school, and then in the larger community. Boys often don't express their anger in healthy ways. They hit, punch, kick, throw stones, taunt, cuss, body slam, and butt heads . . . but rarely do they, or are they encouraged, to use words to express how they are feeling.

Must Boys' Anger Always End in Aggression?

There are many reasons why boys don't use healthy anger expression. One reason is that few people actually know what healthy anger expression is! The three core rules of healthy anger expression are these: When you express anger, 1) it cannot hurt yourself, 2) it cannot hurt others, and 3) it cannot destroy property. Another reason that many boys express anger in unhealthy and harmful ways is that the Pack Rules invariably trump healthier rules. This chapter focuses on how and why this happens, while offering strategies to help boys continue to feel their anger without having it turn into aggression. Aggression is a human behavior. It's not masculine (or feminine). So let's examine why aggression has become associated with masculinity and what can be done to change this.

Superheroes in Waiting

One year, more than a dozen adolescent boys were referred to me for outpatient counseling. They all had the same presenting symptom: difficulty controlling anger. They were aggressive at home or at school. Sometimes both. During clinical interviews, I learned that as younger boys they had been fascinated with action figures, and in their early teens they had been ardent fans of professional wrestling and football. To these boys, such sports exemplified the essence of what being a guy meant. It meant being hulking, fearless, and strong—in the superhero sense.

The magnetism of the wrestlers and other athletes also was seen in the boys' fascination with children's action figures. For nearly a decade now, the same hulking, muscular body type seen on television wrestlers has been molded into little plastic toys that become extensions of the boys' developing egos and bodies. "If only I could be like this," was a frequent wish voiced by the young boys I treated in play therapy. Just as often, they would also proclaim, "Someday *I'm* gonna look like him!"

The Cultural Connection

What do idolizing superheroes, professional wrestling, hulking action figures, and enduring physical pain have to do with boys' anger? There's a connection on at least two levels, and both have to do with culture. The first is the message to boys about aggression, i.e., it's okay to be aggressive. The second is the culture's mandate that boys must be powerful. Most often, this power takes the form of dominance. If a boy is muscular, triumphant, and seemingly indestructible, i.e., if he's a football player or wrestler, then he's okay. This combination of the cultural charge to boys to become as powerful as they can, coupled with tacit or overt permission to be aggressive, is a certain recipe for violence. Yet violence and anger are not synonymous.

Like everyone else, all boys experience anger (unless they've made that feeling disappear). Boys become angry for many of the same reasons that anger everyone else on a daily basis. But when the cultural norm decrees boys must be all-powerful and dominant, boys innocently and incorrectly conclude that it is unacceptable for them to be scared, needy, or vulnerable. Boys think that they cannot *not* be powerful. A common solution boys use to remedy this paradox is, unfortunately, aggression.

Power and Aggression

In the United States and many other cultures, masculinity often becomes synonymous with aggressive behavior for boys and men. This view is unfortunate because (among other reasons) it can obscure our appreciation of many positive aspects associated with masculinity. A comparable gender role for girls is to become beautiful as manifested by body image. Girls internalize media images and are then charged with the cultural mandate to become an *object of beauty*, however the culture defines beauty at that moment. A parallel process appears to take place with boys and aggression. In a culture that portrays men as *objects of power*, it makes sense that boys and men internalize images of being powerful. Unfortunately, when being powerful defines identity, like beauty it becomes a double-edged sword.

For girls who think they must look like models, and for boys who think they must always be powerful, it isn't too difficult to connect the dots and see the bigger picture. Many girls diet, overeat, starve, purge, and distort the simple human experiences of feeling hunger and eating food until they no longer know what simple healthy eating is. Similarly, many boys play and fight past any pain they might experience. They negate an otherwise healthy part of being human, i.e., feeling vulnerable, until they no longer know what healthy anger is.

The process goes something like this. A boy's feelings are hurt or he is physically threatened in some way. Healthy anger is a defense that signals, "Danger—do something to protect yourself!" But if he follows the Pack Rules or other narrow norms for being masculine, he overcompensates for his vulnerability with power. This, by itself, isn't unhealthy or unnatural. But it becomes unhealthy when it is the *only* option he considers, and when it is combined with all the other mandates that boys receive (*win at all costs, aggression is okay, boys will be boys*). Like girls who feel pressure *not to be fat*, boys who feel pressure *not to be vulnerable* can end up sacrificing their real selves. The end result is fewer reasonable options for boys. Talking about vulnerable feelings and learning how to cope without aggression are the alternatives we need to be teaching boys.

In short, a culture can mediate the way that children define who they are and how they present themselves to others. So, when a boy feels sad, hurt, scared, lonely, overwhelmed, stressed, or angry—all of these emotions have only one culturally acceptable outlet. He has one option: be aggressive. Cultural display rules dictate how boys should handle anger.

To be sure, boys' behavior in response to feeling scared or vulnerable will vary across subcultures and settings. Some boys won't ever fight, while some will fight if they have their Pack surrounding them. Other boys fight only when they are carrying weapons (knives, guns), while some boys fight with words and insults, later moving into pushing or punching. If you consider the common thread among these examples of aggression, all of the behaviors are closely tied to a sense of power via dominance, rather than dealing with vulnerability in nonaggressive ways. Thus, boys' physical aggression may be a culturally prescribed defense against feelings of vulnerability. The need for physical dominance and power can become a learned defense against feeling fear. Without changing the norms and challenging the Pack Rules, boys do not have culturally acceptable alternatives to being aggressive and dominating.

Healthy Anger Expression

The view I present in this book promotes the healthy expression of anger. The simple rules for expressing anger in nondestructive ways (anger should not hurt yourself, others, or property) basically describe what healthy anger expression looks like. Boys can learn to feel and express their anger in assertive and direct ways at any age. It is always recommended that healthy ways to express anger be taught to boys early in childhood, simply because such healthy anger expression is more likely to become a natural part of their behavior if it is introduced and practiced early.

Johnny

When I think about the value of teaching healthy anger expression early, I'm reminded of Johnny, a seven-year-old boy whom I worked with a few years ago. Johnny's temperament was "difficult," that is, he was impulsive and oppositional at home, school, day care, and friends' homes. When we first met, I assessed Johnny's ability to name and express positive and negative emotions. I asked him how he felt about typical things like getting a good grade on a math paper or being picked on by another kid at day care. Johnny's response was always framed as a thought: "I think kids shouldn't pick on me," or "I think it was a good math paper," were typical answers. He was unable to identify or express his emotions.

After a few therapy sessions and some practice at home with identifying and expressing his emotions, Johnny got the hang of it. He continued to have a "difficult" temperament, but his acts of aggression decreased significantly. How? Johnny's family became committed to a "zero-tolerance" policy toward aggressive behavior between parents, siblings, and playmates. This meant that the parents changed the norm for themselves as well as for Johnny. They challenged the Pack Rules. Rather than continuing to view Johnny's aggression as typical "boys will be boys" behavior, they said it wasn't healthy and they showed him other ways to express his anger.

Johnny caught on quickly and was very motivated because his parents used a behavior chart to track his progress. They rewarded him with verbal praise (no money, no toys, just "oh-how-wonderfuls"). Another intervention involved the video game with which he had become obsessed. It had lots of violence (superheroes beating up other superheroes, etc.). On my recommendation, Johnny's parents deconstructed his fantasy game. They told Johnny that it was only a pretend game, and that if he continued to practice real "Power Kicks" on his little brother (like the kicks he saw on the video game), then the game would be unplugged for three days. Since he couldn't go three hours without playing it, Johnny understood. Even at very early cognitive levels, kids understand the difference between real and pretend, and cause and effect. "Kick your little brother one more time, and you will not be allowed to play your favorite game for three days," is not a hard concept for a seven- year-old boy to grasp.

Another interesting part of Johnny's anger and aggression pattern was that when I first explained to him that feeling angry doesn't mean he has to become aggressive, he looked as if that possibility had never occurred to him. I used role-plays to show him how anger doesn't have to turn into aggression. I drew it on paper. I showed him how to use his voice instead of hitting, kicking, or yelling.

Johnny had not been *directly* taught ways to express anger other than aggression. Perhaps most boys need such direct instruction because of all the messages they receive from the larger culture that aggression is okay.

Teaching and Learning About Healthy Anger Expression

Anger is a signal. It's a message that communicates a psychological or physical threat is present. It can be a real or perceived threat, but fear is often the common core underlying anger. This fear starts up the "fight or flight" biochemical responses in the body. But the dilemma for boys is that if they have internalized being *an object of power*, they cannot be threatened . . . they cannot feel scared. (The No Fear logo returns again.) If you think about it, this is a dehumanizing paradox . . . to be threatened and not allowed to feel fear. In part, I think this disconnection contributes to the entire cycle of fear, anger, and aggression.

Breaking the Fear→Anger→Aggression Cycle

Although people can become angry because they're frustrated, tired, jealous, and so forth, I've observed a consistent pattern with many boys' anger. It involves a cycle of unprocessed fear, amplified anger, and aggressive behavior that boys find themselves endlessly looping through in relation to others. I call this the Fear→Anger→ Aggression cycle. It appears as a result of the interface between boys' human physiology and the cultural mandate to become objects of power. The human body, at any age, has a fairly predictable response to fear, and anger is part of that response. Viewed in this way, anger is actually a defense. It helps to protect from real or imagined threat.

In most situations, boys don't need to defend their lives. They don't need all that adrenaline pumping through their bodies, heading to their arms and legs so that they can stay and (foolishly) fight the saber-toothed tiger or (more wisely) run away from it. Indeed, in most daily situations boys are reacting only to psychological threats. But if boys are not permitted to feel fear, how can they later realize that they feel safe?

Interrupting the Cycle

Understanding the triggers that set off anger can help you understand where to interrupt the Fear→Anger→Aggression cycle. I don't think that it really matters where in the cycle a change is made (see figure 6.1). As you can see, any point is a point of entry and potential change. If aggression is to be totally prevented, the point of entry immediately after the first awareness of fear provides the first chance to break out of the cycle. For example, when a boy first notices he's been demeaned or psychologically threatened, he then can realize (if he rethinks the event) that he was not threatened in that way at all. He can use self-talk to reassure himself that he was not threatened, that he's safe, and that he need not become aggressive.

Or, if he couldn't stop his anger by rethinking his fear, seconds later when he *becomes aware that he's angry* or that he was aggressive, he can still break out of the cycle. If he *rethinks his aggression* and

Breaking out of the Fear→Anger→Aggression Cycle

A Model to Change Boys' Interpersonal Aggression

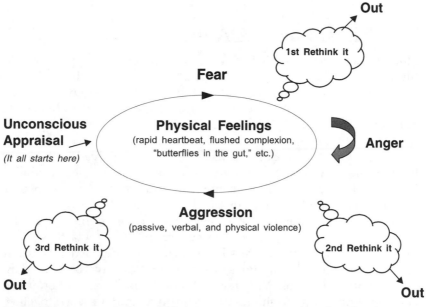

"Rethink it" is the reappraisal process that encourages boys to consider alternatives to aggression and more fear.

1st—Ask yourself whether you are really in danger, either physically or psychologically. Use self-talk, saying to yourself, "I'm okay," or "I can handle it."

2nd—Instead of fighting, throwing, yelling, shoving, etc., say to yourself, "I'm gonna go cool off." (Leave the scene and go somewhere else to cool off.)

3rd—This is the best time to get an objective perspective, so talk to someone! (Also it's the last chance to break out of the cycle before getting trapped into going around again. . . .)

Figure 6.1

realizes that he doesn't want to hurt someone, he can then decide to walk away, rather than inflict harm on this person (empathy definitely aids boys in breaking out of the cycle).

An ongoing aid for breaking out of the cycle requires the boy to observe the physical sensations that he experiences during hostile encounters. When he becomes aware of feeling a rapid heartbeat in his chest or the heat of his flushed face, he may choose to go cool off before doing anything else. Consciously recognizing and understanding the physical symptoms of anger can help boys to feel grounded in their bodies. Recognizing and paying attention to such important physical signals can give them time to think before they act on what they are feeling.

The emotion we call anger has many common physiological characteristics. Because each person is unique, we know there are necessarily many variations between individuals. Consequently, anger can be experienced in many different ways in addition to its commonly shared physiological characteristics.

The Physiology of Anger

Studies have been conducted to determine what happens inside human bodies when anger is felt. Adrenaline (also called epinephrine) appears to be a primary catalyst in the physiology of anger. Or as Carol Tavris (1989) says of it in *Anger: The Misunderstood Emotion*, adrenaline is "the fuel of anger." This hormone, along with noradrenaline (also called norepinephrine), is what signals humans to fight or flee. Both hormones also seem to be involved in the emotions of anger and fear. The two hormones appear to have similar functions, but occur in different amounts and affect different parts of the brain-emotion-behavior circuit.

The ANS (autonomic nervous system) communicates to the adrenal glands and the endocrine system primarily via these hormones and other steroid stress hormones. For a detailed discussion about the anatomy of emotions, see chapter 1 or any good anatomy or physiology textbook. Very few parts of the brain control only one behavior and many hormones and neurotransmitters work together to produce behaviors. This certainly seems to be true for the emotions of anger and fear.

The Feeling of Anger versus the Emotion of Anger

Adrenaline and noradrenaline, as mentioned, appear to play a major role in the feeling of anger. When secreted in large amounts, they may cause the following symptoms: *rapid heartbeat, butterflies in the stomach, heat in the chest or face, and tension in the calf muscles or biceps.* These hormones are released by the adrenal glands and are instructed by the brain to "talk" to the body and prepare it to react. But this feeling of anger is not synonymous with the *emotion* of anger.

Laboratory studies (Ax 1953; Neiss 1988) have shown that a person can be injected with adrenaline, and not necessarily feel anger. Rather, the person feels the physiological feelings of anger (i.e., cardiovascular changes). Thus, the *feeling* of anger doesn't become the *emotion* of anger based on only physiological changes. This distinction between the feeling of anger and the emotion of anger makes even more sense when some of the other functions of adrenaline and noradrenaline are considered. These two hormones also may be responsible for emotional states such as joy, jealousy, anxiety and thrill.

The release of noradrenaline and adrenaline are part of the stress response in the human body and they are released in response to pain, physical exercise, drugs (i.e., caffeine, alcohol, illegal or pre-scribed drugs), and threatening stressors (i.e., being snubbed, giving a speech, being anchor on a relay team). Adrenaline and noradren-aline may also be released when your mind and body are under-aroused or bored. They're at their lowest amounts when the body and mind are comfortably engaged; there's no need for a chemical counterbalance within the body. But when you perceive a threat, the emotions of fear and anger start the chemical ball rolling. Therefore, your perceptions help you distinguish between the physiology of anger and the emotion of anger.

Appraisal and Reappraisal (Rethinking It)

An important aspect of getting the chemical ball rolling in the Fear→ Anger→Aggression cycle is appraisal, or thinking about and "sizing up" an experience. Although appraisals aren't physiological, they are very much a part of the physiological cycle because they mediate the emotions of fear and anger, and the resulting behavioral responses.

There are at least two kinds of anger appraisals. One is the unconscious response or thought that automatically interprets what's happening and "tells" you whether to fight or flee. The other is a reappraisal, or a rethinking. This is conscious. When you rethink an experience, it is no longer unconscious and you are no longer on autopilot. For example, suppose a store clerk treats a customer with disdain. The customer may become irate instantly due to his initial (unconscious) appraisal that he has been intentionally insulted (threatened). Or, the customer may reason (reappraise) the situation and assume that the store clerk is just having a bad day and it really doesn't have anything to do with the customer.

Reappraisal transforms the psychological threat. Anger subsides. The customer no longer feels angry at the physical level (heartbeat goes back to normal, face is not flushed) and he no longer feels the emotion of anger. In this example, the initial reaction is an unconscious appraisal that fuels the physiological response, while the subsequent reappraisal mediates the response of anger.

Another example of how the Fear→Anger→Aggression cycle can be interrupted by reappraisal occurs when a boy becomes aggressive after being picked on. After the trigger (a perceived threat), he has the option of rethinking the situation: "Steve's just being a pain in the butt, I'm not gonna hang out with him." This type of reappraisal is very different from "saving face" or reestablishing dominance after receiving a put-down. It's primarily a conscious, rational mode rather than a physiologically aggressive one.

Given the distinction between the *feeling* and the *emotion* of anger, you can see how vital reappraisals can be to the experience of anger. I hope you can also see how relevant this is for changing the norm for boys' aggression. Boys can learn how to reappraise a situation so that they don't have to respond to triggers with aggression. As illustrated in figure 6.1, the reappraisal can take place at several different points in the cycle. But given the cultural permission for "boys to be boys," a shift must also take place in the manner in which boys are socialized with regard to aggression. Simply put, if aggression were no longer the culturally expected way to establish and maintain power, when threatened, boys would be more likely to rethink threatening situations without being pulled into aggressive behavior as the one-size-fits-all solution.

When Boys' Anger Comes Out "Sideways" as Aggression

Last autumn, I went to the mountains with my family and some friends. Our friends have two wonderful sons. At the time, the older boy, David, was sixteen and large for his age (tall and heavy, muscular). His younger brother, Jimmy, was thirteen and willowy. The boys had been cooped up because of rain, and they had been squabbling on and off for most of the day. While the adults sat talking on the screened-in porch, we were startled by noise from the room where all the kids were hanging out. It sounded like a piece of furniture crashing against a wall. Screams followed the house-shaking thud.

We rushed in and saw David standing over Jimmy. David's face was red with rage. Jimmy was on the floor curled up in a fetal posture, his face red with fear. He was whimpering. Each of the adults felt anger immediately. Seeing the large boy towering over the hurt, smaller boy fired every cell in our sympathetic nervous systems. Especially so, because several young children were in the room and had watched the whole scene close up. Now they were sitting erect like wide-eyed statues, frozen onto the couch. *"Seconds ago, we were watching David and Jimmy play Sega . . . Why? . . . How? . . . What's happening?"* they all asked, without saying a word.

My husband, John, screamed what the children couldn't: *"What happened!?"* Rather than calm things down, his fury was obvious fuel for an inferno.

David's fists were still clenched at the ends of his adrenaline-pumped arms when he answered John, *"What was I supposed to do . . . just stand there and let him get away with it?"* The Pack Rules echoed ritualistically in David's response: *Save face when your power is threatened; win at all costs; be aggressive.*

It turned out that Jimmy had been taunting David all day and David had been tolerating it, not countering with any prosocial responses. He just taunted back. David had never considered telling any of the adults about how his brother was annoying him (that's not in the Pack Rules). He also had never thought to tell Jimmy, firmly, to stop. (*After all, a smaller, younger brother can't really get to you, right?*) Apparently, Jimmy was following the Pack Rules, too. Later in the day, he had decided it was time to surprise David with a hard whack on the back. Perhaps Jimmy saw the moment as a chance to finally prove he had power, especially in front of an audience of smaller children.

After my reappraisal time (it took me about forty seconds), I could see that both boys felt awful about their respective parts in the violence. Once I had reappraised the situation, I no longer felt threatened: *These were "nice" boys, not violent criminals without a conscience.* My fear and anger levels plummeted as I realized that David had acted instinctively rather than with intentional malice. I could see that David was in the grip of the Pack Rules, and that the only option available to him at that moment had been to body slam Jimmy into the wall.

I could tell David had begun to feel badly as he looked at the wide-eyed children on the couch. Getting back in touch with his other feelings (guilty, sad, embarrassed) seemed to help David reappraise the situation and not to cycle back into further aggressive behavior. But he still needed to "save face" in front of everyone, the original appraisal that had triggered his cycle of aggression. The option I chose was to help the boys reconcile and teach the frightened children that when you're angry, violence is not a solution. So my intervention went like this: I told David, in front of everyone, that I understood how and why he had reacted so quickly. Then I told him that I knew he was a good kid and that he had not wanted to scare the children or hurt Jimmy. I paused. He had been staring at the floor as I spoke, but now he lifted his eyes to look into mine. He knew he was being forgiven and he wanted to be. (This is the real way to save face.)

I went on to say there were other ways to handle the kind of "attack" he had experienced. Then, I asked David to say what he could do differently if it happened again. He said, "I'd walk away and not hit him." After this, I asked him to apologize to the children (he did) and to tell them how they shouldn't use violence to solve problems (he did this, too). Then I turned to Jimmy who, although still in pain, needed to take responsibility for his part in the incident. I asked Jimmy to apologize for taunting and smacking his older brother. Like David, Jimmy readily and sincerely did so. It was only after this last apology that the younger children, who were still sitting erect, finally relaxed and leaned back against the couch cushions. This whole incident took about two minutes from beginning to end.

Rethinking Anger, Aggression, and the Pack Rules

This incident captures the essence of the dilemma about boys' anger. The only outlet David had, given all of the biological forces and cultural messages whirling around in his brain, was to reestablish his power by slamming his brother into the wall. In that moment it never occurred to David—or to John—that there were alternatives to physical violence or screaming. In fact, other options didn't even *exist* for them. They had learned the Pack Rules well. To be sure, not every boy (or man) expresses his anger in aggressive behaviors like physical violence or yelling. There are boys who hold their anger in and who don't express it at all. However, "acting out" through aggression and "acting in" by holding on to anger are both unhealthy indications that anger is coming out sideways.

Boys' "Sideways" Anger

To express anger "sideways" refers to the idea discussed throughout this book that if boys do not experience and express their emotions directly and in healthy ways, those emotions will express themselves by means of alternate and unhealthy routes. Anger is one of many emotions that is expressed sideways. You are probably familiar with the term "passive aggression," which refers to the way people express their anger indirectly. For boys, the sideways route is often seen in active or passive-aggressive behaviors, or less frequently, in somatic (physical) complaints. When I use the phrase "sideways emotions" with parents, it seems to make immediate sense to them when they think about their children's behaviors and somatic complaints. It makes sense especially to the parents of boys, since so few boys are coached in expressing their anger in direct and healthy ways.

Andrew's "Sideways" Anger About Divorce

I once counseled an eleven-year-old boy who had suddenly developed a group of somatic problems all at once: headaches, stomachaches, and sleep disturbances. He had also lost interest in playing with his friends and his school grades suddenly dropped. These problems came on so suddenly that Andrew's mother suspected a brain tumor. When all the possible medical causes had been eliminated, his mother realized it was time to visit a counselor. At the first session, Andrew's mother described him as a "sensitive" boy (enter temperament) who, when he was younger, had cried often when hurt or frustrated. He seemed to have outgrown this by early elementary school. He stopped crying so easily and he made lots of friends. She reported that at the present time there were no ongoing risk factors like abuse or neglect.

His father acknowledged that the although the divorce had been sad, it had happened several years ago and now they were all getting along remarkably well. There had been a change in residence at the time, but Andrew had "coped remarkably well" with everything. This is where I zoomed in. Any child who copes remarkably well with a divorce is usually just masking deeply felt emotions remarkably well. When I queried further, both parents replied, "Andrew never cried about the divorce or moving from the big house into an apartment. He was a real trouper. In fact, he helped both of us get through. . . ."

At that point, Andrew's physical problems began to make a little more sense. Perhaps it was a post-traumatic reaction. Indeed, most parents think that if a child doesn't express or display negative emotions, then that child doesn't *have* any negative emotions. In fact, the opposite is true. What happens is that most children are adept at knowing which emotions they can show safely and which emotions they cannot show safely. Furthermore, boys have the added influence of the Pack Rules to guide them into masking their feelings of vulnerability. Andrew had concluded that if his parents were sad about the divorce, he couldn't be sad. He had decided not to upset them further. But by doing so, he gave up his *own* feelings of sadness and anger.

Figuring things out. Not only had Andrew made his own feelings about his parents' divorce "disappear," there was a new stressor for him in the fact that his father had just started dating. It was easy to understand how his parents had missed this stressor. After all, Andrew had "sailed through" the divorce and relocation, visitations were going well, and he was doing well in school. They believed that Andrew had gotten over any emotional fallout related to their divorce. So when Dad started dating for the first time (*just one week before Andrew's symptoms started*), it didn't occur to either parent that the two were connected. After all, Dad's new girlfriend was a nice person and a friend of the family!

In studying developmental psychology, we learn that after a divorce, children always hold on to the possibility that their parents will reunite. Sometimes it is a conscious thought and sometimes it's not. This is true for pre-teens and adolescents, as well. (I have a friend who had been divorced for several years when her seventeen-year-old son called the night before her remarriage to ask: "If Dad calls in an hour to ask you for a date . . . will you please call off the wedding?")

Andrew's therapy. The focus of Andrew's therapy was to help him identify and express the emotions he had caused to "disappear" about the divorce . . . and that were now coming out sideways. The way I did this was to begin in the present and go backwards through time. Andrew was angry with his dad for dating someone else. Not only because this dashed his hopes for reunification, but because his mom wasn't dating yet. Andrew feared that she would feel hurt and lonely. At this age, he also had the insight that he might have to take care of his mom's (imagined) hurt feelings again. He had already "been there and done that" after the divorce. (It's too stressful for any child to take care of a parent's feelings.)

So, another part of Andrew's treatment was to help him and his parents develop healthy boundaries. For Andrew's part, he needed to learn how to empathize with other people's feelings (like his mom's) without confusing those feelings as his own. The treatment also included parent consultations to provide educational and developmental information for facilitating healthy emotional expression at home. One interesting fact emerged here. Andrew's parents found that they didn't need to use their newfound information about children's development with his siblings. They were girls who had been expressing their feelings all along.

Like so many boys, Andrew had learned not to express his negative emotions. Unfortunately, he had also learned to restrict his positive emotions, too. There was little joy or "bounce" in his step. It took his body a while to get back to normal. Support from his family was needed to help Andrew maintain healthy emotional expression. To be sure, his parents learned some important new emotional skills themselves (particularly Dad, who had grown up with the Pack Rules). Andrew's symptoms were totally gone after two months of counseling.

Developmental Perspectives on Anger

Anger expression varies depending on many individual factors, including cognitive and emotional development, temperament, cultural conditioning, and genes. You've probably noticed that most people outgrow throwing temper tantrums and they learn to express anger without hitting, kicking, and yelling. So, what is this developmental progression? And why does the development of boys' anger expression often differ from girls' expression of anger?

Anger Is a Sign of Being a Person

To answer these questions, we must start with the concept of the emerging self and its accompanying ability for representational thought (the ability to distinguish between yourself and another). It has been argued that the emotion of anger cannot be present until a child has a sense of being a separate individual, a "psychological birth" (Mahler, Pine, and Bergman 1975). If anger is indeed related to the experience of being physically or psychologically threatened, this argument makes good sense because a child would have to see himself as separate from, rather than an extension of, another. This representational thought begins somewhere in the second year of life. Thus, while infants can feel frustrated about not being fed or about being in pain, they aren't truly *angry* because they don't know that they even have separate feelings yet (Zahn-Waxler and Smith 1992).

It's not surprising, then, that the onset of temper tantrums occurs about the same time as this psychological birth. Now that a child has his own thoughts and he's told, "No, don't bang the toy on the window," he can really *feel* his anger. All the "no's" threaten his new sense of self. And without many cognitive skills to buffer his rage, a tantrum erupts. If you think about it, children are told "no" for so very many things at this age, most things, actually. It makes sense that there can be an endless wrestling of wills with kids of this age: there are two people in the ring now.

Temperament and Anger

How often you must wrestle with children's anger has its roots in temperament. Most parents have compared stories about how "easy" or "difficult" their child was during the second and third year of life. As little ones begin to explore the world, for reasons of safety, parents must place limits on these explorations. Or as our children's first pediatrician put it, "Children are more mobile than they are intelligent at this age." However, not every parent is bothered by their children's tantrums.

A child who is highly arousable or anxious may have a more intense anger reaction than the laid-back child who recovers quickly after being removed from that window he wants to bang on with a wooden block. But so much depends on the eye of the beholder. Some parents may see anger as a healthy, rather than a "bad," emotion. Indeed, this is how psychotherapists view anger. The following quote by renowned developmental psychologist Alan Sroufe (1978, 56) captures this perspective:

> A child who has a rapid tempo may be seething with anger, hostile to other children, unable to control his or her impulses, and filled with feelings of worthlessness. But a child who has a rapid tempo also may be eager, spirited, effective and a pleasure to others, and may like him- or herself.

Part of what helps children manage their anger and temperamental inclinations is how well the adults in their families understand and cope with their own temperaments and anger management. I once worked with a family who had an "easy" child and a "difficult" child. Each child's temperament mirrored one of the parents' temperaments (the boy had Dad's and the girl had Mom's). Things didn't improve in this family until the parents worked on their own personality styles and examined how this affected the parenting of the child most like them. When children have temperaments similar to their parents', it can be either heaven or hell. Part of what makes the difference is how well the parents accept, cope with, and like their own temperament.

The more parents like themselves, the more they'll like the child who follows in their temperamental footsteps. This doesn't mean that sparks won't fly or that everyone will live harmoniously.

Rather, it means that the backdrop against which daily life unfolds is one in which the child simply feels liked. When parents understand and like themselves, they're better equipped to understand and like their children. Temperament appears to play a large role in this transactional process. Indeed, parents, caregivers, and teachers all play a significant role in whether children like themselves.

It almost goes without saying that self-acceptance is a protective factor for emotional health. Although boys with difficult temperaments may have difficulty regulating strong physiological emotions like anger, it *is* possible to teach them how to do it. Liking these boys may be more than half of the lesson.

Environmental Links Between Anger and Aggression

While temperament plays a role in predisposition, elements in the environment also work to produce or reduce aggression in children. When theorists and researchers examine the prosocial aspects of development (such as empathy, sympathy, and concern for others), they also learn about children's aggression. For example, children who don't display prosocial behaviors often show antisocial behaviors such as lack of empathy or concern for others. Aggression and violent behaviors are examples of this lack of concern for others.

Violence in the Home

Decades of clinical observation and empirical research have linked children's aggressive and antisocial behaviors to having lived in violent homes (Crittendon and Ainsworth 1989; Dodge, Pettit, and Bates 1990; George and Main 1979). This violence may include having witnessed violence or being a victim of violence. Although not all children who grow up in violent homes become aggressive and violent, children who are aggressive usually have witnessed or experienced the Fear→Anger→Aggression cycle in their families. In short, they learned it at home. They learned that adults' anger is uncontrollable, so they learn that aggression and violence are ways to express anger.

These children also learn to become vigilant and how to selectively attend to hostile cues like voice intonation, facial grimaces, and body gestures and postures (Dodge, Pettit, and Bates 1994; Rieder and Cicchetti 1989). This has important applications for boys' anger cycle. Fear, based on the appraisal of threat and perceived hostile cues, can become distorted with boys who have been victimized by violence. This can lead to inaccurate appraisals that eventually lead to aggression, over and over, unless a reappraisal or more accurate "rethinking" takes place.

The Tolerance of Boy's Aggression in Our Culture

Although the connection is established that boys who witness or experience violence in their homes tend to become aggressive when angry, what about boys who grow up in nonviolent homes who also become aggressive? Here, a look at our larger culture, which is tolerant of boys' aggression, may provide some answers.

One study that demonstrates this tolerance asked research participants to observe two children at play (Condry and Ross 1985). Both children were dressed in thick, woolen snowsuits that made it impossible to identify their sex. If the observers were told that the two children playing were both boys, observers "saw" less aggression than when they were told they were watching two girls or a girl and a boy. This study suggests that aggression in boys is more tolerated than it is for girls.

Entertainment and aggression. In addition to the tolerance of boys' aggression, boys in contemporary United States also grow up in a violence-saturated culture. Just look at video games, movies, television, and professional sports. These aspects of culture appear to reinforce boys' aggressive behaviors. The now classic study by Bandura, Ross, and Ross (1963) in which boys watched a violent TV show and then immediately afterwards began pounding the inflatable "bobo" doll was just the beginning of many studies that linked aggression to watching violence.

Boys in the United States are being taught indelible lessons by the World Wrestling Federation and aggressive video games. The lessons state: *Aggression is okay; it's entertainment. Don't worry about how the other guy feels. There is power, dominance, and respect in winning. Crushing your opponent is the way to go.* Furthermore, the younger a boy is when exposed to these lessons ("entertainment"), the less likely he will be to understand that it's not real . . . and that he shouldn't act that way at home or with his younger cousin.

Some of the entertainment industry's initial responses to the terrorist attacks on the World Trade Center and the Pentagon were that toy manufacturers pulled many violent games off the shelf and they redesigned video games, especially those with terrorist themes. Television and movie producers demonstrated similar responses, reducing violent clips in upcoming TV shows and films. I hope that this commitment to reduce violence in entertainment will continue in our culture.

Gender differences in aggression. In regard to gender differences, there are many parallels between the development of empathy and the development of anger. Evolutionary theorists and researchers suggest that for the survival of the human species, females evolved as more caring and empathic (to bear and raise children) and males evolved as more aggressive (to slay mastodons and other large animals for food). The evolutionary perspective emphasizes the role of biology.

The question of whether boys are more aggressive than girls has been examined by psychologists for a long time (Basow 1992; Maccoby and Jacklin, 1974). Cross-cultural studies can be helpful when studying human behavior. Laura Cummings (1991) studied the Cholos, girls who belong to violent gangs in Mexico, to learn more about gender and aggression. Her anthropological research showed that these girls could be just as aggressive as boys. Indeed, the Cholos' aggression involved kicking, clubbing, knife fights and other lethal forms of combat, including shooting. Cummings' study of aggression led her to conclude that the way that girls and boys are influenced by cultural rules can trump any genetic influence on aggressive behavior.

Epidemiological research (large-scale studies conducted to identify the occurrence of specific behaviors, illnesses, etc.) yields additional information about gender differences in aggression. One such indicator is the incidence of heterosexual dating violence (physical and sexual aggression). The 1997 and 1999 Massachusetts Youth Risk Behavior Study, conducted with a combined total of 8,173 public high school students, revealed that approximately one in five female students (20.2 percent in 1997 and 18.0 percent in 1999) reported being physically and/or sexually abused by a dating partner (Silverman, Raj, Mucci, and Hathaway 2001). In an earlier 1995 study, girls were seven times more likely than boys to report being victims of dating violence (Massachusetts Department of Education May 1996). Researchers speculated that boys less frequently viewed dating violence as aggression.

Regardless of one's theoretical orientation, it's difficult to ignore how social and cultural expectations often shape a caring orientation in females and an aggressive orientation in males. It appears that environmental, versus biological, influences account for many of the outcomes in the development of empathy or aggression in children. And it is this perspective that allows parents and boys to interrupt the Fear→Anger→Aggression cycle.

Healthy Ways to Express Anger

So, how can boys move from aggressive behavior to healthy expression of anger? To be sure, it's a lifelong process for boys (for everyone, really). I've worked with adult men and women who were still throwing temper tantrums well into their thirties and forties. One could argue that when people act aggressively because they feel angry, they haven't mastered control of a two-year-old child's way to express anger. Mastering rage is a developmental milestone in everyone's life. Basically, learning how to control your anger involves learning how your anger functions in your body and mind and then learning how to express it in nondestructive, nonaggressive ways.

One outcome of boys' cultural conditioning (that it's okay to be aggressive) is that boys' fear gets buried in their psyches. It stays buried until it erupts like a volcano spewing hot lava. But boys can interrupt the cycle of threat, fear, anger, and aggression. And the best place to start is to intervene at any part of the cycle because *any change at all* changes the cycle.

I believe that conscious reappraisal, or rethinking the situation, is so helpful at any point in the Fear→Anger→Aggression cycle, I focus on this as a major intervention tool. The following suggestions may help boys to rethink their experience and expression of anger. It is always preferable to prevent aggression from taking place at all. But if it can be prevented the second time through the cycle, that's valuable, too. Indeed, anger often cycles through several times before it finally leaves the body.

A General Curriculum for Healthy Expression of Anger

The following suggestions are meant to be general guidelines as you go about changing the rules for boys' aggression in your home, classroom, sports team, Sunday school class, car pool, play group, vacations, and so forth. These generalized suggestions are appropriate for boys of any age. The specific techniques may vary depending on the boys' age and temperament.

★ **Educate boys about anger.** The first step of rethinking anger and aggression involves education. Boys need to know that anger is a natural part of being human. They also need to learn that the behavior of aggression is a choice. Help boys dispel the myths that they "black out" or can't control their anger, and that hiding anger is a sign of strength. Teach boys that healthy anger expression prevents anger from coming out "sideways."

★ **Show boys the Fear→Anger→Aggression cycle and how to break it.** Show them how to choose other options by coaching them how to rethink their unconscious appraisals.

This can be very empowering as it helps to transform anger and fear into empathy, understanding, and change.

★ **Enlist boys' commitment to change** from aggressive anger expression to healthy anger expression. Without a boy's own decision to express anger in healthy ways, he won't change.

★ **Teach boys the three simple rules of healthy anger expression.** The expression of anger *cannot hurt yourselves, others, or property.*

★ **Help boys to identify their anger triggers.** Focus on their feelings of hurt, fear, and their perceptions of threat. Then explore secondary reactions such as feeling unimportant, lost, lonely, jealous, insulted, etc.

★ **Show boys how to identify the physical signals of anger.** Is it in their heads, mouths, chests, arms, legs, guts? Is it warm or cold? Are their hearts pounding? Can they feel pressure anywhere? Explore what else may be unique to their felt experience of anger in their bodies.

★ **Model healthy anger expression at home.** Check in with yourself and observe your anger expression style. If it's passive or active aggression, change it and tell your sons that you're working on it. This is especially true for fathers (and uncles or older brothers) whom boys look to as role models. *Healthy anger expression simply involves putting your anger into assertive (not aggressive) words.* Avoid the phrase, "You make me feel mad." This is an abdication of responsibility. Instead, an "I message" is more accurate and creates less defensiveness: "I'm angry because you didn't clean your room (or the garage or the dog house) as you promised." The focus here is on the boy's behavior rather than an incorrect power attribution.

★ **Confront boys' hidden anger as well as their passive and aggressive anger styles.** Boys, like everyone else, often act on one of three unhealthy behaviors with their anger: (1) Hold it in and try to avoid it; (2) Act it out aggressively in violence (verbal or physical); (3) Act it out passively by withdrawal or the silent treatment (refusing to talk or cooperate and work through a conflict). Each of these behaviors is unhealthy and needs to be confronted. Most boys are likely to act in physically aggressive ways due to the influence of culture (the media, Pack Rules, etc.). Yelling, taunting, hitting, kicking, and punching walls are too often accepted as "normal" boy behaviors.

★ **Offer alternative ways to handle the situation without aggression.** An example with a two-year-old could be, "Johnny, you can't hit me, but you can tell me you are mad with words." With a pre-teen or teen it might be, "Jamie, you can't yell at me, but you can go to your room, cool off, and try to talk to me about it later."

★ **Change gender role expectations for your son and other boys.** Allow boys to feel *vulnerable* and remind them that they don't have to be powerful and dominant to be real.

★ **Don't take ownership of your son's problem when he's angry.** He's trying to cross a footbridge and you have two jobs: Don't stand in his way and don't stand on the other side jumping up and down (out of control with your own anger).

★ **Don't get discouraged if unhealthy aggression patterns return.** Old habits are hard to break. Blend your own fear and disappointment with reasoning . . . look to the future and think about the progress he's made and remember that his behaviors *now* won't be the same as when he's older (i.e., don't telescope). He hasn't finished developing yet!

In the Heat of the Moment: Specific Tools for Parents

★ **Parents must remember to stay calm.** Anger escalates into aggression quicker when both people are out of control (it takes two to have a fight).

★ **Don't punish in the heat of your anger or his.** Wait until you and your son have cooled down.

★ **Allow your son to feel angry.** Use words like, "I understand your anger" or "I'd be angry, too." (You'd be surprised how this often de-escalates certain situations.)

★ **Don't shame his feeling of anger but do set limits on aggression.** Don't say, "You shouldn't be angry," when you really mean, "Don't be aggressive."

★ **Problem-solve** ways to handle the situation without aggression after things have cooled down (sort of like Monday morning quarterbacking).

★ **Be consistent with setting consequences for aggressive behavior.** Don't "let this one pass" because you're tired or overwhelmed.

★ **Monitor progress and praise him.** Give feedback to boys when they do well. Whether it's decreasing physical and passive aggressiveness or increasing healthy expression of anger. It all counts and it all needs to recognized.

★ **Time-outs are good for "twos," "teens" and adults.** Sometimes, all you need to give your son is the *chance* to get himself under control. Whether he's two, ten, or sixteen, he will likely benefit from the space to cool off. Just remember to go back later and process what happened when you're both calmer.

★ **Make your home a place of "zero-tolerance" for aggression.**

In the Heat of the Moment: Specific Steps for Boys' Healthy Anger Expression

The preceding recommendations provide adults with a guide for helping boys to be angry without becoming aggressive. But it isn't enough to simply tell boys what they can't do with their anger; they need to fill the void by doing something else. Simply put, if something is being taken away, in this case, aggression, then boys need to receive something in its place. Boys can learn to do things differently in the heat of the moment using three simple steps, (guaranteed to help interrupt the Fear→Anger→Aggression cycle):

1. **Purposely delay actions when angry.** Tell boys that it's okay to take a time-out. Waiting a few minutes (or seconds) before acting can make a huge difference (counting to 20 is highly underrated). Let boys know that walking away from a bad (hot, explosive) situation can be a sign of good judgment.

2. **Use self-talk when angry.** Tell boys that self-talk is just what it sounds like, talking to yourself, but inside your head. Saying, "I can handle this" in the heat of the moment even helped a forty-eight-year-old CEO and a fifty-six-year-old physicist control their anger. Affirming statements like, "I'm okay," or "I'm doing fine," can get the adrenaline pump to stop flooding the body. Tell boys that the body listens to the

mind. The calming effect that follows self-talk allows reasoning (reappraisals or rethinking it) to become clearer.

3. **Plan—and do—an alternative physical action.** Of course, boys don't always know when they'll get angry. But they can plan ahead by knowing what they'll do when they are angry. If boys have cultural permission *not* to use violence, they'll be more likely to control their physical reaction in the moment and walk away, go running, or work out later in the gym as a way to release the physical tension and rid the body of excess energy.

Conclusion

How anger is ultimately expressed depends largely upon what boys learn. And there is much that boys learn from the prevailing tolerance of aggression in American life. Even considering individual temperament and evolutionary influences, it seems that how anger is channeled, and whether it creates a consistent aggressive response style, depends largely upon what children learn about anger expression. It also seems to matter whether those children are girls or boys.

CHAPTER
7

For Parents: What Families Can Do

Family life is the first school for emotional learning.
—Daniel Goleman, *Emotional Intelligence*

Boys' emotional development is primarily, but not entirely, shaped by family. Much of this chapter draws on theories from developmental and clinical psychology to help parents make connections between family influences, boys' temperaments, and boys' socialization. This information is translated in ways that hopefully will make sense to parents. I offer suggestions for responding differently to boys' emotions with small changes on a daily basis, rather than with a whole new set of foreign responses. My approach is intended to respect already established communication patterns between parents and their sons, while also stretching that communication in a way that will help parents to facilitate boys' emotional skills.

A Snapshot of What Emotional Expression Could Look Like for Boys

You've probably already noticed that I sometimes use comparisons with girls when I talk about boys. These contrasts are used for the sole purpose of describing a fuller range of human expression often denied to boys. Consider the following true story. Molly was sitting on the couch one night. It was getting close to her second-grade bed-time. Molly had been her usual bubbly self that evening. But she suddenly became quiet at the mention of bedtime. When Molly's Dad asked her what was wrong, the child's eyes instantly filled with tears and her face fell. Then she said, "I don't want to ride the school bus anymore, the kids are so loud they never listen to the bus driver. And this afternoon, the bus driver said we're all going to the principal's office tomorrow morning!"

Molly's father listened carefully and he understood the shift in Molly's mood. Apparently, Molly had forgotten about this fear until it was time for bed, which had reminded her of the following day, which in turn reminded her of the impending bus ride. Her father responded by first asking Molly if she had obeyed the bus driver (maybe Molly was just afraid of getting into trouble?). Molly told her father that she had obeyed, just like all the other days. Having ruled this out, he then asked Molly how she was feeling. Molly answered, "I feel scared . . . and mad." Her father reassured Molly that she had done nothing wrong and that Molly's feelings made sense. Molly began to look more relaxed. Then, her father asked her why she felt mad ("because I didn't do anything wrong and I have to go to the principal's") and scared ("because I don't like it when kids don't do what the bus driver tells them to do"). Molly's Dad replied that all those feelings made sense and that he'd feel that way, too, if he were Molly.

Then Molly and her father developed a plan for how Molly would cope the next day on the bus. They also talked about what Molly would do and say if she went to the principal's office. After making this last plan, Molly's somber face returned to its usual grin. She looked as if the weight of the world had been removed from her shoulders. For a second-grader, this is more than just a metaphor; the weight of the world *did* disappear. And Molly fell right to sleep that night.

The Feelings Behind the Behaviors

The scenario described above is replayed countless times in different homes. The problem will differ (a school bully, a big test, trying out for the team, a teen romance ended, etc.), but the need to feel and express emotions, to be understood, and to solve a problem is universal. When sad and mad feelings are overwhelming, children need help from adults in finding their way through their feelings to master the problem. Otherwise, sad and mad feelings can "disappear," or come out sideways, and children don't learn how to express and cope with them in direct and healthy ways.

You may be wondering why I told this true story about Molly. It's because all too often, stories like this have a happy ending, *for girls*. If Molly had been "Mikey," a story like this is less likely to unfold in the same way. If you've read the previous chapters, the reasons are familiar by now: Boys learn it's not okay to say that they're scared (some boys conclude that it's not okay even to *feel* scared), and boys often learn to be aggressive when they're mad or scared (rather than just talk about their feelings).

If Molly had been a boy, the answer to, "What's wrong?" would probably have been, "Nothing." The Pack Rules require boys to mask their vulnerable feelings in the service of being "strong." If Molly had been Mikey, the child probably would have hidden his fear and anger, and it also might have come out sideways in behaviors like silliness, hyperactivity, or not being able to fall asleep that night.

Parents continually face the challenge of how to raise boys who can break social rules (also known as the Pack Rules) when it's healthy to do so. An important part of this challenge is seeing the feelings behind the behaviors and knowing what you can do with them.

Won't I Turn My Son into a Wimp if He Talks About His Feelings?

No, you won't turn your son into a wimp by talking about his feelings. As previously stated in chapter 1, many parents resist boys' emotions because of this specific fear. In its simplest form, the fear is that if your son feels and expresses his emotions, he will somehow be less of a boy or less masculine. This is reinforced by the awareness that he is likely to be rejected by those boys who do follow the Pack Rules if he chooses not to follow them. But what if it could be proven that boys remain "real boys" and strong, even if they are raised to know and express their emotions? To find support for this notion, let's take a look at girls' socialization and behaviors.

In public settings, boys and girls both behave in very similar masculine roles. Both boys and girls know it is important to restrict expression of their emotions in public; girls don't want to be seen crying in school any more than boys do. Girls demonstrate "masculine" characteristics such as confidence, independence, logical reasoning ability, and goal-orientation. Yet families are more tolerant of girls' vulnerable emotions. In other words, girls are permitted to cry but boys are not. Yet how often do you see girls crying in school or at college? How often do you see career women crying on the job? I'm not saying that crying is bad. What I am saying is that parents' fear of their sons becoming "wimps" if their sons' emotions are valued and attended to appears to be largely unfounded.

So, although girls' vulnerable emotions are more tolerated by their parents and more socially accepted than boys' vulnerable emotions, the *behavioral outcomes in public appear to be similar for boys and girls.* These same girls become just as tough as boys with regard to display rules. Girls don't cry and cower all the time. This observation suggests that the painstaking efforts parents put into not permitting their sons to become "wimps" may actually serve to diminish boys' emotional development, rather than "toughen them up" for life.

The Pack Rules Influence Everyone

Over the past two decades, I've worked with hundreds of adolescent girls who display masculine behaviors. Their parents frequently describe how their daughters won't talk about problems ("I don't want to talk about it" is a frequent girls' retort these days, too). Outwardly, contemporary girls appear to be just as "tough" as boys in middle and high school are. Today, girls keep to themselves and they hide their feelings. This may be related to the fact that, although boys and girls' emotions are socialized differently, they are both socialized in a masculine culture. And while girls aren't pressured to follow the Pack Rules in the same ways that boys are, girls (and women) know the Rules and often follow them, because these Rules define how to survive and get ahead in mainstream, corporate culture today.

When transitions and problems come along, girls have access to a broader range of emotional outlets than boys do. And this seems to be due to the different practices in boys' and girls' socialization. While girls *learn* how to display a tough exterior, they are still allowed access to their softer emotions, too. Simply put, perhaps boys also can be taught how to access all of their emotions and still be able to present a "tough" exterior, when necessary.

I offer this boy/girl comparison to enable you to validate and nurture all of your son's emotions. The end result will be that he will know what he feels when he is feeling it, and he won't wind up becoming a wimp. Letting go of this fear is one of the biggest challenges that parents (and not surprisingly, boys) face.

Important suggestions were also provided in the developmental timeline for different ages in chapter 3. In this chapter, I offer more specific ideas and strategies for parents to make small changes in daily life, as well as to assess and monitor your son's emotional development. Most of the suggestions presented are appropriate for boys of any age unless otherwise stated.

An Emotional "Apgar Score" for Boys

Immediately after they are born, all children receive their first assessment, called the Apgar score. This is a medical assessment of basic life functions at one and five minutes after birth. It is repeated at ten minutes if problems are noted in any of these areas: color, heart rate, reflex response, muscle tone, and respiration. (Virginia Apgar is the name of the anesthesiologist who invented this index.) I think there should be an Emotional Apgar Score (EAS) designed to assess and monitor children's emotion skills. This EAS should be conducted *on a regular basis* with boys because their emotional skills are so often neglected. Just as respiration is the lifeline to physical health in the newborn, I think emotions are the lifeline to mental (and physical) health for boys.

The following EAS is not a standardized or norm-referenced test. It's just a set of guidelines that I created to get you thinking about your son's emotional development. I developed it using guidelines from the cognitive development stages of Piaget (1952) and the emotional intelligence skills set described by Mayer and Salovey (1997). Below is an outline of the proposed EAS, along with scoring suggestions and the *approximate* ages that these skills first begin to be observable, or can be developed. (Note: All of these skills should continue to be nurtured throughout boys' lives).

The Emotional Apgar Score

Directions: Read each skill and decide how well it describes your son. Use the following rating scale:

0 = none
1 = present, sometimes
2 = present, regularly

★ **Expresses emotions with facial expressions and words,** ages 1+ or with onset of expressive language (this skill is especially important because other skills build upon this).

★ **Identifies emotions,** ages 2+, with expressive language (Example: "I'm sad, happy," etc.)

★ **Blends positive and negative feelings,** ages 7+ (Example: "I'm angry but I love you.")

★ **Blends thoughts with feelings,** ages 7+ (Example: I'm sad but I understand . . .")

★ **Analyzes emotions,** ages 11+ (Example: understands how emotions are connected and related to thoughts and behaviors.) Analyzing occurs with the onset of abstract reasoning abilities.

★ **Regulates emotions,** all emotions should be controllable by ages 16 to 18, if not sooner. (Example: monitors and controls anger, excitement, motivation, etc.). Regulation varies based on child's age and the type of emotion, and becomes easier as child gets older.

EAS Scoring Guidelines

Ages 2–6, perfect score = 4; less than 4, needs your attention!

Ages 7–10, perfect score = 8; less than 8, needs your attention!

Ages 11+, perfect score = 12; less than 12, needs your attention!

Scoring: You'll notice that I don't include a rating scale for less than perfect scores. This is because a less than perfect score will always need your attention. If you go back to the original Apgar score analogy and your son breathed only "sometimes," he would certainly need your attention! One way to use this EAS is to literally get a pencil and rate your son's EAS. But you can also just use this as a mental checklist for those day-to-day exchanges with your son. Please bear in mind that this is not a standardized "test." It's just a guideline to get you thinking about and tracking your son's emotional development.

The Value of Teaching Emotional Expression to Your Son

Emotional expression is such an important skill that it has its own chapter. (See chapter 4.) Here, I want to specifically address how parents can, and must, be role models for healthy emotional expression. All parents, whether they're single or married, can provide models on how to talk about their feelings.

I don't think there is one "emotional expression gene" that some people have and some people don't. Although folklore and some media reports about scientific research often reinforce the gender stereotype that girls are better at emotional expression than boys, this doesn't mean that such skill is *biologically* based. Rather, it appears to be a socially learned gender difference. Thus, dads and moms, stepdads and stepmoms, single or married, each of you can express your own emotions in ways that will teach your sons how to do it *and* that it is okay to do so.

Despite the reality that both men and women can model emotional expression for boys, same gender role models may have the greatest influence. Although female role models can teach the necessary technical skills of emotional expression, this may not always be sufficient for helping boys to challenge the Pack Rules. Why? Often a boy needs to actually see a man break the Pack Rules and then observe that the man, perhaps his dad or stepdad, is still masculine and unharmed (not rejected or otherwise punished for breaking the Rules). Seeing a gender role model break the Pack Rules helps boys do the same when they need or want to break those Rules themselves.

This following anecdote illustrates the power that fathers have to help their sons express their feelings. Robert Reich was the U.S. secretary of labor in the late 1990s. He rarely saw his sons because of the demanding fourteen-hour days that his cabinet position required. One night Reich's son, Sam, asked to be awakened by his dad when he came home from work that night. His dad declined, saying it would be very late that night. But Sam wouldn't take no for an answer. When Secretary Reich asked him why, Sam said that he just wanted to know that his dad was there. As it turned out, Robert Reich heard Sam's "wake-up call" loud and clear. Shortly thereafter, he resigned his job as Secretary of Labor.

I share this story, as told by Reich, not as a message to parents that they should quit their jobs, but as an example of a son who shared his vulnerability and a father who listened and honored that vulnerability. Somewhere along the way, Sam learned and followed a new rule: *It's okay to be vulnerable and to tell your dad that you need him.* It's not entirely clear how Sam learned to break the Pack Rules, but what *is* known is that Reich validated his son's emotional expression. He also modeled that it's okay to break the Pack Rules (and still be a real guy) by resigning from a powerful career for *emotional* (versus financial, rational, etc.) reasons.

How Can You Keep Your Son's Emotions from Disappearing?

It's important that parents remember to reinforce their son's healthy emotional expression directly. If such expressions are ignored or not commented upon, then boys may internalize shame about expressing their feelings or emotional needs. In Reich's family story, This son's emotional expression was directly and positively reinforced. Although most parents can't just quit their jobs, they can validate their sons' emotional needs. This validation can be done in several ways.

Validate boys' emotions. The direct validation of boys' emotions is especially important because in the larger culture their emotions are so often invalidated, for reasons discussed throughout this book. The steps involved with validation basically involve listening to your son identify or name his emotions aloud to you. You then respond by saying, "That makes sense to me." It's actually very simple when you think about it. You can add other explanations to this such as educating him about how our culture typically ignores boys' feelings, and that you're very aware of how boys are often punished or ridiculed for expressing their feelings. Essentially, this part of the validation is a discussion of the Pack Rules as outlined in chapter 2. You'll probably learn about some new Pack Rules when you talk with your son. While most of the Rules are universal (such as boys don't cry), they can vary from region to region.

Tell stories from your past. Many parents find it helpful to tell stories from their own youth to validate boys' emotions, particularly fathers. It's important in the retelling that you don't present a Utopian or perfect ending. Boys need to hear that other boys and men struggle with emotional dilemmas, and they need to learn how to cope with them in real life. One example of storytelling to validate a jilted son is illustrated by the dad who says, "I remember when I asked Rachel Parker to go out with me and she said no. I was embarrassed because everyone knew I had asked her out. I was also sad because I really liked her." Sharing a story like this is an excellent example of a validation.

Become an emotion detective. Another way to think about validating your son's emotions is to become an "emotion detective." Look for the emotions of fear, anger, sadness, and hurt beneath your son's behaviors, regardless of age. If he's aggressive, look for fear, hurt, or anger; if he looks depressed, look for the same emotions (depression is often anger turned inwards). When teenage boys make demands like, "Why can't I have a car when I'm sixteen, everyone else does!" with a sense of aggrieved entitlement, continue to look for the same emotions underneath the presentation of the entitlement. Sometimes this sleuthing process is hard, but you'll find it's well worth the effort.

When approaching or just talking about your son's feelings with him, experiment with using the phrase "big feelings," regardless of the boys' age, to describe and validate his emotional pain. It often seems that a word like "big" can penetrate through solid defenses to reveal feelings that older boys or men have sealed shut.

Of course, the healthiest way is to prevent this from happening in the first place by talking about feelings and emotional needs, as a part of daily family life. That may be the best form of validation.

Simply remember that boys' emotions matter. If you experience and then express your positive and negative emotions, even in writing, you'll feel better. Pennebaker's (1997) research supports this statement, linking the expressing of emotions to better mental and physical health. This research needs to become more widely known to medical consumers. Talking about feelings isn't just good for emotional health, it also appears to be good for physical health. Keep this in mind as you welcome emotions into boys' lives. It's good for the whole family.

How to Teach Boys to Name and Identify Their Feelings

The quickest and most effective way to help boys know about feelings is to make talking about feelings and emotional needs the family norm. Make it business as usual. If you haven't done this yet, it's never too late to shift in this direction. The best and simplest way to teach your son how to name and identify his emotions is simply to ask, "And how do you feel about that?" At every age. This question is a universal elixir.

However, since many parents and siblings do not express their emotions directly in family settings, talking about emotion needs to become part of the *whole family's* conversation. It's extremely important for boys to see their parents asking this question of each other and their siblings. This is what turns talking about feelings into a family norm.

When boys are younger, they need their parents to provide them with the names for feelings. Some older boys need this, too, especially if they didn't receive much emotional education when they were younger. Putting boys' feelings into words for them when they are infants and toddlers is a form of mirroring (see chapter 3). Furthermore, since receptive language (understanding word meanings) develops before expressive language (speaking words and making gestures), boys can understand messages about their emotions even before they can speak. Thus, early mirroring is critical to the development of boys' emotional intelligence skills. Later on, as boys get older and are well into their teens, that simple question, "And how do you feel about that, Toby?" can reinforce these emotional skills.

Okay, My Son Tells Me About His Feelings . . . What Next?

I always appreciate parents' courage in therapy sessions when they ask me what to do or say after their son tells them how he feels. It's often such a new experience for parents that they're not sure what to do next. The most important rule of thumb when responding to boys' emotions is this: *Parents must respond to boys' emotions without shaming them.* The experience of being shamed for sharing emotions or needs may be the single, strongest deterrent of boys' healthy emotional development. Until the cultural norms change, boys will be shamed nearly everywhere else for expressing their feelings or emotional needs. Thus, it's essential that you make your family and home a safe place for your son to talk about his feelings. Following are some specific ways to respond to your son's expression of emotions.

The universal (and best!) response. While your son is telling you how he feels about something, listen. Then, respond by saying, "That makes sense to me," or, "I understand how you'd feel that way." It's really as simple as that. Of course, if it's a big problem that needs more than just emotional validation, then you'll need to do some problem-solving.

Be prepared. You may have to do some initial preparation if you're uncomfortable talking about feelings or listening to others' feelings. This is often more of a dilemma for fathers since they've had less practice with emotional expression (having been socialized by the Pack Rules, too). However, mothers also have been socialized in the larger culture. Although mothers may have had more practice expressing their emotions, some women are also uncomfortable talking about or listening to others' feelings.

Not knowing what to do or say when your son expresses his feelings and emotional needs is a very common response for many parents. I've worked with many men and women who are comfortable asking their son how he feels, but they feel less confident about responding. I remember a father who desperately wanted to help his ten-year-old son, who was depressed. This dad was one of the brave ones who asked, "What do I say to him after he tells me how he feels?"

Use your own emotions to guide you. Consider your own emotional needs for a moment. When you talk about your positive and negative feelings, you probably do not like being interrupted. You probably do like hearing someone validate what you've said ("I understand," or "That makes sense"). You don't want to be made to feel ashamed about your feelings. If you keep all of this in mind the next time your son needs to talk about his feelings, I'm sure you'll respond in healthy ways.

Practice empathy within the family. This is such an important aspect of emotional experience that all of chapter 5 is devoted to the topic. Read chapter 5 from beginning to end. Then be sure to give and receive empathy in your family.

Practice healthy emotional expression in your home. Anger and fear are two of the toughest emotions to regulate. When parents' anger is out of control in the form of verbal or physical aggression, it can destroy families. But if empathy is practiced regularly, then anger won't get out of control. Empathy is an antidote to aggression, narcissism, and the Pack Rules.

To accomplish healthy anger expression in your home, *examine your own anger style.* Are you passive-aggressive (e.g., using the silent treatment), are you verbally explosive (e.g., yelling, screaming), or are you physically violent (e.g., hitting, kicking, slamming, throwing things). Where did you learn your anger style? Knowing your own style for expressing anger is important because, as with so many other behaviors, you are modeling or teaching your son how to express anger.

So, if you haven't already learned how to control your anger, then you must learn now. Identify your triggers (what sets you off?). Face the fear that surely lies beneath your triggers and deal with it like an adult rather than a two-year-old. One way to get a handle on your anger is to talk out loud as you try to control your temper. (This is also excellent role-modeling.) Saying, "I'm so angry now that I need to go outside for a minute to calm down" is a demonstration of healthy anger expression. Lastly, consider this. When your son becomes angry, are you afraid of his anger? If that is so, why is it so? Does his anger remind you of someone else's? If you're afraid of his anger, you must *work on this.* Your fear will interfere with how you parent him.

Of course, practicing healthy emotional expression in the home must also involve positive emotions. There is a healthy family in my community with two teenage sons. The parents support their sons' emotions (just as they support their sons' athletic and academic skills), and, not surprisingly, these boys are popular, successful, and very nice. Although this family has its ups and downs like everyone else, what stands out most to me about them is the way they smile and laugh together. I frequently see the dad joking with his sons, and they all look *happy.* I share this observation with you to emphasize that identifying and expressing feelings of pride, accomplishment, triumph, or just plain fun are as important as expressing negative emotions.

"Must" Skills and Experiences for Boys' Emotions

Additional skills and experiences are needed, beyond the basics, to promote healthy emotional development in boys. Upon your first reading of the following skills and experiences, they may seem unrelated. But they're actually connected like a web; they work together to support your son's emotional development.

Blending Skills

Discussed throughout this book, blending skills essentially refers to combining emotions that have different valences (i.e., both positive and negative) or combining a thought with an emotion. Here are some examples of emotions with different valences: Jared feels angry at his mother (negative), but he still feels love for her (positive); Ryan feels disappointed about not making the high school basketball team (negative), but he feels relieved about having more free time (positive). Blending also allows boys to receive comfort when sad, or reassurance when scared. The idea here is that one emotion, particularly a negative emotion, doesn't dominate a boy's entire focus and all of his energy. Unfortunately, blending emotions is not a widely known or taught skill.

One study indicated that this skill makes its first appearance around the age of ten (Harter and Whitesell 1989), but I've found that it is easily taught, and learned, earlier in life. I've successfully taught boys how to practice this skill from age four and up. Examples of blending a thought with a feeling are probably more familiar. Six-year-old Kyle is afraid to go on the playground where some of the school bullies might pick on him. But then he remembers and thinks about what his Dad told him about feeling safe. He knows he can find a friend to play with or tell a teacher if the bully hurts him. Simply put, Kyle may still *feel* fear, but he *thinks* about how to stay safe.

Thinking and feeling blended together become especially helpful when dealing with anger, as described in chapter 6. The more a person re-appraises (or consciously thinks about) his or her initial reaction, the more there is someone behind the steering wheel. When left unregulated, anger can steer the best-intentioned of us. This also applies to anger-related emotions such as jealousy, frustration, and fear.

When blending goes awry. Teen "paranoia" is an example of when the blending of thinking and feeling can become unhealthy.

This is important to mention because as teenagers develop the ability to "think about thinking," sometimes they draw inaccurate conclusions. For example, how many times have you heard a teen accuse someone of passing judgment or "talking about him" when, in fact, no such event ever took place? In these situations, it would seem that the teen's fear becomes blended with incorrect thoughts. As many parents know, reasoning with teenagers isn't always successful, and this type of inaccurate blending may explain why reasoning doesn't work. The best approach in this situation would be to validate the teen's emotions first. Then, challenge the faulty thinking or conclusions later.

Another example of when the thinking-feeling blend can go awry involves young children's fears of the dark, bugs, dogs, thunder and lightning, loud noises, doctors, and so forth. These fears are all built upon the same type of blending gone awry; an inaccurate thought (e.g., all bugs are dangerous) is connected to the emotion of fear. One might even argue that some phobias (extreme paralyzing fears) are rooted in this type of blending.

With younger children, their intuitive style of thinking (i.e., what they see or feel is the way it *is*) prevents accurate blending. For example, if one dog scares three-year-old Joseph, now all dogs may be scary to him; or if one thunderstorm scared four-year-old Ryan, now all storms scare him.

How to teach blending skills. The main message about blending is that it should be taught early and continued. Both teens and younger children are on a natural developmental trajectory that eventually will result in successful blending of accurate thoughts with emotions. (So, time is on your side.) The simplest, and most effective, way to teach blending skills is to start as soon as possible and continue right through adolescence. Talk with your toddler and your teen about their different feelings. Ask him how he feels about something and then ask what he thinks about the feeling he has. Other specific ideas follow:

★ When a **young boy** is angry with someone, *remind him* that he still loves or cares for that person. (Don't ask him, *tell him*; this teaches blending). When a **teen boy** is angry, *ask him* if he can still feel positive feelings for the person with whom he's angry. If he says no, *then* remind him about how those feelings are still there.

★ When a young boy is scared, teach him how to create safety. When parents use "go-away monster spray" before bedtime to help bad dreams stop, it works because the child *believes* it works and then he *feels* safe (thus, blending thinking with feeling). Although older children and teens won't believe in monster spray, they have more advanced cognitive skills available to them and they can be coached into rational or reasonable thinking to calm their fears.

★ When a boy of any age only tells his thoughts, ask him how he feels about that person or event. Remember, thoughts and emotions are intertwined like strands of thread in a rope.

The ability to blend different emotions and to blend thinking with feeling is a necessary tool for regulating emotions and for maintaining mental health. Many of the major forms of psychotherapy are rooted in this process. If you teach your son these skills, you may actually help prevent some problems, and, at the very least, help him to cope in healthy ways.

Cultural Deconstruction with Media/ Entertainment (Ages Ten and Up)

Mentioned previously, media deconstruction refers to challenging the assumptions of reality that are presented about boys or masculinity in popular culture (movies, TV shows, MTV). Media deconstruction is a skill that is more easily taught when boys have developed abstract reasoning skills (around age eleven), but some boys may be ready to do this sooner. Using deconstruction with boys is an idea borrowed from Kilbourne (1999) and Pipher (1994), who suggest that girls need to deconstruct cultural messages about girls' body images.

Boys need to deconstruct for different reasons, but the *purpose* of deconstruction remains the same: to learn that reality is what they experience, not what media and entertainment relentlessly splash across the screen. Media deconstruction is especially important with regard to boys' emotional development because, if boys are continuously shown that their emotions aren't important and that "real" men don't talk about their emotions and are "fearless," then it makes sense that boys would think that this construct is reality. In short, unless you help your sons to deconstruct and find the real message behind the created message, they will remain largely uneducated, or tricked, by the mass media.

One way to deconstruct media messages with your son is to say out loud what comes to your mind while watching TV sit-coms, commercials, music videos, movies, or sports that reinforce the macho "man-is-a-machine" type of image. This requires you to monitor and/or spend time with your son in his mass media world.

Another deconstruction technique is to give your son a mini-lecture about the real purpose behind the entertainment business, so that he grasps the notion that the images are really all make-believe for marketing purposes.

Deconstruction seconds. Just a few seconds can also be very effective, especially if your son doesn't like to be lectured. It takes no time at all to say, "Oh, I can't believe they made that man act so aggressive in that scene, real guys don't do that!" Or, "I hate the way that music videos show women just as sex objects: women aren't just for sex!" (Every once in a while, be sure to follow your comments with eye contact, saying, "Did you know that, son?")

Other deconstruction seconds for TV and movies include, "Did you see how that boy looked so invincible in that scene? Any normal human being would have been terrified or run away!" After a while, your deconstruction seconds can be reduced to an incredulous laugh, groan, or a simple, "Can you believe that?" And your son will understand.

One final suggestion is to *reinforce* any real or *healthy* messages about boys' and men's emotions that are displayed in the media. Granted, messages challenging the narrow, unhealthy masculine stereotypes inherent in the Pack Rules are few and far between. But they do exist. This "positive deconstruction" can be done using the same media (TV sit-coms, commercials, music videos, movies, sports, magazines, etc.). You will find few examples of the right stuff. Far fewer than of the macho "ideals," but don't let your son miss them!

To summarize deconstruction techniques, find examples of violence, power, and control that mask boys' and men's true feelings and challenge these examples, so that boys can figure out what's real and what's not real, as well as what's healthy and what isn't healthy.

Encourage Your Son to Spend Time with Younger Children

An excellent way to help prevent your son's emotions from disappearing is for him to spend time with younger children. These younger children can be siblings, nieces, nephews, cousins, friends, or neighbors. The time boys spend with younger children can include playing, baby-sitting, feeding, and yes, even changing diapers. Being with children younger than themselves allows boys to practice nurturing, empathy, and basic emotional connection skills. Greeting and engaging three-year-olds requires more than the monosyllabic Pack response. Spending time with younger children also allows boys to stay connected to vulnerability (like needing help tying a shoelace or a hand to cross the street). So many boys learn to mask their vulnerability, their needs, rather than use social support to cope with this feeling. Seeing vulnerability in little ones is a reminder of the real human condition. Plus, it challenges the Pack Rules.

Discourage Teasing and Taunting of Younger Siblings or Peers

So many parents look the other way when their sons "roughhouse" with each other or with friends. When it's in good fun between equally matched boys, then it makes sense to tolerate it. But when an older or bigger brother teases, bullies, or otherwise tries to intimidate peers or siblings, this isn't good fun. If parents don't intervene, then it's a missed opportunity to help the boys learn to empathize with the feelings of another. ("How do you think your little brother felt when you said that to him? Right. Now apologize!") It's also a missed opportunity to teach boys that being together doesn't mean one boy has to have more power than the other.

Let Your Son Care for Pets

In addition to caring for younger children, boys learn and practice valuable emotional skills by caring for pets. These skills include empathy (feeding the cat when she's hungry or playing with her when she's lonely), emotional identification (talking openly about care and concern for Champ, the family dog), and emotional expression (receiving and giving affection to that family pet). Owning a pet is also often a boy's first experience with grief. From goldfish and hamsters to dogs, pets rarely outlive a boy's childhood. Pets die of old age or get killed in accidents before children become adults. Thus, caring for pets also provides an opportunity for boys to experience sadness and to receive comfort in their time of grieving.

Tell Your School's Guidance Counselor and Teachers to Focus on Boys' Emotions

Elementary schools. I know a very talented guidance counselor who told me an interesting story about a well-adjusted boy in her elementary school. Alex's father told this counselor that he wanted Alex to be in any counseling group offered at school. Alex's mother had died a year ago and his father knew that Alex needed all the emotional support he could get. As it turned out, one day the guidance counselor was doing a class lesson on expressing feelings.

During one of the exercises, a quiet girl in the class said that her grandfather had died over the weekend. The class was silent. A few seconds later, a boy in the back of the room raised his hand and said with a quivering lip, "Yeah? Well I bet no one in here knows that my father died last year." The class was silent again. The boy started weeping and couldn't stop.

This wise and wonderful guidance counselor knew exactly how to facilitate the experience for this class. She looked at Alex, who by now had had lots of practice expressing his feelings, and she gave him a nod. He knew just what to do. Alex went over to the sobbing boy and without a word, started patting him on the back and gave him some tissues that the counselor had slipped to Alex. The class sat in respectful silence as they witnessed these two boys feel the pain of grief and the comfort of a friend.

The guidance counselor told me that before the lesson ended that day, the class had talked about sadness and crying as normal and healthy for everyone, even for boys. When I asked the counselor about any aftereffects this experience might have had for these two boys (did the class later reject them for their display of grief and comfort?), she said that, according to her observations and the classroom teacher's report, the class seemed to have bonded after that event. They got closer. To this day, I can only imagine what the long-term effects will be for these boys. To express grief, to cry in school, to receive comfort—*and for all of this all to be okay.* Every boy should be so fortunate.

Middle and high school. Typically, younger boys don't think of school counseling as "sissy stuff." But counseling can become a violation of Pack Rules in middle and high school, when gender stereotypes become so rigid. Yet as boys grow older, their emotional expression needs don't change. As I write this, I recall a counseling group I co-facilitated in a high school. The purpose of the group was to intervene with "high-risk" students who were failing their classes or who had alcohol or drug violations at school, or both. That particular group had ten students, all boys. During weekly group meetings, the boys discussed everything from their grades, parents, and girlfriends, to their alcohol and drug problems.

At the last session, the boys unanimously agreed that they had liked the group (and not only because it got them out of the classroom). As each boy named aloud the reasons why he had liked the group, they seemed surprised. They said that they had actually liked sitting and talking to each other about important stuff, even without drugs or alcohol. One boy, Bubba, was silent as the others talked. He had stringy, shoulder length hair and tattoos. He said, "I was really mad at first about being in a group that did 'sissy' stuff." He paused and then continued, "But getting into trouble was the best thing I've ever done . . . because it got me into this group." It seems that even rough-and-tough high school guys not only need, but also like this "sissy" counseling stuff. I co-facilitated a grief group for middle school boys with similar results. They all liked the experience of just being able to talk Boy Talk with other boys and adults.

The Importance of Physical and Psychological Boundaries

Psychological boundaries involve how you think and feel. They are rooted in emotional needs. Psychological boundaries may be harder to understand than physical boundaries because you cannot see the psychological. But you can feel when someone crosses a psychological boundary: the person tells you or asks you something that just doesn't *feel* right. The same is true for physical boundaries, which is, essentially, your personal space. You feel uncomfortable when a physical boundary is crossed, when someone touches you when you don't want to be touched (sexually or nonsexually), or when someone stands too close while talking with you.

Babies and young children have very few boundaries. Their identities are still merged with their parents. But as they grow into childhood and adolescence they individuate, or become more their own person, by creating and maintaining psychological and physical boundaries. Psychological boundaries help children individuate, in part, by defining their uniqueness.

Physical and psychological boundaries also help keep children safe from harm. As children grow older, they're able to say, "I don't want to hug or kiss Aunt Jasmine anymore." Indeed there are social customs as to the physical and psychological boundaries for both children and adults, including how close to stand when talking with someone, or whether the parents decide their child's future career or mate. Clearly, these boundaries vary from culture to culture. Indeed, in India, people put their faces so close they almost touch when greeting each other in the street. And in Vietnam today, children are still their parents' social (financial) security. In short, culture may define our boundaries for us and establish group norms, but we still get to decide whether these are ultimately harmful or beneficial for us as individuals.

One way that boys' physical boundaries can be compromised is through physically aggressive sports or other violent rites of passage that involve ignoring physical pain and danger. Military training (such as boot camp) provides another example of how physical boundaries are violated, although in that situation, the people involved have given their consent. But in boys' day-to-day lives, they don't really give consent to having their physical boundaries compromised. They just absorb the mandates that saturate our culture: boys must get hurt, not object to the hurt, and certainly not *feel* the hurt. These messages may have roots in the "man as warrior" or "man as defender of his country" roles. But when physical dominance is not needed to survive, it seems unfair that we still charge boys with the stoical role of ignoring their physical pain. If this cultural norm changed to respect boys' physical boundaries, boys would be more likely to respect other people's physical boundaries.

Teaching Physical Boundaries

Feedback to boys about their behavior can help them to learn about their own boundaries and the boundaries of others. For example, Eric may not understand that hitting is wrong. He feels mad, so he whacks his younger brother. What's the problem? Left unattended, Eric doesn't learn that his behavior crossed a boundary. His little brother has the right to be free from physical harm.

As boys become older, they develop empathic skills and learn social rules. Their behaviors are more apt to naturally reflect physical boundaries between themselves and others. (Unless, of course, they're taught a different set of rules that disregard these boundaries.) Thus, like so many skills, learning about physical boundaries begins with understanding your own. These skills are all rooted in the basic philosophy of respect for the human body.

Parents can begin teaching boys about physical boundaries from the time they are toddlers and continue reinforcing these boundaries throughout childhood. As boys internalize these boundaries, they'll not only act in safer ways for themselves, but they will also act respectfully toward others. Some suggestions for teaching physical boundaries follow:

★ Teach your babies and toddlers about why others shouldn't hit or hurt them.

★ Let older boys know that they don't have to "be tough" and get beaten up by anyone. Teach them that paying attention to pain and avoiding it are human needs that everyone has.

★ Teach boys about sexual boundaries. Although they are less often sexually victimized than girls are, boys are victims of sexual abuse, too. Help boys know about the private parts of their bodies and about "good touches" and "bad touches" and not to keep "secrets."

★ Teach boys to know their physical strengths and limitations. Some boys will be more muscular and stronger than other boys: most boys will be stronger than most girls (after pubertal development is complete). Show boys how to handle their strength and not use it to dominate or hurt others.

★ Most boys lack the experience and skill of gentle touch. As babies, they were caressed and hugged, but somewhere in late childhood, boys' physical "affection quota" drops off (largely due to parents' fear of "feminizing" their sons). If you want your son to show affection, you'll need to keep showing affection to him!

Teaching Psychological Boundaries

Psychological boundaries are a felt sense that helps you know where your thoughts and feelings begin and end, and where someone else's begin and end. For example, if eight-year-old Danny's father comes home angry from work one day, it's obvious that Danny isn't responsible for his father's feelings. (But Danny may not know this and he may feel that somehow he has angered his father.) Or if Danny's father says, "Danny, you should become a stockbroker when you're older," it's clear that Danny's own thoughts are being ignored. Although these may seem to be innocuous examples, the point is that younger children are susceptible to absorbing the thoughts and feelings of others because younger children's boundaries are more permeable. When a child is told that he is responsible for another person's feelings or is told how to think and feel—or not to think and feel—then that child's psychological boundaries are crossed.

Boys' experiences and perceptions can become distorted when they're told not to think or feel a certain way. As discussed in chapter 5, boys' empathic abilities can become affected when their boundaries are violated, resulting in too much or too little empathy. Although boys and men have always had the privilege to express their public thoughts (writing the Constitution, recording world history, making scientific discoveries, etc.), there has been less permission for boys and men to express their intimate thoughts and feelings. I think this contributes not only to boys' restricted emotional expression but also to boundary confusion. Boys learn to move their psychological boundaries so far inward that their own thoughts and feelings may be eclipsed.

The following "do's and don'ts" are basic guidelines that can help teach healthy psychological boundaries to boys at any age:

★ Ask boys how they feel and think; don't tell them how they (should) feel or think.

★ Listen to boys; don't overpower them with your own thoughts and feelings.

★ Validate boys' thoughts and feelings, never shame them.

★ Help boys understand that they can think and feel differently from you, and that's okay.

★ Help boys learn how to empathize with others without taking on the other person's identity or dilemma. Boys must learn how to comfort someone in pain without feeling as if it is their responsibility to fix things (unless they were part of causing the pain). Encourage boys to celebrate someone else's good fortune without needing to compete toe-to-toe.

Summary

This chapter provides specific tools for parents who want to promote their sons' healthy emotional development. These tools include validating boys' emotions, teaching boys blending skills, encouraging them to spend time with younger children and to care for pets. The importance of deconstructing media messages about masculinity and the relevance of psychological and physical boundaries in emotional development are also discussed. As parents, you are charged with the task of encouraging schools to pay attention to boys' healthy emotional development. Because both the Pack Rules and the code of silence about boys' emotions are continually affecting boys, it is extremely important that families teach boys how to have and handle their emotions. If boys don't learn these healthy emotional skills in their families, where will they learn?

CHAPTER
8

For the Other Adults in Boys' Lives: Practical Ways to Support Boys' Emotional Development

Never doubt that a small group of thoughtful, committed people can change the world.
Indeed, it is the only thing that ever has.

—Margaret Mead

Many different adult men and women can provide help that will foster boys' emotional development. This help can range from subtly asking boys how they feel about something to directly telling them that it's okay to have feelings. Or the help may involve educating parents about the need to pay attention to their boys' emotional development. The teacher who describes a boy during a parent-teacher conference as having a "brilliant mind and a tender heart" is using a subtle approach, just like the coach who talks about his team of boys as being "caring and competitive." A more direct approach would be the grandfather who tells a concerned father, "You know, son, I wish I had been there for you when you were growing up; your son needs you . . . show him you understand how badly he's feeling right now."

As a therapist and professor, I use the direct approach. I come right out and say that boys' emotions are important and that far too often adults ignore or dismiss our boys' feelings. I quickly add that ignoring boys' emotions is not healthy for boys, and that everyone has a role in changing this pattern. Then I talk about the Pack Rules, that narrow and unhealthy code of behaviors that boys often follow in an attempt to be masculine (see chapter 2 for the rules). I use the direct approach because I figure the more people who know about all of this, the better our chances will be for changing things for boys.

It Will Always Take a Village

Although the entire book was written for parents of boys and other adults interested in boys' emotional development, this chapter focuses exclusively on the roles that other adults play in boys' lives. Parents also will benefit from reading this chapter because it offers a systematic view of who these other adults are and how they can contribute to boys' emotional development. This chapter contains practical guidelines and specific suggestions to help boys develop in healthy ways, especially with regard to emotional expression skills. But before reading any further, there's an important question that must be addressed for all of the adults in boys' lives. That question is: *Won't a boy turn into a wimp if you support his emotions?*

The Wimp Factor

The answer to the above question is no, you won't turn boys into wimps, sissies, wusses, or mama's boys by supporting the expression of their emotions. Unfortunately, most people don't believe this. And that fear contributes to the cultural resistance to boys' expression of emotions. In its simplest form, the fear is that the boy who feels and expresses his emotions will be "less" of a boy and he will be rejected for not following the Pack Rules (described in chapter 2). But the truth is this: *Honoring boys' feelings doesn't create wimps; it creates humans.*

As discussed in the previous chapter for parents, although girls' emotions receive more support in our culture than boys' emotions (especially the vulnerable emotions), behavioral outcomes in public appear to be similar for boys and girls. Think about how rare it is to see boys *or girls* cry in public. Indeed, girls don't want to show their vulnerability in school or on the ball field anymore than boys do. I believe that the way adults try to prevent boys from becoming "feminized" by teaching boys not to talk about their feelings merely serves to reduce boys' emotional expression. The "toughen him up" approach may be good for warriors, but it is not good for boys' emotional development.

Who does or doesn't cry in public isn't the real issue, of course. The issue is this: When faced with challenges or conflict, girls have access to a broader range of emotional skills than boys do. And this isn't fair. Thus, boys need to be taught how to feel and express their emotions and know that they are still "real" boys. It's essential for the adults in boys' lives not only to tolerate, but to validate and nurture boys' emotions. The end result is that boys will know how they feel and they *won't* wind up as social outcasts. Letting go of the "wimp fear" that is so firmly rooted in the culture as a corollary to the Pack Rules is probably the biggest challenge that many adults (and, not surprisingly, boys) face.

Foster Parents

The role that foster parents play in helping boys to develop healthy emotional expression is similar to the role that birth parents have. But foster parents have the additional challenge of having much less time to help with this aspect of development and to do so without a secure attachment relationship. Foster parents have another added challenge. Their foster son has been emotionally hurt in some way. If he didn't experience abuse or neglect, then he is experiencing the pain of grief because of the separation from his parents.

Grief and Stress Have No Age or Gender Limits

From two-year-olds to teens, loss is loss. Although very young babies are less likely to have conscious verbal memories of losing their parents, they are aware of a disruption in their attachment to others. Foster children benefit greatly from having aid given to them by someone skilled at facilitating the grieving process, especially boys who can mask their feelings so well. If these boys also experienced abuse and neglect (often the case with foster children), then their grief may be complicated by post-traumatic stress (PTSD) symptoms.

I strongly encourage foster parents to read books about grieving (and PTSD if that applies). Books specifically written for foster children and grief would be best, but almost any book about children's grief is recommended; examples include Emswiller and Emswiller's *Guiding Your Child Through Grief* (2000) and Mundy's *Sad Isn't Bad: A Good-Grief Guidebook for Kids Dealing with Loss* (1998). You'll notice as you read these books that their major focus involves emotions. Helping children of any age express emotions is part of their healing, but especially so for boys whose feelings may be neglected. Otherwise their emotions may come out "sideways," disguised as anything from physical symptoms and flashbacks to an empty longing inside. Aggressive behaviors and clinical depression are other common sideways expressions of emotions.

I also recommend that foster parents read chapters 2, 3, 4, and 7. These four chapters combine to provide a solid developmental background about boys' emotions and what to do with them. When reading the chapter about boys' emotional development (chapter 3), it's important not to just zoom in on a foster son's current age. Even if he's ten years old, read the entire chapter. It provides information about earlier stages of development and emotional skills that he may still need to master. It also describes the emotional skills he'll need in the months and years ahead.

How Does Attachment Affect Emotions?

Attachment is an important aspect of a foster child's emotional development. Attachment refers to that special bond or attunement between humans, most often associated with the parent-child relationship. In its purest sense, attachment is really about emotional survival. For the child, attachment requires a feeling of safety and security, being understood and cared for, and being able to give caring in return. The attachment process is a two-way street between foster child and foster parent; however, sometimes only the child or parent attaches.

I've observed that when a boy attaches to the foster parent and the foster parent doesn't attach to the boy, boys can still develop healthy emotional skills in this *temporary* setting. This is not, however, the case with *permanent* foster care arrangements. Attachment needs to be present or developing in permanent foster care relationships. Thus, it is recommended that foster parents be honest with a foster son about how long he'll stay with them. Some boys will be told they're staying only a short time, but they decide to call their foster parents Mom and Dad anyway. Foster children do this because they *need* to be attached to someone.

Sometimes the foster parent attaches to a foster son, but the boy doesn't become attached due to post-traumatic stress, an attachment disorder, or because he's old enough to realize this is a temporary relationship. He also may not attach because he doesn't want to risk the pain of more loss. Or he may still be attached to another caregiver or to his biological parent(s). Regardless of the reason, I've observed that the foster parents can "carry the relationship." In such a one-way attachment, the adult invests more emotional risks, sharing, and caring than the child does. There are fewer tangible rewards (hugs, kisses, compliments, and caring) for the adult. But the relationship can still "work" and be helpful to the boy's emotional development.

Emotional Expression Prevents Boys' Emotions from Disappearing

Although attachment is a complicated and important aspect of healthy emotional development, the most basic rule of thumb for promoting a foster son's emotional development is to help him identify and express his emotions. This helps with the grief process, PTSD, and general emotional development. The ultimate goal for boys (anyone, really) is to put their feelings into words with someone they trust. Thus, this is not only about teaching boys to master an emotional skill, it's also about experiencing a healthy relationship, one in which emotions can be expressed.

A few words to foster dads. By many standards, you're considered the gender role model due to the fact that you and your foster son are the same sex. Thus, you need to keep in mind the fact that your foster son is watching you for clues about how to be a man. (Just the way you watched your father or the other male figures in your life.) What you say or don't say about your own emotions will be noticed; what you say and don't say about his emotions will also be noticed. If you agree with the main ideas in this book (that boys' emotions matter and that expressing those emotions is every boy's birthright), then trust your natural instincts about what to say and do about his emotions . . . and yours.

A few words to foster moms. Due to biological sex differences, you are not considered a gender role model. But you are still an incredibly important role model for being human. If you believe that your foster son's emotions matter and that feeling and expressing them are healthy for him, have confidence that what you do and say about his emotions (and yours) will be helpful to him. Although he'll be looking to male figures for clues about "how to become a real man," he's also looking for clues about how to be healthy and how to relate to others. I remember a fourteen-year-old foster boy who said that his foster mother was the first one to teach him that his feelings were important. He described her as being like a light, a light shining in a dark cave.

Grandparents

Familiarity with the pressures of being a parent makes being a grandparent an even sweeter experience than it would be by itself.

Over and over I hear boys talk about how much their grandparents mean to them. Especially grandpas. And this is true not only for the boys who actually live near their grandparents. Distance doesn't seem to hamper the grandparent-grandchild relationship; that very special relationship seems to transcend both miles and time.

I counseled a ten-year-old boy, Tim, for aggressive behaviors at school. He had never known his father, and his grandfather lived thirteen hours away. Yet this grandfather remained important, on a daily basis, to this boy. How did this happen? It seems that when the two of them were together, they experienced "power time." Tim felt totally respected, understood, and loved by his grandfather. It didn't matter *what* they did together, it was *how* they were together. When Tim tried to put into words what his grandfather meant to him, he cried. This power isn't limited to grandpas. Grandmothers also provide a source of unconditional love, the kind that is a soothing balm for any kind of self-doubt.

What Grandparents Can Do to Help Boys' Emotional Development

Grandparents are not in the position to set rules or curfews. And they don't carry the unspoken anxieties that parents do. (Am I doing things right? How can I help my son do better in school? How can I keep him from making the same mistakes I made? If I support his emotions, won't he be considered a sissy and be rejected?) Thus, grandparents are in the perfect position to help boys to develop their ability to express their emotions. Free from parental anxiety and armed with "broader views" grandparents know what is real, what is possible, what matters, and what doesn't matter at all. Drawing from their years of experience and the wisdom of age, they can whittle down a confusing conflict to its essence.

Steven's grandparents. Whenever Steven and his parents got into a fight (about using the car, going to the mall, or similar issues), he'd usually go to his room, lock the door, and blast his stereo. Unfortunately, once Steven cooled down, he never went back to his parents to work things out. The way Steven saw it, his parents were focused on "ruining his life." Naturally, his parents saw things differently. They were just restricting his time at the mall and not letting him drive whenever he wanted to. As is often the case, parents and teen were locked into a power battle; in such a case it often takes the help of an objective person to straighten things out.

This is where Steven's grandparents helped. They were able to see (and respect) all the emotions that all the participants in the power struggle were feeling, including those that Steven couldn't see in his parents and vice versa. Steven was struggling with being socially popular and growing up. He was *afraid* that he'd lose his friends if he didn't go to the mall, drive around, and stay out past his curfew. He was also stressed about balancing his part-time job, keeping up with his schoolwork, and paying his part of the car insurance. These are all growing-up issues. Yet Steven's parents were afraid that if they allowed Steven do everything he wanted to do, that would be both unhealthy and unsafe.

Steven's grandparents saw all of this. Since they lived nearby, Steven would go to their house whenever he felt like it. Not surprisingly, he went there several times a week "just to check on them." They were getting older and Steven had started doing some chores for them. When his grandparents didn't have a chore (which they would sometimes invent), they'd just sit and talk. They'd listen to Steven talk about his frustrations and social anxieties and say, "That makes sense to me," or, "How embarrassing to have to check in earlier than your friends do."

They were careful not to undermine his parents' power or their good intentions. In fact, they gave Steven just the perspective he most needed: "Your parents aren't doing this to ruin your life, even though it may feel that way; they're just trying to keep you safe and healthy." Indeed, hearing this perspective clearly stated helped to straighten out some of Steven's sideways anger expression.

So, during the difficult teenage years, grandparents can act as buffers to conflict while also validating boys' emotions. But grandparental emotional support doesn't have to wait until adolescence. In fact, the more you support your grandson's feelings early on, the better! Helping him to tell you how he is doing, from the time he can talk, is excellent preparation for helping him during his adolescence. One could speculate that if Steven had had more emotional expression practice as a youngster, he might have been better able to tell his parents that he was feeling scared or angry with words, rather than with his behaviors.

So, if your grandsons follow the Pack Rules, explain to them that, in the long run, the Pack Rules actually may end up hurting them more than helping them. (Grandfathers can speak from their own experiences about this.)

Grandparents as parents. If you or someone you know is parenting a grandson, because his parents are gone or otherwise unable to take care of the boy, then reading this whole book probably will be of value to you.

Teachers

Whenever I talk with teachers, I make it a point to tell them that in their students' eyes, they are second in importance only to parents. Some teachers nod in a knowing way. Others are surprised but also pleased. Outside of a boy's family, teachers are the grown-ups with whom he interacts more than any other adults. *That's important.* And although teachers have different personalities, different areas of expertise, and different styles of interacting with students, they can all provide a similar respect for boys' emotions in their classrooms. This respect is sorely needed.

The Pack Rules and boys' emotions in the classroom. One way to challenge the Pack Rules (see chapter 2) is to encourage boys to identify and express their emotions. This will be hard if you don't like to talk about emotions. But teachers know only too well about how emotion is tied to learning. The emotional aspect of learning isn't about being "mushy" or "touchy feely" in the classroom. Rather, it refers to including the *affective* element in the *academic* experience.

The following classroom list is a guide for teachers who want to make room for boys' emotions in their classrooms. These suggestions essentially challenge the Pack Rules:

For Elementary and Middle School Teachers:

★ Use emotion words, "You look happy . . . sad . . . proud . . . curious . . . angry . . . frustrated . . . excited" with boys when talking with them about their schoolwork, or on the playground, about their social experiences. Boys must be able to use their emotional skills, just as much as they use their cognitive skills.

★ Establish zero-tolerance for boys and girls who make fun of boys who show their emotions. For example, when children call a boy a *crybaby* or *sissy* for showing tender feelings, let it become an instant lesson about how *all* feelings are normal and healthy. Let it be known that bullying is not tolerated in your classroom!

For High School Teachers:

★ High school can be the time to correct the rigid gender roles that boys learned in middle school. What you do in your classroom can reinforce, challenge, or actually change those roles for boys.

★ There isn't any reason to tolerate bullying or hazing of boys in high school. Make your classroom a place of zero-tolerance for aggression, including verbal aggression such as sarcasm. Model that it isn't okay to exploit power through aggression to establish dominance. This forces boys to find assertive ways to keep their individual power and express anger. You can model this in your classroom simply by *not* using sarcasms, put-downs, or physically intimidating gestures. (Sometimes teachers do these things without even knowing it.) When a person in power treats those who are less powerful with respect, the issues of dominance and subordination become less salient.

★ Use feeling and emotional words as much as you can. Reflect boys' emotions as described above, "You look angry, proud, curious, pleased, frustrated, etc." Say this even if you teach a seemingly unemotional course like math or physics. Students are human and boys are, too. There is clearly a lot of satisfaction in solving complex algebraic equations or in investigating theories of relativity and physical laws. Talk about these feelings.

The suggestions above are relevant to wealthy and poor students, urban and rural, Christian and non-Christian, native-born Americans and immigrants. Emotions don't observe a color line. They are not racist or prejudiced. Emotions are human.

Teachers also can support boys' emotions indirectly by talking with the parents of the students about boys' emotions. A teacher might be the one to introduce parents to the idea that boys' emotions matter (or introduce them to this book). Teachers are not only incredible role models, they actually *create experiences* for their students in their classrooms. When these experiences help boys to become fully human, rather than stoic robots, these teachers will have indeed taught another valuable lesson.

Principals

Because principals usually have only brief contacts with students ranging from disciplinary matters to bestowing honors, the majority of a principal's influence with students is indirect, via the teachers. Here, I want to discuss both the contacts the principal has with students, as they relate to boys' emotional development in K-12 schools, and the influence the principal has in creating a climate in which teachers feel supported in their efforts to help boys to develop their emotional natures.

Principals' encounters with boys. What a principal says to a student is remembered, in part, because of the power the principal represents. Furthermore, male principals have the role not only of administrator, but also of masculine role model. Thus, when a principal breaks the Pack Rules, boys notice it.

For example, suppose a male student is sent to the principal for fighting and the principal says, "I'd be scared and angry, too, if that kid had said that to me . . . but that's no excuse for losing control and becoming violent. Violence isn't acceptable." This single statement would do two things: it would validate the boy's feelings and it would challenge the Pack Rules. Boys need to hear messages like this from men in power.

Women principals, too, can and must give the same message to boys. Although the boys won't identify with a woman principal as a *biological* masculine role model, they will identify her with the "masculine" role of power.

The second equally powerful contact that principals have with students involves positive emotions associated with the bestowal of academic or athletic awards as public events. These events offer opportunities to support boys' emotional development by highlighting the positive feelings that accompany receiving student honors. Remarks about feelings of pride and happiness would be not only natural, they would also be helpful to boys and their parents. (Making a big deal about positive experiences is not reserved only for girls.)

The principal's greatest influence. The school climate (or environment) that principals create for teachers and staff is extremely significant and this climate clearly trickles down to the students. Although principals can't force teachers to act or speak in specific ways, they can create a faculty and staff climate that is respectful of boys' emotions. Such respect takes place not only through school policies, but through the students' interactions with teachers. If principals follow the Pack Rules, overtly or covertly, the Rules will permeate all of the school's activities. If principals challenge and break the Pack Rules, it's more likely that boys' humanity and emotional development will be supported.

Early in my career, I had a friend who worked in a school in which the male faculty "rated" the women faculty's bodies. The principal was involved in this sexist rating system. You can image what the climate of that school felt like. Although my friend liked and respected this principal in many other ways, it was clear that he had been successfully socialized by the Pack Rules. In this particular situation, the principal experienced professional consequences for observing the Rules. One of the female faculty filed a sexual harassment complaint and he was professionally reprimanded.

The principal's leadership can create a professional and respectful school climate for everyone (or not). In the preceding situation, if an eighth-grade girl had brought a sexual harassment charge against an eight grade boy in that school before the principal was reprimanded, it probably wouldn't have been seen as a problem!

Breaking the Pack Rules and promoting boys' healthy emotional development doesn't mean turning the school into a "warm and fuzzy" place. It does mean creating an environment in which teachers and students are respected. And that often involves challenging the Pack Rules. It would have been very powerful, indeed, if that principal had exercised his leadership role with the male faculty and challenged the Pack Rules rather than going along with them. (As a rule, men seem to have one of two reactions when the Pack Rules are challenged; they either feel relieved or become defensive.)

Changing the Pack Rules in school. What does a school look like that doesn't follow the Pack Rules? Principals can make it known that boys don't have to follow the Pack Rules. The best way to do this is to offer alternative rules for boys. Make it clear to faculty, staff, and students that: it's okay for "boys to be boys" (but it's not okay for them to be hypersexual via the telling of smutty jokes, sexual harassment, etc.); it's okay for boys to be angry (but it's not okay for them to express their anger with violence); it's okay for boys to be scared or vulnerable (but it's not okay to shame them for showing their fear or vulnerability); it's okay to be a good sport (but not always the winner); it's okay for boys to be on the same level as everyone else (they don't have to be all-powerful); and finally, it's just plain *not okay* to bully other boys or girls. Bullying demeans both the victim and the bully.

If a school truly embraces respect for each other "from the top down," then boys' emotional development will flourish right along with girls'. In any school, the principal's leadership (whether male or female) decides whether the Pack Rules or humanity rules.

Coaches

The role that coaches play varies from boy to boy. Part of this depends on whether the boy is a recreational athlete who plays in community leagues, a serious athlete who plays on school teams, or an elite athlete who plays sports year round with sights on an Olympic or a professional career. Thus, coaches' roles range from the coordinator of a fun time, to technical advisor, to father figure/mentor. The more serious a boy is about his sport, the more likely it is that he will look to his coach for technical knowledge, motivation, and athletic discipline.

For all boys, however, there are some common denominators in the coach-athlete relationship, regardless of the seriousness of the athlete. One common denominator involves the quality of the coach. My definition of a "good" coach is this: A good coach is one who has a complete command of all of the technical knowledge of the sport and who motivates athletes on the team with respect rather than shame. When coaching boys, showing them respect rather than shaming them is especially important if the Pack Rules are to be changed.

Sports and the Pack Rules

It may be tempting for coaches to uphold the Pack Rules because the "win at all costs" attitude can seemingly lead to more wins. Indeed, the Pack Rules also legitimize physical aggression, at the core of sports like football, hockey, boxing, and basketball. Sports and athletics, in turn, also seem to influence the Pack Rules (no pain, no gain). The more coaches abide by the Pack Rules themselves, the more likely it will be that they'll reinforce the aggressive aspects of certain sports.

The Pack Rules are closely related to another common denominator in boys' relationship with coaches. Sports are a gateway to masculinity. Therefore, coaches convey what masculinity is and isn't, in what they say and how they say it to boys. There are subtle and not so subtle ways to shame boys when they break a Pack Rule. The subtle way is to ignore boys' emotions and needs silently. This invalidates their experience. The direct way is to verbally shame the boy; tell him he's being a sissy or playing *like a girl*. Either way, when coaches tell boys that their emotions and basic needs don't matter, this reinforces the idea that boys should be more like machines than people.

In the context of sports, this "be tough" philosophy can make sense from the coach's point of view of winning the game at all costs. But to a boy, the "be tough" attitude can become an experience of numbing, dissociating, or otherwise cutting off his emotions from his experience. This attitude can become toxic for boys if no one explains that being tough is okay only *during* the game, and it is not appropriate off the field, or that it's only a game and not the end of the world.

A Word to Coaches About Being Boys' Role Model

Another obvious influence of male coaches is that of gender role model. Boys scrutinize male coaches. If you cuss, they'll think it's okay to cuss. If you lose your temper and become aggressive, they'll think that's okay. If you make fun of girls or talk about girls only in sexual ways, they'll think that's okay, too. If you tell them to win at all costs, that will be their focus. All of these are variations of the Pack Rules.

Consider the alternative. You can teach boys something different from the Pack Rules, something healthier. You can talk about boys' emotions and use their feelings to motivate boys. Or you might honor the competition without having to make the opposing team into an enemy fit only for annihilation. (And your team can still win.) Indeed, the elite coaches at the top schools know how to use their athletes' emotions to enhance performance. This is very different from the Pack Rules, which ignore emotions, particularly fear. There is obviously a respectful way to play sports that honors the emotions of fear, competition, and winning, without turning boys into machines that can't feel pain or bodily sensations such as thirst. A clear focus is quite different from numbing out feelings. Male and female coaches, alike, must begin to consider paying attention to boys' emotions and using them in productive ways.

Medical Doctors

As most of us know, doctors' roles have changed drastically in America over the past several decades. (I remember how our family doctor still made house calls in the 1960s.) Today a physician's contact is often less intimate and personal. House calls are rare and office visits are brief. This change in medical care has also changed the physician-patient relationship. But regardless of this shift, when doctors meet with a boy, they have his undivided attention. And similar to the other adults in boys' lives (grandparents, teachers, coaches), if you're male, you're automatically a masculine role model. These factors combine to make doctors an ongoing influence in boys' lives (an influence that can help loosen the grip of Pack Rules), especially with regard to boys' emotional development.

Doctors Are Important to Boys' Emotional Development

A family physician or pediatrician may be the only health professional (other than orthodontists and/or dermatologists) who gets a close look at boys. This is due, in part, to the social stigma about seeing a mental health professional that still exists in many parts of our country (especially for boys and men). So physicians may be the only ones who can do "mental health" checkups. The Emotional Apgar Score in chapter 7 can be a reference for evaluating boys' overall emotional health. There are important links between emotional and physical health. Indeed, practitioners of behavioral medicine and pediatric psychology closely consider these links when evaluating and treating their patients.

If a boy visits your office complaining about vague symptoms of malaise, stomach or headaches, sleeping or eating problems, and/or attention or hyperactivity problems, be sure to ask him if he feels worried, scared, sad, or mad about something. I cannot tell you how many young boys and teenagers keep some of their really big feelings bottled up inside themselves. These suppressed feelings often result in physical symptoms that ease up just as soon as their ability to express these emotions increases. This is a fairly common pattern for boys whose parents have divorced or remarried, as well as for boys whose parents are contemplating divorce or remarriage.

In short, I'm recommending that when a boy comes in for an office visit, whether for a physical complaint or for an annual physical or wellness checkup, doctors should also consider doing an "emotions checkup" at all ages. If it appears that a boy's emotions are in danger of disappearing or have already completely disappeared, encourage the boy to talk about his feelings with you, and then encourage his parent/guardian to talk more with him about his feelings at home. Recommend this book or counseling with the school guidance counselor or a private counselor. If medical doctors ask boys about their feelings, then those feelings will be legitimized in a way that would otherwise go unnoticed. Perhaps physicians' cultural influence hasn't lessened after all?

Religious and/or Spiritual Leaders

Several years ago, I attended a professional training session about emotional self-care. The first presentation was by a Native American leader who talked glowingly about her father, an Indian chief. One of her comments was that this wonderful man never, ever got angry. I sat there and thought about how he must have felt anger at times; after all, he was human and alive. What this devoted daughter might have said that would have been more accurate was that she never saw her father become aggressive. Unfortunately, many different religions convey the same inaccurate message: feeling angry is bad (thus they confuse anger with aggression). Needless to say, my idea of healthy emotional self-care values the message that anger brings to us.

How Organized Religions May View Emotion

Emotions are frequently confused, as in the anger versus aggression example cited above. Depending on the particular religion and set of beliefs, feeling frightened or angry may be considered sinful and weak. Although adult Christian, Jewish, Muslim, or Buddhist individuals may appreciate what "human weakness" means in the abstract, young boys are concrete thinkers. They hear only that being afraid or angry is bad. They also hear that being bad means being weak or sinful. They may hear these concepts and absorb them whole, without any gradations. Due to their cognitive development, younger boys tend to think in black and white. If they think that showing their feelings is sinful, the fear of being a sinner may cause them to cut themselves off from their feelings almost as efficiently as following the Pack Rules.

Religious leaders can play many roles in boys' lives. They can be role models, they can help shape boys' experiences with faith, they can minister to boys in time of need, and they can introduce boys to spirituality. But in terms of boys' emotions, perhaps the most important role spiritual leaders can play is to *help boys integrate their healthy, natural emotions with their spiritual development.*

Tucking emotion into the shadows. You've probably observed adult religious leaders who have tucked their natural needs and emotions into their shadows as a way to cope with their earthly imperfections ... their "weak" emotions. In the pursuit of being more godly here on earth, these people end up neglecting their emotions, only to have their natural human needs come out sideways in hurtful behaviors and addictions.

I once worked with a twenty-six-year-old man who was raised in a conservative, Christian religion. His addiction to pornography had begun when he was seventeen. His shame about his addiction had become so huge in the intervening years that he could see very little that was good about himself; indeed, he saw only a weak sinner.

When we explored what had been going on in his earthly, human life at the time he started looking at pornography, he confessed that he had been feeling sad, angry, and confused about his parents' divorce. He had not talked with anyone about these powerful emotions at the time he was experiencing them. He had been taught to "rise above" his emotions and pray to God for help.

While I have no doubt that prayer can be both helpful and miraculous, it was clear to me that this boy also needed people here on earth to minister to his earthly emotions when he was in a great deal of pain. Some might say that one important way that God or the Great Spirit answers prayers is through human help. Nevertheless, the pornography addiction appeared to be a symptom of this man's unattended, human emotional needs.

Regardless of a faith's particular religious tenets, it's extremely important that boys' emotions remain a healthy part of their humanity while they explore their spirituality. Too often, humanity and spirituality become mutually exclusive. Or, at least, that's how some spiritual concerns are translated to young children who lack the ability to handle abstract thought. Let boys know that their emotions are an essential, healthy part of who they are here on earth.

Therapists and Guidance Counselors

I frequently introduce myself to children as a "feelings doctor." This is not a novel idea, others therapists do the same. But for me, it isn't just a cute way to introduce myself either. I really mean it. I see one of my primary roles as a psychotherapist as validating people's feelings. This validation occurs in several ways, described below. Overall, I stay focused and committed to children's emotions and family member's emotions throughout the course of therapy.

Validating Boys' Emotions

Because boys' emotions are so often invalidated in our culture, for all of the reasons discussed previously, validating their emotions in a therapeutic setting is especially important. Basically, the steps involved with validation include helping a boy to identify and/or name his emotions, and then helping him to express those emotions to me and to others he trusts (parents, friends, teachers, etc.). This is a frequent goal for boys' treatment.

The next layer of validation includes educating boys about how the larger culture typically ignores their feelings and how boys are often punished or ridiculed for expressing feelings. This is, essentially, a discussion of the Pack Rules. I then talk with boys about how to cope with all of these pressures not to feel and especially not to express their feelings, without having to surrender to stoicism or to give up feeling their true emotions.

Assessment and treatment. One approach to assessing and treating boys that therapists may find helpful is to become an "emotions detective." When a boy of any age presents as aggressive, I look for the primary emotions of fear, anger, sadness, and "hurt." When boys of any age present with depression symptoms, I look for the same emotions. When older (teen) boys present with entitlement issues, I still look for the same emotions. Even with more complex disorders, such as Post-Traumatic Syndrome Disorder or Obsessive Compulsive Disorder, I look for these underlying basic emotions, the ones that haven't been fully expressed or attended to, and come out sideways.

Another way of approaching or perhaps just talking about boys' feelings is to use the adjectives "big" and "powerful" to describe and validate boys' feelings, especially the painful ones. I even use these adjectives with adult men. It seems that a childish word, like "big," can open up the feelings that boys may have sealed over when they were younger, and the word "powerful" can help boys tap into the idea that they can handle their feelings.

A comprehensive way to work with boys' emotions is a clinical approach I developed, called Cognitive-Emotional-Behavioral Therapy (CEB-T). Just as it sounds, this treatment approach involves assessing and intervening at all three levels: thinking, feeling, and behaving. It doesn't matter which level is accessed first, as long as all three areas are included in the assessment and treatment plan.

Generally, my CEB-T protocol begins with the boy's strongest area (the one he has the most awareness of), and then my questioning branches out from there. I often find that the process is circular, rather than linear. For example, a thirteen-year-old boy may recognize his bullying behavior, but be clueless about *why* he picks on his sister so much (the *cognitive* aspect) or the *feelings* that trigger his behavior (the emotional process). With a boy like this, I would begin by learning more about his behaviors and then help him understand the psychological connection between his bullying, his emotional needs, and his thinking patterns. If we don't identify these connections the first time through, we go around again and again (the circular process) until we do. Then we make a plan to change the problem behavior while addressing the cognitive and emotional levels at the same time.

If solutions aren't reached via direct dialogue, I use other methods such as play therapy (with younger boys), asking boys to keep a journal between sessions, and including family members in sessions. As mentioned, you may find yourself circling through the CEB-T process, but the circularity is good because it allows you to go back and make connections to previous information or sessions. Therapists and counselors are invited to consider how important it is to use a multilevel approach like this and not to focus on just one area, i.e., only thoughts *or* behaviors *or* emotions. Making the cognitive and behavioral links to boys' emotions can be very valuable in treatment, because boys may not get that experience elsewhere.

Family emotions. As indicated throughout this book, boys' parents and the surrounding culture significantly influence boys' ability to express their emotions. Therefore, whenever you work with children, you are also working with the family. Thus, therapists and counselors need to assess how emotions are expressed (or not expressed) in the family. As you know, parents often may totally ignore their boys' feelings, for fear of turning him into a sissy. Or they may try to "toughen him up" so that he will be able to cope with the "real world." It's important to keep in mind that many parents and siblings also don't express their emotions directly in family settings. So promoting emotional expression in the whole family is important when trying to support boys' emotional expression.

Parents can help their younger and older sons express their emotions. The more simply this concept is explained to parents, the better. Therapists may find it helpful to read chapter 7, the parenting chapter, for detailed ways to do this. But, in general, as a therapist, make sure that parents are aware of at least three critical skill areas:

1. *Parents must understand that boys' emotions are real and important.* (See chapter 1 for an overview.)

2. *Boys must be able to identify and express their emotions to their parents to stay healthy.* Mirroring boys' emotions, having parents role-model their own emotional expressions, and asking boys directly about how they feel are all examples of being able to identify and express emotions.

3. *Parents must respond to boys' emotions in healthy ways, without activating the shame embedded in the Pack Rules.* Saying, "That makes sense to me," or, "I understand how you'd feel that way" are two tried and true ways to respond to boys' emotions.

I've worked with parents who nod their head enthusiastically when I tell them about points 1 and 2. Then they look hesitant with the third point. Brave parents will ask me how to respond to boys' emotions. I remember a father who desperately wanted to help his ten-year-old son who was depressed. Knowing that parents often don't know what to say to their sons, I usually give them the examples above. ("That makes sense to me," and "I understand how you would feel that way.") The simpler and the more familiar the response, the easier it is for parents to respond.

Prevention and intervention. In Susan Gilbert's (2001) book, *A Field Guide to Boys and Girls*, this comprehensive researcher summarizes the results from much of the sex and gender research that has been done in the last decade for parents. She dispels previous beliefs (and research) that girls become depressed more often than boys. It turns out that boys become depressed just as often, they just mask it in ways that others can't see. John Lynch and Chris Kilmartin's (1999) book, *The Pain Behind the Mask: Overcoming Masculine Depression,* describes this exact same phenomenon in adult men. A similar book needs to be written for boys.

Since boys often don't directly express the emotions that precede depression, and they often don't express their situation by saying, "I'm depressed," they are at a double disadvantage in terms of the progression of the depression. First, they lack the experiences that would prevent some depressions, i.e., talking about their "big" feelings of sadness, fear, anger, and hurt. Second, they hide their emotional pain behind masks of silliness, aggression, irritability, and sometimes hyperactivity. Anytime a therapist works with boys, he or she is accomplishing both intervention and prevention. If boys heal in the moment (intervention), and they learn ways to express their emotions now and in the future, then later mental and physical health problems most likely will also be prevented.

Measuring progress. Tracking boys' emotional development is often a good barometer of boys' progress in therapy. You can use Mayer and Salovey's (1997) list of emotional skills (outlined in chapter 1) as a checklist of sorts. I usually rely on the following checkpoints to know whether boys have made progress in therapy, particularly with their emotional development. (Note: The following items are accurate markers for boys of any age, unless noted otherwise.)

★ Does he express his feelings directly in therapy and at home? (Children under three may have fewer names for feelings, but they still can identify feelings with words, if they've been taught.)

★ Does he have a friend with whom he can talk about *anything*?

★ Does he have empathy for himself? (Easier to observe behaviorally after age four.)

★ Does he have empathy for others? (Easier to observe behaviorally after age four.)

★ Can he regulate or control his anger?

★ Can he regulate or control his excitement?

★ Does he demonstrate nurturing behaviors toward others?

This list is certainly not a complete one, but if the answers to these questions are mostly "yes," then I'd say that this boy has made significant progress in his emotional development. If his parents can maintain this progress at home, then the prognosis for continued emotional development is positive.

Mentors

A mentor is someone who guides a younger or less experienced person through specific life experiences. These life experiences may involve mastering a skill (for a job or career) or navigating through a personal relationship or life stage. Mentors can be formal, professionally trained adults who make a regularly scheduled time commitment with a younger and/or less experienced person. Mentors may volunteer or be paid for mentoring; they can be teachers, coaches, neighbors, or college students. Basically, anyone can be a mentor to boys. In the 1990s, many schools, community mental health centers, and social service agencies began recommending formal mentors to children and teens in need, especially to boys with absent fathers. The prevention department of the community agency in my county provides a mentoring program for boys called Boys to Men. There are other similar mentoring programs around the country.

Whether you're a formal mentor who spends scheduled time with boys or an informal one (neighbor, family friend, aunt or uncle), you can be a significant influence in boys' emotional development. It is likely that you will be male, since most (but not all) mentors follow gender role assignments. Assuming you're male, it's important that you read chapters 1 and 2 of this book, and that you consider how the Pack Rules have influenced your own emotional development. The chances are good that if you're a volunteer mentor, you have broken free of at least some of the Pack Rules. That will be helpful for the boy whom you're mentoring. Most boys need to see and know a biological masculine role model (i.e., a man) who challenges those Rules, in order to break free themselves.

Reading the chapters on empathy, anger, and emotional expression is also recommended. Each chapter zeroes in on important aspects of boys' emotional development. The boy you mentor may choose you as the one to whom he will confide important stuff . . . like his feelings. Simply put, be prepared to be a good listener and to validate the boy's emotions. The three steps listed in the section for therapists will also be helpful to you.

Media and Entertainment Professionals

I debated with myself about whether to include this section since it addresses corporate entities rather than people. However, if members of these entities read this book, I decided it was worthwhile since the media are *everywhere*: television, movies, videos, magazines, newspapers, etc. Media professionals can have such an important impact on boys' emotions, especially boys' emotional expression.

The chief way that media professionals can help boys develop in healthy emotional ways is this: Challenge the Pack Rules and other narrow or unhealthy stereotypes of masculinity that tell boys how to be "real boys" or how to become men. Weave these challenges into your plots, sound bites, anchor stories, real-life dramas, news reports, and advertisements. Let boys' emotions be part of your lyrics, stories, and character's lives. It can't hurt. Plus, in our current culture, it will be a novel marketing angle.

Resources

American Association of Retired Persons, Grandparent Information Center, 601 E. Street NW, Washington, DC 20049. 202-434-2296. Resources for grandparents raising grandchildren.

Bennet-Goleman, T. 2001. *Emotional Alchemy: How the Mind Can Heal the Heart.* Harmony Books. Provides a Buddhist perspective to help adults understand their own emotions which, in turn, can help boys.

Cain, B. 2000. *Double-Dip Feelings: Stories to Help Children Understand Emotions.* Second Edition. Washington, DC: Magination Press. Helps children identify basic and complex feelings. Can be ordered online: www. Maginationpress.com

Childswork Childsplay: A Guidance Channel Company. 1-800-962-1141. Resource for various games, books, and videos on emotional development and health.

Emswiller, M., and J. Emswiller. 2000. *Guiding Your Child Through Grief.* New York: Bantam. A very useful book for helping children express emotions related to loss.

Gurian, M. 1999. *A Fine Young Man: What Parents, Mentors, and Educators Can Do to Shape Adolescent Boys into Exceptional Men.* New York: Tarcher/Putnam. Parents praise this book and its practical "how to" approach.

Mundy, M. 1998. *Sad Isn't Bad: A Good-Grief Guidebook for Kids Dealing with Loss.* St. Meinrad, IN: Abbey Press. Another good book written to help children express feelings related to loss.

Neville, H., D. Johnson, and J. Cameron. 1997. *Temperament Tools: Working with Your Child's Inborn Traits.* Seattle, WA: Parenting Press. A practical reference guide for parents who don't want to read an entire textbook about temperament.

Pollack, W. 2000. *Real Boys' Voices.* New York: Random House. This best-selling author has written a second excellent book, filled with what boys have to say about their thoughts and feelings.

Thompson, M. 2000. *Speaking of Boys: Answers to the Most-Asked Questions About Raising Boys.* New York: Ballantine. The co-author of *Raising Cain* wrote this easy-to-read guide.

www.healthemotions.org. This is an excellent database of current brain-emotion-behavior research.

www.nurturingfathers.com. This is a website that is exactly what it states, a resource for fathers who nurture.

References

Ainsworth, M. 1973. The development of infant-mother attachment. In *Review of Child Development Research*, Vol. 3. Edited by B. Caldwell and H. Ricciuti Chicago, IL: University of Chicago Press.

Ainsworth, M., M. Blehar, E. Waters, and S. Wall. 1978. *Patterns of Attachment.* Hillsdale, NJ: Earlbaum.

Ax, A. 1953. The physiological differentiation between fear and anger in humans. *Psychosomatic Medicine* 15:433–442.

Bandura, A., D. Ross, and S. Ross. 1963. Imitation of film-mediated aggressive models. *Journal of Abnormal and Social Psychology* 66: 3–11.

Basow, S. 1992. *Gender: Stereotypes and Roles*. Third Edition. Montery, CA: Brooks/Cole.

Benson, H. 1975. *The Relaxation Response*. New York: Avon.

Borkowski, J., and R. Ramey. In press. *Parenting and the Child's World: Influences on Academic, Intellectual, and Socioemotional Development.* Hillsdale, New Jersey: Earlbaum.

Bowlby, J. 1969. *Attachment and Loss*. New York: Basic Books.

Brothers, L. 1989. A biological perspective on empathy. *American Journal of Psychiatry* 146:10–19.

Button, A. 1969. *The Authentic Child.* New York: Random House.

Carey, W. B. 1999. *Understanding Your Child's Temperament*. New York: IDG Books.

Carlson, N. 1992. *Foundations of Physiological Psychology.* Second Edition. Boston, MA: Allyn and Bacon.

Cicchetti, D., and V. Carlson. 1989. *Child Maltreatment: Theory and Research on the Causes and Consequences of Child Abuse and Neglect.* Cambridge: Cambridge University Press.

Colburn, D. 1996. Suicide rate climbs for older Americans. *Washington Post Health,* Jan. 23, 5.

Coltrane, S. 1998. Theorizing masculinities in contemporary social science. In *Questions of Gender: Perspectives and Paradoxes,* edited by D. L. Anselmi, and A. L. Law. Boston: McGraw-Hill.

Condry, J., and D. Ross. 1985. Sex and aggression: The influence of gender label on the perception of aggression in children. *Child Development* 53:1008–1016.

Courtenay, W. 1998. *Better to Die than to Cry?* A longitudinal and constructionist study of masculinity and the health risk behavior of young American men. Doctoral dissertation, University of California at Berkeley. Dissertation Abstracts International #9902042.

Courtenay, W. 1998. Constructions of masculinity and their influence on men's well-being: A theory of gender and health. Under review. *Social Science and Medicine.*

Crittendon, P., and M. Ainsworth. 1989. Child maltreatment and attachment theory. In *Child Maltreatment: Theory and Research on the Causes and Consequences of Child Abuse and Neglect,* edited by D. Cicchetti and V. Carlson. New York: Cambridge University Press.

Cummings, L. 1991. Fighting by the rules: Women street-fighting in Chihuahua, Mexico. Paper presented at the annual meeting of the American Anthropological Association. Chicago, Illinois.

Damasio, A. 1994. *Descartes' Error: Emotion, Reason, and the Human Brain.* New York: Grosset/Putnam.

DiCamillo, K. 2001. *The Tiger Rising.* Cambridge, MA: Candlewick Press.

Dinnerstein, D. 1976. *The Mermaid and the Minotaur: Sexual Arrangements and Human Malaise.* New York: Harper & Row.

Dodge, K., J. Bates, and G. Pettit. 1990. Mechanisms in the cycle of violence. *Science* 250:1679–1683.

Dodge, K., G. Pettit, and J. Bates. 1994. Effects of physical maltreatment on the development of peer relations. *Development and Psychopathology* 6:43–56.

Duck, S. 1991. *Understanding Relationships*. New York: Guilford.

Dworetzky, J. 1996. *Introduction to Child Development*. Sixth Edition. St. Paul, MN: West.

Eisenberg, N., and P. Miller. 1987. The relation of empathy to prosocial and related behaviors. *Psychological Bulletin* 101:91–119.

Emswiller, M., and J. Emswiller. 2000. *Guiding Your Child Through Grief*. New York: Bantam.

Frederickson, B. 2001. The role of positive emotions in positive psychology: The broaden-and-build theory of positive emotion. *American Psychologist* 56:218–226.

Freedman, B., and W. Knoedelseder. 1999. *In Eddie's Name: One Family's Triumph Over Tragedy*. New York: Faber and Faber.

George, C., and M. Main. 1979. Social interactions of young abused children: Approach, avoidance, and aggression. *Child Development* 50:306–318.

Gilbert, S. 2001. *A Field Guide to Boys and Girls: Differences, Similarities: Cutting-Edge Information Every Parent Needs to Know*. New York: HarperCollins.

Goleman, D. 1995. *Emotional Intelligence: Why It May Matter More Than IQ*. New York: Bantam Books.

Greenspan, S. 1993. *Playground Politics: Understanding the Emotional Life of Your School Age Child*. Reading, MA: Addison Wesley Longman.

Greenspan, S., and N. Greenspan. 1985. *First Feelings: Milestones in the Emotional Development of Your Baby and Child*. New York: Viking Press.

Greenspan, S., and J. Salmon. 1996. *The Challenging Child: Understanding, Raising and Enjoying the Five "Difficult" Types of Children*. Reading, MA: Addison Wesley Longman.

Gross, J., and R. Levenson. 1993. Emotional suppression: Physiology, self-report, and expressive behavior. *Journal of Personality and Social Psychology* 64: 970–986.

———. 1997. Hiding feelings: The acute effects of inhibiting negative and positive emotion. *Journal of Abnormal Psychology* 106: 95–103.

Gross, J., and R. Munoz. 1995. Emotion regulation and mental health. *Clinical Psychology: Science and Practice* 2:151–164.

Gurian, M. 1996. *The Wonder of Boys: What Parents, Mentors and Educators Can Do to Shape Boys into Exceptional Men.* New York: Tarcher/Putnam.

———. 1999. *The Good Son: Shaping the Moral Development of Our Boys and Men.* New York: Tarcher/Putnam.

Harris, J. 1998. *The Nurture Assumption.* New York: Free Press.

Harter, S., and N. Whitesell. 1989. Developmental changes in children's understanding of single, multiple, and blended emotion concepts. In *Children's Understanding of Emotion*, edited by C. Saarni and P. Harris. New York: Cambridge University Press.

Herrenkohl, R., and E. Herrenkohl. 1981. Some antecedents and developmental consequences of child maltreatment. In *Developmental Perspectives on Child Maltreatment*, edited by R. Rizley and D. Cicchetti. San Francisco: Jossey-Bass.

Izard, C. 1982. *Measuring Emotions in Infants and Children.* New York: Cambridge University Press.

Kadusan, H. 1998. *Short-Term Play Therapy.* Harrisonburg, VA: Virginia Association of Play Therapists, Annual Conference.

Kagan, J. 1978. *The Growth of the Child: Reflections on Human Development.* New York: W. W. Norton.

Kagan, J., J. Reznick, and J. Gibbons. 1989. Inhibited and uninhibited types of children. *Child Development* 60:838–845.

Kagan, J., and N. Snidman. 1991. Temperamental factors in human development. *American Psychologist* 46:856–862.

Katz, L., and J. Gottman. 1995. Vagal tone protects children from marital conflict. *Development and Psychopathology* 7:93–116.

Kilbourne, J. 1999. *Deadly Persuasion: Why Women and Girls Must Fight the Addictive Power of Advertising.* New York: Free Press.

Kilmartin, C. 2000. *The Masculine Self.* Second Edition. New York: McGraw Hill.

Kimmel, M. 1987. *Changing Men: New Directions in Research on Men and Masculinity.* Newbury Park, CA: Sage Publications.

Kindlon, D., and M. Thompson. 2000. *Raising Cain: Protecting the Emotional Life of Boys.* New York: Ballantine Books.

Klimes-Dougan, B., and J. Kistner. 1990. Physically abused preschoolers' responses to peers' distress. *Developmental Psychology* 26:599–602.

Lamb, W. 1998. *I Know This Much Is True.* New York: HarperCollins.

LeDoux, J. 1992. Cognitive-emotional interactions in the brain. In *Development of Emotion-Cognition Relations*, edited by C. Izard. Chichester, England: Wiley.

LeDoux, J. 1996. *The Emotional Brain: The Mysterious Underpinnings of Emotional Life*. New York: Simon and Schuster.

Levant, R. 1995. *Masculinity Reconstructed: Changing the Rules of Manhood at Work, in Relationships, and in Family Life*. New York: Plume.

Lynch, J., and C. Kilmartin. 1999. *The Pain Behind the Mask: Overcoming Masculine Depression*. Binghamton, NY: Haworth Press.

Maccoby, E. 1990. Gender and relationships: A developmental approach. *American Psychologist* 45:513–520.

Maccoby, E., and C. Jacklin. 1974. *The Psychology of Sex Differences*. Stanford, CA: Stanford University Press.

Mahler, M., F. Pine, and A. Bergman. 1975. *The Psychological Birth of the Human Infant*. New York: Basic Books.

Main, M., and C. George. 1985. Responses of abused and disadvantaged toddlers to distress in age mates: A study in a day-care setting. *Developmental Psychology* 21:407–412.

Massachusetts Department of Education. 1996. Executive Summary of the 1995 Youth Risk Behavior Survey Results, accessed August 4, 2001.

Masten, A. 2001. Ordinary magic: Resilience processes in development. *American Psychologist* 50:227–238.

Masterson, J. 1993. *Emerging Self: A Developmental, Self, and Object Relations Approach to the Treatment of the Closet Narcissistic Disorder of the Self*. New York: Brunner/Mazel.

Mayer, J., and P. Salovey. 1997. What is emotional intelligence? In *Emotional Development and Emotional Intelligence*, edited by P. Salovey and D. Sluyter. New York: Basic Books.

Mundy, M. 1998. *Sad Isn't Bad: A Good-Grief Guidebook for Kids Dealing with Loss*. St. Meinrad, IN: Abbey Press.

Neiss, R. 1988. Reconceptualizing arousal: Psychobiological states in motor performance. *Psychological Bulletin* 103:345–366.

Neville, H., D. Johnson, and J. Cameron. 1997. *Temperament Tools: Working with Your Child's Inborn Traits*. Seattle, WA: Parenting Press.

Nolen-Hoeksema, S. 1994. An interactive model for the emergence of gender differences in depression in adolescence. *Journal of Research on Adolescence* 4:519–534.

Olweus, D., S. Limber, and S. F. Mihalic. 1999. *Blueprints for Violence Prevention, Book Nine: Bullying Prevention Program.* Boulder, CO: Center for the Study and Prevention of Violence.

Patrick, C., B. Cuthbert, and P. Lang. 1994. Emotion in the criminal psychopath: Fear image processing. *Journal of Abnormal Psychology* 103:523–534.

Pennebaker, J. 1997. Rev ed. *Opening Up: The Healing Power of Confiding in Others.* New York: Morrow.

———. 1995. Emotion, disclosure and health: An overview. In *Emotion, Disclosure and Health*, edited by J. Pennebaker. Washington, DC: American Psychological Association.

Pert, C., and D. Chopra. 1997. *Molecules of Emotion: Why You Feel the Way You Feel.* New York: Scribner.

Piaget, J. 1952. *The Origins of Intelligence in Children.* New York: International University Press, Inc.

Pipher, M. 1994. *Reviving Ophelia: Saving the Selves of Adolescent Girls.* New York: Ballantine.

Polce-Lynch, M. 1996. Gender and self-esteem from late childhood to late adolescence: Predictors and mediators. Doctoral dissertation. Virginia Commonwealth University, Richmond, Virginia.

Polce-Lynch, M., B. J. Myers, C. Kilmartin, R. Forssmann-Falk, and W. Kliewer. 1998. Gender and age patterns in emotional expression, body image, and self-esteem: A qualitative analysis. *Sex Roles* 38:1025–1048.

Polce-Lynch, M., B. J. Myers, W. Kliewer, and C. Kilmartin. 2001. Adolescent gender and self-esteem: Exploring relations to sexual harassment, body image, media influence and emotional expression. *Journal of Youth and Adolescence* 30:225–244.

Pollack, W. 1998. *Real Boys: Rescuing Our Sons from the Myths of Boyhood.* New York: Holt.

Powers, S., D. Welsh, and V. Wright. 1994. Adolescents' affective experience of family behaviors: The role of subjective understanding. *Journal of Research on Adolescence* 4:585–600.

Radke-Yarrow, M., and C. Zahn-Waxler. 1984. Roots, motives and patterns in children's prosocial behavior. In *Development and*

Maintenance of Prosocial Behavior: International Perspectives on Positive Morality, edited by E. Staub. New York: Plenum.

Real, T. 1997. *I Don't Want to Talk About It: Overcoming the Hidden Legacy of Male Depression.* New York: Scribner.

Real, T. 1999. *Male Depression.* Richmond, VA: Richmond Clinical Society of Social Work. Annual Conference.

Richards, J., and J. Gross. 2000. Emotion regulation: The hidden cost of keeping one's cool. *Journal of Personality and Social Psychology* 79:410–424.

Rieder, C., and D. Cicchetti. 1989. Organizational perspective on cognitive control functioning and cognitive-affective balance in maltreated children. *Developmental Psychology* 25:382-393.

Robinson, J., J. Kagan, J. Reznick, and R. Corley. 1992. The heritability of inhibited and uninhibited behaviors. *Developmental Psychology* 28:1030–1037.

Salovey, P., and D. Sluyter. 1997. *Emotional Development and Emotional Intelligence: Educational Implications.* New York: Basic Books.

Sameroff, A., and M. Chandler. 1975. Reproductive risk and the continuum of caretaking casualty. In *Review of Child Development Research,* Vol. 4. Edited by F. Horowitz. Chicago: University of Chicago Press.

Scarr, S., and K. McCartney. 1983. How people make their own environment: A theory of genotype—environment effects. *Child Development* 54:424–435.

Seligman, M. 1998. *Learned Optimism: How to Change Your Mind and Your Life.* Pocket Books: New York.

Seligman, M., K. Reivich, L. Jaycox, and J. Gillham. 1996. *The Optimistic Child.* New York: Harperperennial Library.

Shaffer, D. 1999. *Developmental Psychology: Childhood and Adolescence.* Fifth Edition. Pacific Grove, CA: Brooks/Cole.

Silverman, J., A. Raj, L. Mucci, and J. Hathaway. 2001. Dating violence against adolescent girls and associated substance abuse, unhealthy weight control, sexual risk behavior, pregnancy, and suicidality. *Journal of the American Medical Association* 286:572–679.

Smolowe, J. 1993. Sex with a scorecard. *Time,* April 5, 41.

Sommers, C. 2000. The war against boys. *The Atlantic Monthly,* May, 59–74.

Sroufe, A. 1978. Attachment and the roots of competence. *Human Nature* 1:50–57.

———. 1983. Individual patterns of adaptation from infancy to preschool. In *Minnesota Symposium in Child Psychology*, Vol. 16. Edited by M. Perlmutter. Hillsdale, NJ: Erlbaum.

———. 1997. *Emotional Development: The Organization of Emotional Life in the Early Years.* Cambridge, MA: Cambridge University Press.

Stern, M., and K. Karraker. 1989. Sex stereotyping of infants: A review of gender labeling studies. *Sex Roles* 20:501–522.

Taffel, R. 2001. *The Second Family: How Adolescent Power Is Challenging the American Family.* New York: St. Martin's Press.

Tavris, C. 1989. *Anger: The Misunderstood Emotion.* New York: Simon and Schuster.

Thom, A., G. Sartory, and P. Johren. 2000. Comparison between one-session psychological treatment and benzodiazepine in dental phobia. *Journal of Consulting and Clinical Psychology* 68:378–387.

Thomas, A., S. Chess, and H. Birch. 1970. The origin of personality. *Scientific American* 223:102–109.

Werner, E. 1993. Risk, resilience, and recovery. *Development and Psychopathology* 5:503–514.

Whalen, P., L. Shin, S. McInerney, H. Fischer, C. Wright, and S. Rauch. 2001. A functional MRI study of human amygdala responses to facial expressions of fear versus anger. *Emotion* 1:70–83.

Zahn-Waxler, C., and J. Robinson. 1995. Empathy and guilt: Early origins of feelings of responsibility. In *Self-conscious Emotions: Shame, Guilt, Embarrassment and Pride*, edited by K. Fischer and J. Tangney. New York: Guilford Press.

Zahn-Waxler, C., and K. D. Smith. 1992. The development of prosocial behavior. In *Handbook of Social Development: A Lifespan Perspective*, edited by V. B. Van Hasselt and M. Hersen. New York: Plenum.

Zahn-Waxler, C., P. Cole, J. Welsh, and N. Fox. 1995. Psychophysiological correlates of empathy and prosocial behaviors in preschool children with behavior problems. *Development and Psychopathology* 7:27–48.

Mary Polce-Lynch, Ph.D., is a developmental psychologist, psychotherapist, and researcher. Over the past twenty years, she has worked in public education, community mental health, and higher education. Polce-Lynch is the Assistant Director of the Center for Counseling and Career Planning at Randolph-Macon College, where she also teaches Psychology of Gender as a Visiting Assistant Professor of Psychology. She has published professional articles throughout her career and is currently directing her writing toward general readers, especially parents. She has a private clinical practice in Richmond, Virginia with Westhampton Family Psychologists. She lives in Ashland, Virginia.

Michael Gurian is a family therapist, educator, and author of fourteen books including the national best-sellers *The Wonder of Boys, A Fine Young Man*, and *Boys and Girls Learn Differently*. He has served as a consultant to school districts, families, therapists, community agencies, churches, and policy makers, traveling to approximately thirty-five cities a year to lead seminars, consult, and keynote conferences. Gurian's training videos for parents and volunteers are used by Big Brothers and Big Sisters agencies in the U.S. and Canada. He lives in Spokane, Washington.

Some Other
New Harbinger Titles

The 50 Best Ways to Simplify Your Life, Item FWSL $11.95

When Anger Hurts Your Relationship, Item WARY $13.95

The Couple's Survival Workbook, Item CPSU $18.95

Loving Your Teenage Daughter, Item LYTD $14.95

The Hidden Feeling of Motherhood, Item HFM $14.95

Parenting Well When Your Depressed, Item PWWY $17.95

Thinking Pregnant, Item TKPG $13.95

Pregnancy Stories, Item PS $14.95

The Co-Parenting Survival Guide, Item CPSG $14.95

Family Guide to Emotional Wellness, Item FGEW $24.95

How to Survive and Thrive in an Empty Nest, Item NEST $13.95

Children of the Self-Absorbed, Item CSAB $14.95

The Adoption Reunion Survival Guide, Item ARSG $13.95

Undefended Love, Item UNLO $13.95

Why Can't I Be the Parent I Want to Be?, Item PRNT $12.95

Kid Cooperation, Item COOP $14.95

Breathing Room: Creating Space to Be a Couple, Item BR $14.95

Why Children Misbehave and What to do About it, Item BEHV $14.95

Couple Skills, Item SKIL $15.95

The Power of Two, Item PWR $15.95

The Queer Parent's Primer, Item QPPM $14.95

Illuminating the Heart, Item LUM $13.95

Dr. Carl Robinson's Basic Baby Care, Item DRR $10.95

The Ten Things Every Parent Needs to Know, Item KNOW $12.95

Call **toll free, 1-800-748-6273,** or log on to our online bookstore at **www.newharbinger.com** to order. Have your Visa or Mastercard number ready. Or send a check for the titles you want to New Harbinger Publications, Inc., 5674 Shattuck Ave., Oakland, CA 94609. Include $4.50 for the first book and 75¢ for each additional book, to cover shipping and handling. (California residents please include appropriate sales tax.) Allow two to five weeks for delivery.

Prices subject to change without notice.